CONQUERING THE DARKNESS

CONQUERING THE DARKNESS

•

*One Woman's Story of
Recovering from a Brain Injury*

•

Deborah A. Quinn

PARAGON HOUSE
St. Paul, Minnesota

Published in the United States by

Paragon House
2700 University Avenue West
St. Paul, Minnesota 55114

Library of Congress Catalog-in-Publication Data

Quinn, Deborah A., 1954-
    Conquering the darkness: one woman's story of recovering from a brain injury / Deborah A. Quinn.
      p. cm.
      ISBN: 1-55778-763-8 (alk. paper)
      1. Quinn, Deborah A., 1954---Health. 2. Brain damage--Patients-Florida--Biography.
I. Title
RC387.5.Q56   1998
362.1'968'092--dc21
  [B]   98-14373
                                              CIP

This book is dedicated to all my family members, friends, doctors, nurses, physical therapists, and speech therapists, that helped me through my difficult time.

Each and everyone of you know who you are and fortunately, for me, too numerous to mention in this dedication.

CONTENTS

•

INTRODUCTION

•

When I first moved to Florida six years ago, I lived a charmed, almost a dream fairy-tale life. I was 34 and had just gotten married only nine months earlier to a man named Bob I loved and cherished. I came from a wealthy and supportive Massachusetts family, where my father made his fortune in real estate. I was following in his footsteps by becoming a real-estate entrepreneur myself, was very ambitious and assertive. I had already acquired several properties with my father, and had gotten a few on my own. All were thriving in an expanding real estate market. In addition, I had launched an expanding Mail Boxes franchise, one in Massachusetts, and I was planning to set up several more in three counties in Florida.

Personally and socially, everything seemed wonderful too. My new husband and I were about to begin a new adventure—heading to Florida to begin a new life. I had a large circle of friends I adored, many whom I had known since high school and college. I enjoyed an active social whirl filled with travel, visiting, dinners, parties, sailing, theater, and art openings. I could easily take off for Hawaii or Bora Bora for a delightful tropical vacation when I wanted for a few days, even a week or two, during a lull in the real estate business.

Just about the only storm cloud that occasionally appeared on the horizon was a mother-in-law who resented my marriage to her son, because I was Catholic and he converted from their Lutheran faith to marry me. Also, she often tried to tell Bob what to do. But Bob and I thought the move to Florida would resolve that. We would be on our own, totally free of her influence at last.

Then, on that trip to Florida in February 1989, everything changed. I was in a nearly fatal car crash, when the car my husband was driving careened off the road after a tire blew out. The car went rolling over four times and ended up in a ditch. When I came to in a hospital several days later, I gradually came to learn that my husband was dead. Soon I realized I would never be the same either, because I had suffered a tremendous brain injury. Everyone at first thought I mainly had some physical healing to do. But as I healed physically, I began to discover numerous ways in which I could no longer think or remember clearly, although I had once had a razor sharp mind.

As this realization hit, I went through months of depression dealing with everything I had lost. Not only Bob, but the whole life I had enjoyed was gone, because I could no longer do so many things I once did. Not only couldn't I manage my business, but I could barely get up and dress myself, since once I got out of bed, I had to wear a huge cage-like contraption on my head to keep my neck from breaking while my spine healed. I suffered from all sorts of pains, and often became dizzy.

Over the next months, my charmed life turned into a nightmare of doctors, lawyers, insurance agents, and creditors. Meanwhile, some friends I had long trusted took advantage of me, thinking I wouldn't survive or function normally again. One was a friend of over 30 years who embezzled over $40,000 from my business and caused its bankruptcy.

Then, making everything even worse—much worse!—my mother-in-law turned into my enemy, since she wanted to blame me for the accident by claiming I was driving. As a result, almost all of the insurance settlements I expected to get for my injury were placed on hold, as my lawyers fought her lawyers in a two- year battle over Bob's estate and settlement money. In the process, I saw the $2 million estate I had built up over 10 years dwindle to nothing, and I became nearly homeless.

So life became a struggle for survival. And while these legal battles raged, I still tried to keep my business alive and endure ongoing physical, psychological, and rehabilitative therapy, so I could regain as much as possible of my normal functioning. Meanwhile, my friends and family members didn't understand why everything was so difficult for me, because I appeared to heal physically after a year, so outwardly I seemed fine.

But like many brain injured patients, I wasn't. My mental functioning was far below what it had been, though this wasn't obvious to others. But I knew when I forgot, was confused, and got dizzy. I knew when I suffered excruciating headaches, couldn't understand things, and forgot what people had just told me or what I just read within minutes. I knew I wasn't the same.

Yet, somehow, by force of will and my deep faith, I kept going, determined to overcome what had happened and become self-sufficient again. In many cases, this meant learning new ways to think and do things. For example, I found great help through brain injury support groups, new computer devices, and a software program called the Captain's Log, which was specifically designed by Dr. Joseph Sandford for brain injury victims. I discovered personal strategies to help me remember and organize my life and business activities. I also became interested in doing what I could to help other brain injured patients to show them the way back too.

Conquering the Darkness tells my story. It describes the tremendous darkness and pain I first experienced and how I overcame this to become who I am today. It has been a long struggle, and I know I will still have to keep working at overcoming my injury and moving on. But the more I do to learn, to be active, to think—and to help others do the same, the more I improve. *Conquering the Darkness* has been part of this process—and I hope it helps others with brain injuries and their families as much as it has helped me to write this. I hope it will help others understand, as well.

PART I:

WAKING UP TO TRAGEDY

CHAPTER 1

•

WAKING UP TO TRAGEDY

When I woke up after the car accident that killed my husband and tore my world apart, I had no idea what had happened. I just felt groggy and the area around me only gradually came into focus. I was in a hospital bed in the intensive care section of the Naples Community Hospital, and the first thing I saw was my brother standing at the end of the bed.

Although I didn't know what happened, I could see the pain and anguish in his eyes. At the time, I couldn't understand why. I could only see the pain. Then I drifted back into unconsciousness, and over the next few days I was in a state of almost total blankness. It was like being in suspended animation, as I floated in and out of being conscious.

This state like suspended animation went on for about a week, while I was in intensive care and the doctors weren't sure if I would regain my ability to think or talk again. Meanwhile, my parents, relatives, and friends came to visit, though I was unaware of most of these visits. They came and agonized by my beside, concerned if I would pull through.

* * * * * * * *

Basically what had happened was that I was in a car crash on Alligator Alley, a narrow country road through the Florida Everglades. I was with my husband of nine months, Bob, on our way to the closing of a new house I had recently purchased on the West Coast of Florida. I had bought it shortly after buying a new Mail Boxes franchise, and Bob and I saw the move as a way to start a new venture and new life together in Florida.

I wanted to go there, because I felt a strong desire to do something completely on my own after being involved in several joint-ventures with my father. He had been very successful in real estate in Massachusetts, and he had helped me get started in the field. But now I wanted to show I could do something myself. Also, I saw the move as a chance to break away from my mother-in-law Shirley Raymond, who had always resented my marriage to Bob. Again and again, Shirley tried to tell Bob what to do, or she put me down in Bob's eyes.

But finally, Bob and I had made the break, and the trip was like an extended honeymoon and reaffirmation of our love for each other. We were going to have a new business, a new house, a new life together.

The last thing I could remember later, after months of therapy, was getting into the car with Bob. I remembered I was holding a bouquet of dried flowers in my lap. Bob was driving as usual, and I put the flowers in my lap, as he stepped on the gas and took off.

Then everything went blank until I ended up in my hospital bed and started piecing my life back together again.

* * * * * * *

As best as I can put it together from the police, medical, court and other records that were collected, what happened is this.

Bob and I were whizzing along in our bright red Mercedes to the real estate closing on our new house about 7:30 in the morning, as several attorneys waited there for us. It was a bright sunny day, about 67 degrees, and as usual, Bob raced along at about 75 to 80 miles an hour, since he always liked to drive fast. It gave him a sense of exhilaration, like flying free.

Then, suddenly a tire blew out, and the car went careening across the road. Bob quickly jammed on the brakes. But it was too late. With the sudden jerk of the brakes, the car spun out of control. In seconds it was tumbling over and over, sliding down the grassy shoulder on the side of the road. As it did, I was thrown out of the car. A few moments later, Bob was hurled out, too. According to the accident reports that came out later, the car flipped over four times, and finally came to rest near Bob's body, a total wreck.

A passing truck driver, George Kendrick, who had seen us zoom by about 20 minutes earlier, saw the wreck after he noticed skid marks on the roads and looked to his left. In the trees by the side of the road, he saw our car bent like an accordion, its lights on and smoke coming from the hood. He couldn't stop immediately because a car was directly behind him. But after he made a brief stop for a delivery, he called the sheriff's office and returned to the scene to describe what he saw.

Meanwhile, in response to his call, Trooper Stuart K. Whiddon, a Traffic Homicide Investigator, appeared on the scene soon after 8 a.m. and began assessing the grim carnage. Almost immediately, he could tell Bob was dead—it's even painful now six years later for me to write those words, but I seemed to be still breathing. So Kendrick called for Emergency Services. Soon other medical and police personnel began arriving to pick up the pieces and write up their own assessments of what happened. Later, all these reports would become the basis of a bitter battle between me, my mother-in-law, and various insurance companies over who was actually driving, whether the tire manufacturer was at fault, and who would therefore pay who for what happened.

The police all agreed that Bob was driving. That's what truck driver George Kendrick reported he saw when we passed him on the road. That's also what Trooper Whiddon said in his homicide report, and what an accident reconstruction expert, later called into the case, agreed. That's also what I vaguely remembered before my world went blank.

However, when the paramedics were strapping me onto the gurney, about to put me in the helicopter to go to the hospital, one of the Emergency Technicians, Susan LeMay, asked me the question that would later start the legal nightmare—"Were you driving?" I remembered almost nothing of this conversation after the accident, nor do I now. According to various accident accounts, she arrived in the Emergency Services helicopter, just around the time the Medical Examiner had concluded that Bob's injuries were fatal, and the funeral services van was on its way to pick up Bob.

LeMay, a heavy set woman in her 40s, was the senior crew member in charge of the paramedics. She came over to me while I was lying on the ground writhing in pain, lapsing in and out of consciousness. She quickly assessed my situation, noting that I could barely move, had injuries to my neck and shoulders, and was in great pain. Next she asked me a series of questions about what happened.

I could barely understand or answer, because I was only minimally conscious—and I sometimes wasn't conscious at all. So I gave disjointed and rambling answers. At least I was able to tell her "My name is Debbie," say I was thrown from the car, and give her the date of my birth and current year. But I did not know what day it was or the time or location where we were.

Then, LeMay asked me that question: "Were you driving?" Groggily, I managed a quiet "Yes." But did I really understand the question? Did I think "driving" meant going driving with my husband to the closing? Driving on some other day in some other place? Able to drive at all? I'm not sure either then or now what I was thinking when she asked me the question—except that I know my "Yes" didn't mean I was actually driving the car myself.

At that time LeMay wrote down my "Yes," even though she noted I could barely understand or respond to anything else. In fact, she even wrote in her report that: "Patient responds to voice, has inappropriate answers. Does not remember time, place or what happened. Patient will sometimes answer correctly, then sometimes not."

Yet, despite these explanations, that little "Yes" made all the difference. That's because that half-conscious statement was what my mother-in-law would later use to try to blame the whole accident on me when she filed a wrongful death suit accusing me of causing Bob's death. Once she did file it, her suit led to the almost complete collapse of my already fragile world, as I tried to recover from what had happened.

However, I'm getting ahead of myself. Let me first tell you what my world was like when I woke up in the Naples hospital and started my long struggle back. This process included keeping a diary of what was happening in my life and how I felt about what was going on. By way of introduction, let me tell you a little about myself and what my world was like before the accident. It was almost a story-book dream life, because everything seemed so wonderful and idyllic, especially after I met Bob.

CHAPTER 2

•

THE WAY IT WAS

MEETING BOB

When my magical life with Bob began in the spring of 1985, I was in my early 30s and had thrown myself into the world of real estate with a passion. I was still feeling burned by the end of a marriage to a man who had cheated on me, and I was concentrating on developing myself professionally instead of trying to date and find another husband. And I was becoming very successful. My real estate investments were doubling, even tripling in value, and I was acquiring more properties. So I was not even thinking about starting a new relationship.

Then my sister-in-law Cindy introduced me to Bob. She thought Bob and I would make the perfect pair. For months, she tried to get the two of us together. She kept telling me: "He's such a nice guy". Both Bob and I held her off repeatedly saying: "We don't do blind dates; we don't do blind dates."

Finally Cindy told each of us: "Look, I'll take the two of you out, and we'll have a couple of drinks. Then, if you don't hit it off, fine. We'll go our separate ways."

So that's how it started. Cindy set up the meeting, and one night in March, 1985, I accompanied her to a restaurant in Peabody, Massachusetts called the Hardcover. We sat down at a small table by the bar, and as we sat there waiting, the waiter appeared with two drinks. "They're from an admirer," the waiter said, and a few moments later, I learned they were from Bob, who was sitting across the bar. He had come in shortly before we arrived to "check me out" before we met.

A few minutes after the drinks arrived, so did Bob. As he walked over, I was immediately impressed by his strong good looks and friendly open smile, and Bob was similarly drawn to me. So from the beginning, we both felt an immediate mutual attraction.

Ironically, I didn't think I wanted a man in my life at the time, because I had so much going for me professionally, due to my success in real estate. Also, I hadn't fully rebounded from my previous bad experience with my ex-husband. But now meeting Bob, I felt a new sense of aliveness.

Cindy could sense this, too. As a result, after we finished our drinks and left the restaurant, Cindy gracefully excused herself and went home, and Bob took me to the Cherrystones, a cozy cocktail lounge, for a nightcap. There we talked on and on about what we wanted to do in life and about our families and friends. I found it so easy to talk to Bob. I felt I could tell him just about anything and he would understand. So I went home that night feeling a warm glow of excitement, like something special and uplifting had just come into my life.

On our first date about a week later, Bob took me to Cape Cod, which he loved. We drove down, picking up his sister's son on the way, and once there, the three of us walked along the beach. Bob had brought a kite, and we took turns flying it. I felt like a kid again, it was so much fun.

A few days later, on our next date, we went to a beautiful romantic restaurant, Rosalie's, in Marblehead, Massachusetts. It was one of the first of many dinners in cozy, romantic settings, because as Bob told me early on: "I'm a real romantic. I love romance."

He also had an old-fashioned sense of chivalry which captivated me. On the way to Rosalie's, Bob walked outside near the curb, and he remarked that a gentleman should always walk there, because "That's the chivalrous thing to do to show you respect women." Then, he explained how in the past, wagons would drive by on muddy roads and the splashing mud could get the person walking on the outside all wet and muddy. So men started walking on the side by the curb to protect women from getting splashed. I thought it was a sweet, gentle touch, and I started falling in love with Bob at that moment.

Later, as we sat down in the restaurant and the waiter took our order, both of us were strangely nervous, perhaps because we each realized this could be the start of something very serious. I felt oddly shivery and tingly all over as I sat watching Bob order. Meanwhile, Bob, who was a real connoisseur of wines, couldn't even order correctly. He pointed to one of the wines on the menu, and after the wine steward came over to pour the wine into Bob's glass so he could smell and taste it, Bob quickly said: "Oh, that's fine. It's absolutely wonderful."

Later, about half-way through dinner, when I looked at the bottle, I realized the wine wasn't the type that Bob had actually ordered. At that moment, Bob looked at the bottle too, and when he realized the mistake, he was so embarrassed, he blushed from ear to ear. It was a silly little error, but as a "wine expert" he was deeply embarrassed. In turn, I just laughed at his blushing, and it was one of those funny endearing things that helped me fall in love with Bob even more.

Then, too, I liked the way he had old fashioned romantic values and treated me like a lady he cherished and respected. So there was no pressure to have sex right away, and I didn't want that. In fact, we didn't make love until we had been together for six months, and afterwards, Bob told me he respected me so much because I chose not to have sex early on in our relationship. That's why I loved Bob so much—because he didn't ask me to choose.

BECOMING CLOSER AND CLOSER

Over the next few months, we became closer and closer. Soon after that first real date, we began touring the Cape for several months. Frequently, we visited my parents in New Hampshire. Looking back now, I see this period as a magical time as our romance blossomed.

One especially magical occasion was when we went to Puerto Rico for my brother Paul's wedding. We sailed around the Caribbean in a sailboat, and one sunny day, when I was standing at the helm of our sailboat, as I looked down at Bob, I knew I loved him and wanted to marry him.

Afterwards, like in a dream, the romantic times continued, especially since it was a time of weddings. Besides my brother, several good friends tied the knot, and they chose faraway romantic locations to celebrate the nuptials and flew their guests to the wedding site. So along with 50 to 150 other people, Bob and I went jet setting between the Bahamas and Puerto Rico for these glamorous occasions.

After Bob and I knew each other a year, Bob moved in with me, and we lived together for about two years before we got married, about 9 months before the accident. Feeling so close to Bob made what happened later so much harder.

Besides Bob, so much else was good about those years. Economically, this period from 1985-1988 was something of a boom time, and I was working hard during this time trying to build my business. I looked for properties with potential as an investment to buy, rent, or live in myself, and I negotiated a half-dozen real estate contracts for these new properties.

Meanwhile, as a release, I looked forward to those times when Bob and I could get away from it all. Often we did so by borrowing a limo from a limo business I shared with my father. Then, we headed almost anywhere we wanted within a day's drive of Boston. Sometimes when we took a limo bus with a kitchen, a young woman came along to make the drinks and appetizers. I felt like royalty when we took that limo. Sometimes we arranged for special entertainment when we stopped. One time, for example, at a small celebration for Bob's birthday with my father and three close friends, my father and I arranged for a belly dancer to entertain us. As we sat having brunch at a restaurant on the water in Rye Beach, New Hampshire, a belly dancer appeared swathed in silk and danced around Bob like Salome of the seven veils.

Bob and I also had two places which we regarded as a retreat, as well as the beginning of a nest-egg. One was a house in Topsfield, Massachusetts; the other, a condo on the East Coast in Florida in Hillsboro Beach. Both were places of wonderful memories. Though they might seem very ordinary now, thinking about them helped me get through the many periods of despair that came after the accident.

For example, I remember how we hid eggs at Easter at the Topsfield house, and Bob turned into a little kid running around the yard looking for them. I also recall how Bob came down to visit me in Florida from time to time, when I went there as a retreat from all the business activities in Massachusetts. When he visited, we explored the Florida coast, turning his visits into a glorious vacation. Besides driving around, we went sailing and scuba diving, walked on the beach, went surfing on the waves, and made love by the pool of my condo.

Sometimes Bob did wonderfully ironic funny things. For example, several times, when he went out to get take-out dinners for us, he spent $100 on a bottle of wine, and picked up two cheeseburgers at MacDonald's to go with the wine. Then, when he returned, we had a good laugh about the crazy contrast—like combining the ridiculous and sublime.

In turn, I tried to surprise Bob, too, like a kid being playful in a game. For instance, on Valentine's Day in February 1986, I came home early, and as a surprise, put a dozen roses in a silver vase on the table and soft satin sheets on the pull-out couch in the family room. After I set out some crab canapes for appetizers, among Bob's favorites, I called him at his office and told him urgently: "You've got to come home right away. I have something important to show you." But though he asked, I wouldn't explain. When he came home, brimming with concern and curiosity, I was lying on the satin sheets completely naked. I had a bottle of champagne propped up between my knees and was holding a rose in my hand. When he walked in the door and saw me, the look on his face was so funny—a mixture of surprise, shock, and excitement. And then we made love.

These little fun things helped to make our relationship so special. We even did everyday things like this. One day, for instance, I would open the refrigerator door and see a card from him on a shelf saying something like "I love you" or "I'm thinking of you". And then I'd do the same thing for him, sometimes leaving the notes in the refrigerator or on the window of his car.

We surprised each other with trips, too. For example, in March 1986, after a friend gave me some extra tickets to Washington, D.C.,

I told Bob to meet me at the airport, without telling him where we were going. So he didn't know until we got to the line at the gate. But, like me, Bob loved the spontaneity and adventure of such trips. Then, after we got to our destination, we celebrated with a special dinner with rare wine, and enjoyed the following day relaxing in bed and seeing the city.

I was also charmed by the way Bob always seemed to put me first, putting his own concerns aside, whether the situation involved just having fun or taking care of business or the house. For example, Bob put aside his own fears when I invited him to go hot air ballooning at the Topsfield Fair in the summer of 1986. I didn't know at the time that Bob was afraid of heights, and he didn't want to tell me. So he just joined me in the balloon's gondola and never mentioned his fear, as we drifted blissfully up in the clouds and gazed down on the buildings and fields below. But later, when we saw the pictures a friend took, I noticed the mixture of excitement and fear in his eyes, and when I asked, Bob explained that he didn't want to spoil the event for me. So he just went along, even though he was scared to death.

LIVING A FAIRY-TALE

For three glorious, romantic years, it was like living a fairy-tale with Bob, though like many fairy-tales, this had it's wicked witch—my mother-in-law—who did what she could to derail our relationship. She didn't succeed, though, at least then. Instead, Bob and I came to realize we wanted to make our relationship permanent, and in part our decision to move to Florida was to get away from the wicked witch.

We started thinking about making it permanent after I made several trips to Florida and Bob couldn't get away to see me there. That's when we both began realizing how much we missed each other. One time, Bob sent me some flowers with a card that said: "You are missed." Then, on his next trip to Florida, in early January 1987, we started discussing marriage, deciding that we really did want to have kids together.

A month later, in February, when we were both in Massachusetts, we got engaged, on the 13th, a day before Valentine's Day, and Bob turned it into a dramatic, special occasion. Ironically, it started the night before Bob proposed when we went to our favorite Italian restaurant near Topsfield, the Ponte Vecchio. One of the waiters who served us many times began singing "I'm getting married in the morning."

I didn't make the connection at the time, but the next evening, at a catered dinner at my house, Bob proposed, turning his proposal into a mysterious surprise. Initially, it seemed like we were just having an ordinary dinner with a wonderful four course meal with house specialties like lobster ravioli and chicken piccatta. Then, Bob brought out a special white cake from the kitchen with a solid silver ring case on top. When I opened it, there was the engagement ring. At once, I jumped up, threw my arms around him, and gave him a big kiss. Of course, my answer was a resounding "Yes!" Then, to celebrate, we headed to Montreal, where a limo whisked us to a penthouse suite.

Also, six months later, our engagement party in August was like a fairy-tale. We held it at an old Irish country club surrounded by a golf course with rolling meadows in Salem, Massachusetts, where my parents were members. We had a traditional celebration for 150 family members and friends, since both of us had been married before. Also, we wanted a large engagement party, so we could keep the wedding itself small and intimate.

Then, for the next six months before the wedding, Bob became more and more part of my own family and business, though increasingly I felt the tension between Bob's mother and I. Instead of recognizing our coming marriage, the closer Bob and I got, the more she seemed to want me out of his life.

Although, I tried to push my concerns about her aside, since after the engagement, there was so much to do to plan for the wedding. This included flying to the California wine country a few times to make arrangements, since we decided to get married there. Meanwhile, Bob became increasingly close with my father, and even took over one of his businesses. Bob and I also planned various real estate ventures together, and I bought a Mail Boxes, Etc. area franchise to cover three counties in Florida. So it was a busy, hectic, but wonderful time, when I felt more than ever like I was part of the jet set, flying here and there for both business and pleasure.

A few trips were especially memorable. One was a cross-country skiing trip in New Hampshire in February 1988, where Bob and I stayed with a long-term friend, who would be my maid of honor, and her boyfriend. Though I had gone skiing downhill since I was three, this was my first time going cross-country skiing and Bob's first time on skis. Still, he was game to try, just as he had been to try ballooning and show he was fearless.

I wasn't quite as confident of myself, though, when Bob persuaded me to learn to scuba dive on another trip we took to Florida in March before the wedding. There was something deeply frightening to me about diving far down under the surface of the water with strange, even dangerous fish like sharks, even though I had felt fine about skydiving. So I insisted: "No way. One thing I won't do is scuba dive." But Bob was determined I would, and one day when we were sitting by my pool, I kiddingly remarked: "Oh, what a shame I can't get certified now." I thought that would be the end of the discussion, because we were just in Florida for a long weekend, and I didn't think I would have enough time to be certified. But a few minutes later, when I returned from taking a shower, Bob announced he was taking me for a surprise drive, and about 30 minutes later we pulled up at a Fort Lauderdale dive shop. Then, despite my resistance, Bob used his boyish charm to convince me, telling me with a big grin: "Oh, no problem. You can be certified by Sunday afternoon. I've already signed you up for a crash course starting this Friday."

So finally, I agreed to try, and afterwards, I came to love diving. Once I got in the pool, with the instructor beside me, showing me he had the confidence I could do it, I began to feel better and got over my fear. Later, ironically, diving became my favorite sport, because on our honeymoon, we went diving in some of the most spectacular places in the South Pacific. It was another example of how Bob influenced me to conquer my fears and work hard to do something new—an influence that stayed with me and helped me after the accident, as well.

GETTING MARRIED

Then, in May we got married. We organized a special five-day celebration at a wine-country hotel with traditional old-world charm, the Auberge du Soleil in California's Napa Valley, and we invited 50 of our closest friends and family members. Though we had been living together for about three years, Bob moved out of our room the day before the wedding, because he had this old superstition— 'Don't sleep with your fiance the night before the wedding'. So he wanted to honor that.

The morning of the wedding, when I woke up, I discovered that Bob had sent a dozen red roses to my room at the hotel with a note telling me how much he loved me. I thought it was such a sweet touch, so characteristic of Bob.

After the wedding, we had an exotic reception filled with rose petals, streamers, and champagne in the hills overlooking the Napa Valley. Then, we floated away in a hot air balloon—a romantic, dramatic touch. After we hovered over the reception area, watching the guests below for several minutes, the wind picked up and we drifted to an open field about three miles away.

Later that night, as we made love for the first time after we had married, I felt Bob shivering as he held me and said: "I love you so much." I felt closer to him than ever then; it was as if we had become totally part of each other in that moment. I felt so totally loved and cared for by someone I loved so much, I couldn't imagine ever being apart.

Afterwards, our honeymoon continued this magical relationship in a tropical paradise before reality set in. The day after the wedding, we flew off to Bora Bora, an island in the South Pacific. We landed in Tahiti around four in the morning, spent the rest of the night talking to a couple from L.A. in the airport, and as the sun came up, we boarded a small motor boat. After the boatman steered it from the dock, we sped across the bay. About a half hour later, we landed on the beach. It looked like a brilliant white crescent of sparkling sand with palms in the distance, and I instantly fell in love with Bora Bora. It seemed so blissful and peaceful, like a place out of time from a romantic past before modern conveniences were invented.

After a tiny bus took us along a windy dirt road to our hotel—a rustic hideaway with a thatched roof and walls by the ocean, we checked in and had a breakfast with exotic fresh fruit on the veranda. As we sat eating, overlooking the shimmering green water, we heard parrots and other birds twittering nearby. Later, after we dropped off our bags in our bungalow which was on stilts over the water, we walked around the hotel and stopped in the bar for a nightcap.

The next few days became a glorious collage of memories that helped sustain me through the darkest moments after the accident. The first day, we explored the island on a little moped. After we stopped at a small bungalow which sold beautiful shells and black pearls from the tide pools, we put on our diving gear and slid into the water. Besides feeding the fish with crusts of bread, we took underwater pictures of the colorful swarms of fish that sped by. And later that day, we chartered a boat and glided through the maze of islands, as the couple who owned the boat pointed out different sites. Along the way, they invited us to a native luau on a nearby island, Raitia, where no one spoke English, and the Polynesian girls danced barefoot and in grass skirts. As I saw them dance, I fell in love with the South Pacific. It was a culture where the grim realities of modern life did not yet exist, as the native dancers recalled a magical wonderland of the past.

The following week, we cruised on a 55-foot sailboat with a captain and cook—a wedding gift from my parents—seeing the other islands in the chain. One high point was going to a tiny restaurant at a small village where we docked. Inside were just a few tables in a thatched cottage, lit by a small generator since there was no electricity. It was so peaceful and romantic—another glimpse of a world out of time.

It was likewise romantic a few weeks later on the island of Kauai in Hawaii, when Bob and I got all dressed up—me in a long black gown, Bob in a sleek black suit—and we went to dinner in a horse drawn carriage. As we sat at the table and dined with a candle flickering, Bob had the piano player play our wedding song. Again, I was flooded with so much happiness and emotion. I felt like a princess the way Bob treated me with such thoughtfulness and care.

The next day, Bob seemed like my protector when he put aside his fear of heights so we could ride on a helicopter to see Kauai from the air. We glided over the coast, valleys, and waterfalls; then stopped in a remote spot in the middle of the island near a swimming hole. There, we picnicked on cornish game hen and champagne under the palm trees, and afterwards we swam in the nude in the swimming hole. It felt so freeing to swim there—like being native Hawaiians ourselves and imagining the modern age was a world away.

To end the trip with a last touch of glamor, on our way back we stopped at the Beverly Hills hotel. We arrived by limo and stayed in a special luxurious suite, with the smell of gardenias everywhere. The next morning, as we sat by the pool, with phones at every chair, Bob picked up the phone and playfully acted like he was a big film producer, who was talking to a business partner and was about to close some big deals now that we were back. It was so funny to hear him try this act on my parents and a couple of friends, when he called them and they joined him in this grand outrageous joke.

So while it lasted, our relationship was like a fantasy—too good to be true. And since we were both monogamous, we had this sense of perfect trust in each other. We felt like we were becoming a part of each other—like perfect soul-mates, which made losing him so hard.

BACK TO REALITY

After this paradise-like honeymoon, it was back to work in New England and Florida. Back to reality. I went to Florida to get my new Mail Boxes area franchise established and spent most of the next few months down there, with occasional trips back to Boston. I had a lot of paperwork and legal and financial arrangements to take care of. Meanwhile, Bob tried to wrap up things at the bowling alley he managed, so he could hire a local manager, become an absentee manager himself, and move to Florida.

As a result, we spent the next months flying back and forth, seeing each other when we could. Mostly it was a time of long hours of hard work for both of us, though we celebrated a few special occasions in Florida—like our six month's anniversary in November 1988. To make it really special, Bob took me to a charming restaurant, the Grill Room at the Ritz Carlton Hotel in Naples, which had a look of old-fashioned elegance, with white lace tablecloths and waiters in tuxes. When, the waiter came over and presented me with a bouquet of fresh flowers from Bob, it was a reminder of our special relationship, despite the hard everyday work of relocating to Florida.

Such romantic gestures, in turn, helped me keep up my spirits during the difficult days of getting my new Mail Boxes store going. I was understaffed and swamped from the first day with dozens of new customers. So I ended up working from about seven in the morning until 11 or 12 at night six days a week until the last few days before Christmas, when things slowed down for awhile. Meanwhile, with Bob still winding up his business affairs in Massachusetts, we mostly talked on the phone for long hours, though I made an occasional trip north for a few days to see him. Somehow, none of the separation, none of the problems seemed to matter, because we imagined that soon we would be together forever and ever. We had found a beautiful villa in Naples, Florida, and in early February 1989 the sale would be final. Then, like a dream castle, that would complete the dream.

I remember that last weekend in January in Boston, a week prior to the accident, just before I was planning to return to Florida. After Bob and I had spent a quiet weekend together, Bob hugged me and said, "Guppy" (that was my nickname), "I love you." When we made love, it was like we were on our honeymoon again, as he held me tight and trembled, saying as he did before: "I love you! I love you so much!"

"How could anything be more perfect?" I thought.

STORM CLOUDS ON THE HORIZON

Yet, while everything seemed so perfect, there was a storm cloud on the horizon that would turn into a raging whirlwind after the accident. It was Bob's mother, Shirley Raymond. She not only tried to interfere in our marriage when Bob was alive, but later as executrix of the estate, she tried to get everything she could—and nearly destroyed me in the process.

I only wish I did more to heed the early warning signs. From the beginning Bob warned me to stay away from his mother, saying she was no good. I was shocked to hear him say it, since he always said such good things about others, and this was his mother. But I soon began to see her angry, manipulative, dominating side.

For example, in the four years I knew her, I never saw her with a friend, and Bob said she didn't seem to have any. When Bob and I began getting serious, and she invited her only brother and sister-in-law over for dinner to meet us, I could sense the hostility between them. This feeling descended over the table like a curtain as we talked, which made me nervous. I didn't understand why at the time, though later I came to believe her brother and sister-in-law might be angry, because when Shirley's father died, she grabbed most of the estate, much as she tried to go after the settlement money from the accident after Bob died.

Shirley also seemed distant from her husband George, who was a nervous socially awkward person, who had trouble making ordinary social conversation. But, Bob told me, they stayed married, because divorce was not socially acceptable. Instead they adjusted by living essentially separate lives, including taking separate vacations, and when together, Shirley dominated and manipulated George. She ordered him around and insulted him freely, much as she tried to do to me and Bob, if we let her. As a result, Bob had trouble respecting his father, because he didn't stand up to her. It was a major reason that he wanted to get away from her by moving to Florida after we got married.

I soon felt her hostility towards me, too. I believe she came to resent me because Bob decided to convert to Catholicism, although

I never asked him to do so. It was his free decision. He felt very close to the deacon, whom we saw for the pre-marriage counseling classes, and as a romantic, he loved the ceremony. So he wanted to convert for himself.

I began to notice warnings in the way Shirley treated others in the family, too, trying to take over and direct their lives. For example, she tried to marry off Bob's sister Honey and buy a house for her, though she actually controlled it. She did so because when she bought the house, the deed stated that Honey only owned one third, while Shirley and George owned two thirds. Then, around the time Bob and I got married, Honey was engaged to be married, too. But the marriage never took place, because one day, while Honey was away traveling for her work, Shirley insisted that her finance Ray come over to the house and have dinner with her, since George was out of town on business, as well, and he did. But soon after the dinner, Honey's prospective husband backed out, telling Honey, "I'm not marrying you. I'm marrying your mother." And he called off the wedding.

So early on, Bob and I decided we wouldn't let the problem of his mother's interfering happen to us. In Florida, we would be thousands of miles away and out of her control. So that was a major reason we decided to move there—along with the prospects for a new business opportunity in a growing state.

THE BEGINNING OF THE END

Ironically, though, the day that was to be the beginning of our hoped-for dream—the closing sale of the new villa we recently bought as our home—was the beginning of the end. That day, February 9th, changed everything, for that was the day of the accident.

It happened after I spent a wonderful weekend with Bob in Massachusetts.

I returned to Florida, and spent the next few days packing everything at my condo on the East Coast in Hillsboro Beach, so I would be ready to move everything to our new villa on the West Coast. Finally, by February 8th, when Bob flew in, everything was set.

That night, I drove to the airport and picked him up, and as I saw him standing there in this bright pink jacket, looking so good and vibrant, I realized how much I loved him all over again. After we stopped at the Cove for dinner and listened to a steel band playing as we dined, we returned to my now almost empty condo. All that was left was a big inflatable bed for our last night there. We collapsed on the bed around 10 p.m., because we had to be up early to meet the movers and go to the closing.

The next morning, we got up about 5:30 a.m. The last thing I remember is getting in the car, holding a bouquet of flowers on my lap. As we drove off I remember trying to look for the moving company because they were supposed to head off that morning with all of the things I had packed.

Then it all went blank, until I woke up a few weeks later in the hospital room, seeing flowers everywhere and wondering why there weren't any from Bob.

PART II:

THE LONG STRUGGLE

CHAPTER 3

●

THE STRUGGLE BACK

The accident changed everything. I woke up briefly the following day in a hospital and didn't know where I was. Mercifully, I didn't remember anything of the accident and was mostly drifting in and out of consciousness and incoherent for about a week. But perhaps that was for the best, because I don't think I could have handled it if I knew what had happened and I knew Bob was dead. It would be too painful, because he had been so much a part of my life. It was like we had become one. But now all that was gone. I probably would have died had I known, since I was hovering on the border between life and death anyway.

Besides all the physical damage, I had also suffered a severe brain injury, although the doctors who initially treated me weren't aware of this, and I wasn't in any condition to know anything. In fact, as I would eventually discover, this brain injury not only helped me forget the painful things, but many of the skills I once had. So I had a long slow recovery and healing process ahead—physical, neurological, and psychological. Then just as I started to recover a little, I found myself in a legal quagmire that took over 5 years to sort out.

It would be a long and difficult way back—and even now as I write, some lingering problems of all types remain. I still have both short and long-term memory loss; feel a little dizzy at times from vertigo; and the reoccurring pains in my neck and back are reminders of the accident. Otherwise, though, I feel I'm finally back. But in the first weeks after the accident, no one, least of all me, realized how long and difficult the road to recovery would be. Nor did I realize that the charmed and luxurious life I had lived would now be over, or that many of the people I had once trusted and loved would take advantage of me when I was most vulnerable. It would truly be a learning—and relearning—experience in all areas of my life.

THE FIRST DAYS BACK

In the first week after the accident, I was in a state of almost total blankness. It was like being in suspended animation, as I floated in and out of being conscious. Meanwhile, as I lay there, drifting in and out of consciousness, the doctors began the first of their examinations and operations. As I learned later, they noted I had experienced multiple injuries, including fracturing my spine and rupturing my spleen. As a result, after performing an emergency splenectomy to remove my spleen, they put me in a thick felt collar, called a Philadelphia collar. This was supposed to hold my neck in place to ease the tremendous pain I felt in my neck and keep me from moving my head, so the fractures would heal.

The way back began when I finally opened my eyes in the intensive care section of the Naples Community Hospital. This is where the doctors sent me to recover from the splenectomy and where I briefly gazed at my brother at the end of my bed looking at me with pain in his eyes. Then, I faded back into unconsciousness, and for the next week, I drifted in and out of this state, not really knowing what was happening around me.

Sometimes I'd wonder about Bob and where he was. At other times, I had a dim, barely conscious memory of being in or by a car, answering a question, and I vaguely recalled saying 'No, no, no, you have it wrong'. Or maybe I was just thinking that, but wasn't able to get the words out to explain that something I said was wrong. Afterwards I felt deeply frustrated that I couldn't get the words out or explain, and nobody could understand. I felt like I was in a fuzzy, almost blank box, where I couldn't move and could barely stay in touch with my own thoughts. They seemed to pass by in fragments, until I drifted back to sleep.

Then, finally, at the end of another week, when it appeared I would live, the doctors removed me from intensive care and transferred me to a private room. When I woke up there, I looked around my room, I saw flowers everywhere. They were all over the floor, on the shelves—and I kept wondering why there weren't any from Bob. I couldn't understand it.

Though I was somewhat more alert now, I was still very confused. My doctors, family members, and attorneys thought this confusion was only natural. But I began to get some foreboding warnings of the extensive brain injury I experienced as I began to become aware of memory lapses as people came to visit.

These visits began once I was out of intensive care and well enough to receive visitors, as family members and friends all around the country learned of the accident. Soon, there was an outpouring of flowers and phone calls from all over the United States, which pleased and amazed me. I felt so much love and support, and I'm sure that helped me heal, just knowing that these people who meant so much to me were behind me, rooting for me. At one point, there were so many flowers, that it was impossible to see the floor of the room. Just colorful sprays of petals everywhere.

I kept asking for Bob, each time my mother or a doctor walked in the room, knowing in the back of my mind something was terribly wrong. Though my mother and the doctors told me again and again, "He's dead, he's dead," as my mother explained later, I didn't want to believe it. Or I didn't want to accept it. In either case, I couldn't comprehend what they told me at the time, because of my head injury or because I wanted to deny what had happened. Thus, in those first days, I kept waiting for Bob, thinking he would be by my side any moment. It was too hard to believe he wasn't coming back.

The first indication that something was really wrong, though I didn't realize it then, occurred when a friend from New Hampshire, Rick Denver, arrived holding a bouquet of flowers. As he stood in the doorway, he commented: "How's your property in New Hampshire?" For a few moments, I looked at him blankly, because I had completely forgotten I owned a property in New Hampshire, due to the head injury. Finally I asked: "What property?" Without answering, Rick looked at me very strangely, and after we talked briefly, he wished me well in getting better and left. At the time, I didn't realize this forgetting was very significant. Over the next few days, as I recognized I had forgotten more and more things I thought I should know, I began to realize that something very serious had happened, and I felt my first taste of fear that mentally I wasn't all right.

A few days later, the first of a number of people began to take advantage of me, though I didn't realize it until much later. Even now, thinking back, it angers me to discover how the very people one trusts can take advantage when one is down. The first to do this to me were some of the emergency crew members. One of them came into my room soon after I was moved out of intensive care. I woke up hearing the door of my room opening or closing. As I looked up, moving my head slightly, I saw the helicopter pilot who had flown me on the emergency flight to the hospital. I didn't know who he was, since I wasn't conscious during this flight. But after I acknowledged him by slightly moving my head, he said: "Hi, I'm the helicopter pilot. I just stopped by to see how you were doing."

At the time, I just smiled slightly and went back to sleep because I was so drugged up. Now I think he came back to return my pocketbook which disappeared after the accident and was originally reported missing. Then it mysteriously showed up on my hospital room floor in a plastic bag a week after the accident—right around the time the helicopter pilot appeared. All my identification and credit cards were still in the bag when a nurse found it. But all the cash—about $5000—was gone, though the police said they found it strewn around the car after the accident and put it in my purse. Then, they put the pocketbook on the stretcher with me in the helicopter, and I believe he and others on the crew took it. My husband and I had this money in large bills, because we had to pay in either cash or a cashier's check at the closing, and we brought cash. Afterwards, the money was gone. Of course, there was no way to prove this, since all the missing money was cash. So I couldn't even make a claim that anything was missing. I barely understood what had happened myself.

THE RETURN OF REALITY

Over the following days, I gradually began to understand generally what had happened. I came to realize that there had been an accident and my husband was dead. This realization about Bob's death was especially painful, because besides feeling alone and recalling the glorious times with Bob I would never have again, I felt some guilt, too. That's because as memories of the past began to return, I recalled some of our problems, such as our inability to have kids and our separate business activities. This difficulty had led us to split up over the Christmas holidays for a month. Since we loved each other so much, we decided to try again; and Bob agreed to move to Florida, so we could spend more time together. That's why Bob had flown in, so we could move to our new home. As I thought about how Bob came to be in Florida that day, I began to wonder if I was therefore somehow to blame for his death and I felt tremendous pangs of guilt as I considered this possibility.

When I spoke to a psychiatrist in my first weeks in the hospital, Mary Ann Foures, she agreed that my feelings of self-blame contributed to my feelings of hopelessness and guilt, especially when I looked ahead to the future. As I did, I saw only a dark hole where so much hope for a new life with Bob had once been. Then, too, as she noted in her report, besides wanting to discuss my husband's death, I said I wished I was dead. That's why she recommended that I should participate in ongoing counseling for grief as well as physical rehabilitation. I said I would give anything to change places with my husband. Also, she noted that I had needed medication to go to sleep, didn't feel like eating, and had difficulty concentrating. Even more worrisome, she observed "signs of retrograde amnesia." What this meant is that I had lost the memory of about a third of my life.

Also, now that I understood my husband had died, I felt very sad and alone, because I couldn't be at the memorial service for Bob that was put on by my mother-in-law. I felt deeply disappointed that I wasn't there to say good-bye. When I told my mother and doctor about this, the doctor suggested I might do this myself in a cremation ceremony for my husband's body after I was out of the hospital. But did I want to do this? I wasn't sure and said I would think about it and decide what to do in a few days. I was uncertain because once I began thinking about formally acknowledging Bob's death, this triggered such painful feelings.

Unfortunately, as I later learned, these feelings contributed to making the effects of my brain injury even worse, because any kind of stress increases the trauma. But I had no way to control these feelings at the time, and no one recognized the seriousness of my brain injury back then. As a result, the trauma got worse, and it took years of work to overcome these feelings in therapy, besides going through all sorts of physical and neurological rehabilitation, before I could really begin to heal.

It was like I had ended up in the hospital like a broken jigsaw puzzle, and I needed help in putting all the broken pieces back together. Making the process even more difficult, no one knew exactly how large that jigsaw was supposed to be and what pieces were missing. And worse, as time went on, all sorts of outside forces began messing up the pieces and trying to take what was left away—like the lawyers who swooped in as the lawsuits began, along with the other people I trusted who exploited me and took what they could.

For now, however, it was time to start the healing process, as difficult as it proved to be.

GOING HOME

I didn't realize how difficult the healing process would be until I returned to stay with my parents at their vacation home in Naples, Florida. The final hospital report from the Naples Community Hospital when I left on February 21, made it sound like everything would be fine. It said I just had a few minor fractures, some "weakness" in my shoulder, and some "mild headaches" which I could treat with painkillers. Supposedly, I was "generally doing well." In fact, that's why the hospital discharged me to go home and advised me to take only a few follow-up precautions—continue wearing my Philadelphia collar for awhile, take some Percocet to relieve the pain in my neck and back, and take it easy with limited activity, as I felt comfortable. I could even eat a regular diet. Supposedly all would now be well.

Soon, the more I tried participating in everyday activities, the more I discovered I couldn't do. This is what often happens with a brain injury. On the surface, one seems fine, but then one discovers one can't do the everyday things one takes for granted. For example, I was used to doing a couple of things at a time, like reading a newspaper, making a phone call, and having an ordinary conversation simultaneously. But now I could barely do one thing at once.

It quickly became increasingly apparent that I couldn't simply go home and be okay. I had to overcome many serious and lingering problems first.

The growing realization began the first day. This occurred when I fell at home several times. I had fallen a few times in the hospital because my left side was completely numb and my left ankle kept collapsing. At home, this happened again. Repeatedly, I felt myself go off balance, and I couldn't hold myself up.

Soon I found I couldn't watch TV either. I tried watching it, laying my head on a pillow to rest it, because of the head injury. But once I did, I had double vision. I saw two images of the screen dance by in my head, so I couldn't follow anything. I couldn't read either because I was in such a daze.

Also, it was hard for me to speak clearly and for people to understand. I discovered this after several people who had called me at the hospital, though I don't remember them calling, told me they still couldn't understand what I was saying. They claimed I was still slurring my words badly. At other times, when I tried to talk more, I couldn't complete sentences. So the problem became even more obvious.

Worse, I acted like a zombie lost in a mystery world of my own, which is a blank to me now. At the time, I did this to retreat from all the agony and pain I had experienced and didn't want to face. Also, the brain injury contributed to this zombie state, because it erased so much of what had been me. For example, my mother later told me that for the first few days after I came home, I walked from room to room holding my tea cup. In each room, I put it down, picked it back up, and walked to another room, where I did exactly the same thing—over and over like a caged animal in the zoo. They do the same thing repeatedly, rotely, because they are imprisoned in a small caged world.

It was very unnerving for my mother and family to see me this way, not knowing if I would ever get better or not. I had once been so bright—I could do a dozen things at one time and hold the most complex financial real estate data in my mind. Now I seemed to know almost nothing, like my mind had been emptied out and gone blank.

I realized how bad the problem was a few days after I left the hospital, when my parents arranged to complete the closing on the villa, where Bob and I were going when the accident happened. They asked me to go with them, and I put on a dress and high heels to dress up as I usually did. Once I was dressed, however, it was a struggle to walk and stay upright. After we got to the closing, it was even worse. Since my left arm was in a sling due to my broken shoulder bone, I could barely sign my name, much less read or understand the closing statement. Previously, I had gone through this process at over 100 real estate closings before I moved to Florida. Now as I scrawled my name on the dotted line, I had no idea of what was going on. I just signed, since my parents and the attorney kept urging me to do so.

After the closing, I mostly spent my days lying down in bed or sitting around the house doing nothing, staring ahead blankly, because doing anything was such agony. Even getting in and out of bed was extremely painful. I nearly cried every time. Whenever I tried to go from a lying to a sitting position or vice versa, the room spun around me for two or three minutes. Each time I tried to stand, the left side of my body felt so weak, I was afraid of falling as I had many times before. Additionally, I still felt dazed and in shock from grief over what happened; and I could still barely talk and complete full sentences. It was like living in a world stuffed with cotton.

Then, too, I was so severely depressed, that I usually didn't want to get out of bed either. So I just lay there, though many times my mother came into my room and told me: "Deb, you gotta get up, you gotta get up." When she did, I would pull myself up for awhile and go sit in a wingback chair by the fireplace in the family room. Sometimes I sat there for hours, just staring at the wall. Mostly my mind remained blank or I began thinking about Bob, now that I recognized his death and felt so desolate and alone. I just wanted to retreat into nothingness, because reality was so painful.

Soon I felt increasing real pain, too. When I ran out of pain pills, I felt a strong stabbing pain in my neck that became excruciating. It had been masked by the pain killers before.

THE IDES OF MARCH: BACK TO SURGERY AND REHAB

After a month of these experiences, I told my parents and doctors that something was very very wrong. My local doctor, Dr. Kapp, doing follow-up tried to dissuade me, saying no further medical procedures were necessary. In turn, my parents kept saying, "Listen to the doctors. These things take time." But I was sure there was a serious problem and wanted another opinion. "I want to go to Boston," I told them, since that's where I knew several doctors.

So finally my mother agreed and took me back to Boston in mid-March to see a specialist. My mother gave me a few of her pain pills, so I could make the trip, and she pushed me in my wheel chair from plane to plane, until we arrived. A few days later, on March 21st, I met with a neurosurgeon, Dr. Cox, who looked shocked when he saw me. As I walked into his office, wearing my Philadelphia collar, he exclaimed: "My God, who put that collar on you? It's much too big. It's too loose to do much good." Dr. Cox also asked if anyone had done an MRI or Magnetic Resonance Image test of my neck. When I said "No", he was amazed, saying it was standard operating procedure in a spinal cord and head injury case. Then, he explained that the MRI is a test that involves taking a 360 degree X-Ray of the bone, so the doctor can see it as a 3-D picture and look at the bone from different points of view. "Then, it's possible to see if anything is broken or otherwise damaged." He arranged for me to have the test done immediately.

A week later, when the results came back, Dr. Cox told me, "We're going to have to go and fuse three vertebrae together, because that's what's causing the excruciating pain each time you move your neck."

So a week later, in early April, I went to another hospital—the Holy Family Hospital near Boston—for him to do the fusion surgery. He began by taking a rib out of my rib cage. Then he put the rib in my neck and fused that and several other bones in my neck together.

Unfortunately, when I went through this fusion procedure, the problem turned out to be even worse than they thought. As a result, instead of just fusing three discs together, he had to fuse five of them, so the operation lasted ten hours, instead of six as usual. At least I didn't feel it, since I was unconscious during the whole procedure. He and the assisting surgeon shaved the back of my head and sliced into my back to take out a rib. Afterwards, they put me in a halo—a large ugly metal contraption with long steel bars—which I would have to wear for three months. This device is commonly used in neck surgery cases to prevent a patient from moving his or her neck, so the injured bones can fuse.

As Dr. Cox put it on, while I was unconscious under heavy anesthesia, the halo made me look like I was wearing a heavy upside-down hoop around my head. Then, he attached this large wire hoop to a heavy plastic vest lined with a soft sheepskin which he strapped around me. It fit tight, like a straightjacket, and later, Dr. Cox explained that I could never remove this, not even to take a bath or shower, until the halo was taken off.

Finally, to secure the halo to my head, Dr. Cox tightened it with four set long screws that he inserted into holes he had drilled and bolted them to my head to keep the halo in place. Then, he attached four long posts that projected downward to the non-removable vest. Later when I woke up, I felt like I was trapped in a cage for the next three months—wearing this Frankenstein-like device that could never come off. I even had to learn to sleep in it sitting up, since I couldn't lie down, because flying flat would put too much pressure on the screws in the back of my head.

Though I felt like I was in traction with my halo on my head, I later learned how important this immobile device is in helping neck injury patients heal. It was invented by a man whose daughter broke her neck, and she was in a Stryker frame for several months. This is a large metal frame which holds a person in a rigid position on a bed, and he or she remains stationery until flipped from time to time to help with circulation and prevent bed sores. But since his daughter didn't move around at all during this time, all of her muscles atrophied. So he invented the halo, so a patient can get up and walk around.

That's what they did at my hospital. As soon as possible after surgery, the doctors get their patients up and walking so their muscles don't atrophy. Still, I found it really painful and uncomfortable to lug this 9-pound device around on my head. I felt like I was wearing a massive rock day after day. It was awkward and excruciating, but I knew I had to wear it to get well.

LEARNING TO FUNCTION AGAIN THROUGH REHAB

With this new contraption on my head, I was ready to take the next step in the healing process—going through rehabilitation—or "rehab" for short. I began this long slow process at the North East Rehabilitation Hospital in Salem, New Hampshire, where I spent the next two weeks learning how to walk again. I had to do this to be able to maneuver and balance myself with this heavy cage on my head. Otherwise, without this training, I could easily fall over.

It took awhile to adjust at this new hospital. At first, I was still full of painkillers. The doctors gave me Demerol, and for two or three days, I was so groggy and depressed, I couldn't get out of bed. To cheer me up, the hospital staff had another halo victim come in to see me and describe his own experiences, which is a common way of helping halo victims adjust to wearing this contraption—by learning how others do it. As the man walked in to my room, I was still lying groggily in bed, and my first reaction was: "He looks like some kind of space alien from another planet. I can't believe what he's got on his head." I didn't realize that I had a halo on, too, since I couldn't see myself. Then, the man explained that I was wearing one, and he wanted to reassure me that everything would be okay. "Just hang in there," he said. Then, after asking: "Any questions?", he answered my many questions about what it was like to wear the device. Later, when I felt better and could walk around myself, my nurse asked me to talk to other halo victims in the same way, and I did.

After about a week of lying in bed or sitting in a wheelchair I had healed enough from the fusion operation, so I could get up, and the nurses wanted me to do so as soon as possible. This way my muscles wouldn't atrophy. Also, the nurses felt that becoming active would help me feel less depressed and heal faster. First I had to show I could handle getting in and out of my wheelchair, as well as maneuvering it around. Then I had to show I could walk. Once I showed the nurses I could, they put me in an all-day physical therapy program, in which I had all sorts of exercises to do. Many of these were designed to make my legs and arms much stronger, so I could move around and function with the halo on, which is very difficult, because of the nine extra pounds on my head.

I literally had to learn to walk again and keep my balance wearing the halo. Besides the nurses, the hospital assigned several people to work with me, including a physical and occupational therapist, head injury specialist, neuropsychologist, and social worker. At various times, these different people guided me or observed me to make sure I could get up, walk around, and participate in various activities with the halo, without falling on my face.

For example, they watched me as I tried to walk to the bathroom unaided, wash myself, and eat a meal. I had to practice dressing, too, which was sometimes difficult, especially when I put on a skirt or slacks, because I had to bend over slightly. At first I had trouble putting on my shoes and socks, using an extra long shoehorn to help me. Again and again I practiced until I could. The nurses helped me grooming my hair, as well. The experience was like learning to walk and get dressed like when I was a baby.

Then, after mastering these basics, I had still other exercises to practice: walking up and down the stairs, moving from a sitting to a standing position, lying down and getting up, and getting from my bed to my wheelchair and back. I also had to show I could roll ahead and maneuver in my wheelchair.

Despite the hard work, this exercising was the first thing after the accident I actually liked doing. That's because before the accident I had always loved to exercise and had spent hours doing aerobics and weight lifting.

I had to learn how to take care of the pins in my head, too. My nurse explained that I not only had to clean them everyday so they wouldn't get infected, but I would have to have them tightened each week after I left the hospital by an orthopedic specialist. As I came to learn, this is a very painful procedure, but unfortunately, all halo wearers have to do this. It is necessary to have the screws tightened each week, because moving around tends to loosen them. At least I didn't have any complications with the halo, which happens to some wearers when the doctors are installing the screws and hit a nerve. Then, the wearer can potentially lose his hearing. Or the procedure can damage one's facial nerves, causing the eyes or face to droop. Fortunately, these problems didn't happen to me.

PARTICIPATING IN A REHAB PROGRAM

Once I was finally up and around, I found the hospital structured the program to keep everyone very busy—and to compensate for the memory deficits that often occur with head injury. This meant assigning me a full schedule and writing it down where I would see it repeatedly. I had a complete schedule from morning to night, and one of the hospital staffers wrote it down for me on a chalk board in my room. She listed everything I was supposed to do and where I was supposed to be at what time from 8 in the morning to 8 at night. And if I forgot where to go, I soon became conditioned to return to my room to look at the schedule.

This schedule included all sorts of things—physical education, physical therapy, occupational therapy, group therapy, and seeing one of my many doctors. They included a psychologist, psychiatrist, head injury doctor, spinal cord doctor, and my overall rehab doctor. Each day, I got up at 7:30 a.m. and found whatever I ordered for breakfast on a tray by my bed. Afterwards, starting at 8 a.m., my full schedule of activities began with only a brief break for lunch in my room. Then it was back to classes or examinations, until about five or six with a break for dinner. By eight, I was dead tired and ready for bed. Nine was about the latest I stayed up.

With all these activities, I didn't have time to think about much of anything. And if I found myself wandering through the hospital wondering where I was supposed to be, I would go back to my room and check the chalk board. It was a simple thing to remember, and after a few reminders from the nurses, I learned to remember to go there.

Soon my various doctors designed a specific rehab program for me. They used tests to decide what I needed, just like they do in examining and assessing every brain injury patient to create a personalized program. I started off by seeing a head injury doctor who determined the physical damage and deficits I had suffered. Afterwards, he sent me to a psychologist who gave me a neurological and psychological exam and sent the results back to the head injury doctor. Then, together, they came up with a plan of activities to help correct the deficits they found. Typically, as with most brain injury patients, this meant giving me activities to improve my memory and concentration.

Also, in rehab, as with many patients, they gave me additional exercises to help me become stronger physically through physical therapy, using upper body and leg movements to further strengthen my body. They tried to get me ready to go home and do things on my own, too. They wanted to make sure, for example, that I could cook a dinner, bathe, and even take my medication properly.

As I worked with these exercises, I soon started seeing gaps in what I could do and had to find ways to compensate, which is a way that brain injury patients adjust. For example, I had a real problem taking too much or too little medication, because I couldn't remember when I took something and when I didn't. So the hospital staffers conditioned me to make a list every day of what medicines I had to take. Then, each time I took anything, I checked it off on the list. I remembered to use this list, because I learned to keep it in the bathroom, where I saw it many times each day.

I also had to learn how to cook a meal again. The hospital had a small kitchen, and the physical therapist showed me how to do things I had once done automatically but had to relearn. For example, once when I made brownies, she gave me a box of mix to start with, and after I poured in some water, she showed me how to stir the mixture so it was smooth. Next, she showed me how to put the pan in the oven and take it out of the oven without turning it over and dropping the brownies on the floor. We normally take such things for granted. I was like a child learning these very basic things again, as well as how to adjust my movements to compensate for the halo.

I even had trouble remembering what to do when if there were more than two or three steps to a task, so I learned to compensate by writing down each of the steps on a sheet of paper or on a set of post-it notes. I discovered this in the hospital, and later, after I left the hospital, when I tried to cook my first complete meal at home about a month later, I had to write and put a post-it note on every pan explaining what to do when. Then it took me three to four hours to cook the dinner, because I had so many post-its to read. I had one note that said, at 6:25 p.m., turn on the oven to 350 degrees; at 7 p.m., turn the oven on to medium; at 7:30 p.m. add some water, and so on. I needed all this detail to remember what to do. Otherwise, I couldn't have made the dinner.

Then, I began an occupational therapy program to work on discovering what I could and couldn't do to help me go back to work. Could I go back to running my own business again? That was the big question. From time to time, when I was in the hospital in Naples, I had called to find out what was going on at the Mail Boxes franchise I owned, while others were taking care of sales and operations. I had also asked my father about the status of some of my real estate properties, which he was handling. But even though I had asked, in reality, I understood little of what people were telling me. Now as I continued occupational therapy in rehab, it was becoming more and more obvious that I couldn't run my businesses and had to start thinking about doing something else.

I discovered this because in occupational therapy, the therapist gives the patient interest and skill tests to help determine what he or she likes and can do to suggest an appropriate direction for future work. In my case, however, it was tough to know what I should do, because I had my own business. However, after testing me and talking to my doctors, my therapist decided I couldn't handle my own business again. So instead, she tried to show me what I might do in working for someone else. I had never done that in my life before, so it was hard to think about doing this now. Since the tests I took showed I had a very strong love for the arts, she tried to direct me towards getting into something artistic, like photography.

She also sent me to a neuropsychologist, Dr. Glenn Higgins, who had me take all sorts of neurological and psychological exams to determine what skills I had left. Some of these tests were designed to identify the parts of the brain that were damaged by testing how well I performed various functions. These tests are based on the premise that when you can't do something or can't do it well, that's a sign the part of the brain which controls that function is damaged.

For example, to test my memory, Higgins showed me a picture of something for several seconds, then took it away. Afterwards, I had to redraw the picture as best I could. In another test, he gave me a box of blocks of two different colors—some were all red, some all white. Then, he took the blocks out of the box and threw them on a table, instructing me to put them together to make a picture with them. In a third test, he gave me a board with blocks in three different shapes—a star, a circle, and a square. Then, after blindfolding me, he removed the blocks leaving a space on the board, and I had to put the shapes back in the appropriate place, using just my hands.

Afterwards, he analyzed the results of these tests to determine what parts of my brain had been damaged. He used these very specific tests which can even pinpoint exactly what area of the brain was injured and the effects of that injury. For example, in my case, my neuro-psych exam showed I scored much higher in one area of the test than anyone my therapist had tested in this area. It also indicated that I had a much better retention rate if I read something than if I talked about it. The reason I did so well is because my reasoning ability, which was always high, was never damaged. This ability is located in the forehead area, and there was no injury there. By contrast, the ability to remember is located on the top of the head, which is where I was affected by the accident. So that's why my memory was so bad.

I felt some comfort in realizing my situation could have been even worse, after I shared a room for a time with a woman who had been in a snowmobile accident. In the course of sharing about what we each lost and our hopes for the future, I learned she was happily married and had a child, but she would never walk again. Though I felt it was worse for me in some ways, because I had lost my husband, at least I could walk, in spite of my spinal cord and head injury.

Meanwhile, as I worked on getting better through rehab, my medical records, which would become central to a dispute between my insurance companies, lawyers, and mother-in-law, accumulated. In time, they came to be studied and fought over to determine who caused the accident. Initially, though, I was unaware of any of this. I was still barely aware of anything except the physical, emotional, and mental pain I experienced everyday, and I was not yet fully aware of the seriousness of the brain injury I suffered.

However, my doctors' reports about my physical condition hinted at this in noting headaches and memory and attention problems. For example, back in mid-March, after I first met with my a neurosurgeon, Dr. Cox, he had noted I still had a post concussive syndrome, which included "short term memory difficulties, easy fatigability, and headaches." Also, though the accident had occurred over six weeks earlier, he warned that my brain could still be swelling from the trauma of the injury—a problem many accident patients and their families often aren't aware of. They only realize this swelling has happened much later, weeks after the physical healing seems well under way, when they discover continuing deficits in certain areas of activity. Then, when I saw him again in April, Dr. Cox felt I should get further counseling and supportive care, because I still felt so depressed about losing Bob.

Part of the problem was that on top of the physical pain, I began to experience increasing psychological and psychic pain as the protective blankness that first surrounded me wore off. As it lifted, like a dissipating fog, it left me with haunting memories, fears of the future, and guilt about what happened. I kept wondering: "Was the accident some kind of punishment?...Did I do something wrong to cause this?" Also, I began to recall some hints of problems that disrupted my glowing recollections of my relationship with Bob. It was painful to acknowledge these returning memories, and it made me feel more at fault and guiltier for thinking such negative thoughts about Bob.

I was glad I could meet with a psychology consultant, Dr. Robert A. Moverman, as part of my rehab to discuss these concerns. I started seeing him in late April 1989. He seemed so sympathetic and supportive, as I poured out my feelings and described past experiences and family relationships that might affect how I was feeling now. He told me the goal of our sessions was to try to understand how I felt about what happened, and use this understanding to help me heal.

One contributing factor to my feelings of guilt and depression that soon came to the surface was that my father was very distant. Another possible factor was that my first husband had been both physically and verbally abusive to me, slapping me around and yelling at me to put me down. Then, too, I had been experiencing some problems at times with Bob. While he was much kinder and concerned about me than my first husband, there were some conflicts under the surface of our many romantic times together. I had tried to deny their importance at the time, but now, in therapy, they began to come to the surface.

For one thing, we discovered we couldn't have our own children together. Secondly, I always had a strong streak of independence and I wanted to work hard in my own business to get ahead, so we had little time together. This was part of the reason we had separated for several weeks after the Christmas holidays before we tried to reconcile by moving into a new home together in Florida. As these issues became clearer and clearer in therapy, my hope that our move was to be a new beginning made it even harder for me to adjust to the trauma of the accident and the loss. Although I told Moverman I saw myself as something of a "survivor," I felt the loss of my husband so intensely, because this was the first time in my life that anyone close to me had passed away. And since I had been a "workaholic," who had tried to do too much work over the past year, not having any work now left me feeling a vast emptiness.

Also, as the reality of what I lost sank in, I began to ask those "Why?" questions more and more, which brought even more pain. These questions came up now, because I didn't have the ability or time to think about my physical condition or loss of my husband in those first weeks. But now it began to hit me even more, and I felt really guilty and scared. I wondered if perhaps I was being punished because I had been impatient and intolerant towards Bob. Or was this accident a punishment, because I was to intent on building my business and didn't think enough about Bob? Worse, with Bob gone, I wasn't sure if I could survive. Even though I had once told Dr. Moverman I was a survivor, the future loomed like a big black hole, and I felt very afraid. It helped me to stay busy with the many rehabilitation exercises the hospital put me through and to pray. Also, since I have always been a fighter, that helped, too.

However, since I was used to being independent, it disturbed me that I now had to be dependent on others for everything. There were so many things I had I once taken for granted doing, but now I had to have others do them for me—everything from driving to going to doctor's appointments to washing my hair. Also, I didn't like people worrying about me, so that weighed on my mind, too. I felt so powerless, so desperate. Everything seemed so hopeless and bleak, and I felt myself somehow to blame or maybe being punished, because of what had happened.

Dr. Moverman was the first person I had ever talked to about such things, because I wasn't used to letting my feelings out to someone else. But I felt such a desperate need to talk to someone that I opened up to him very quickly, and within a few minutes of first speaking to him, I began crying about my despair. As I told him, it was so difficult to realize that I was getting better, but I could never return to my former married life...or to the work I had known and loved. It was so hard not to be the independent person I had once been. Bob, the whole world I had known, was dead.

That's why, I told him at one session that I didn't care whether I was alive or dead anymore myself. Yet, I didn't feel any desire to voluntarily end my life due to my religious beliefs. I knew I could never go to heaven, never have a chance to see Bob or my family again if I did.

Then, in April, as I continued to adjust well physically, I continued to discover even more hidden damages due to the brain injury. They were so difficult for others to spot because in many respects I seemed to be functioning normally. In other areas, lapses turned up—which is often the case in a head injury, since the damage may affect different parts of the brain that control different functions. As a result, while certain functions might be damaged, others might seem perfectly fine, camouflaging the effects of the injury. However, when one tries to do something and finds one can't, these lapses appear. This is why when one is first recovering from a serious injury, one might not be aware of such changes, because one is not engaging in activities that challenge one's mental functioning. But once the challenges begin, the damage is revealed.

As I continued to meet with staff neuropsychologist, Dr. Higgins, he noticed some of these things—this mixture of loss and apparently normal functioning—as he put me through still more tests to determine what I could or couldn't do. This time, the tests including recalling a series of digits he had just showed me from memory, repeating a series of phrases after he said them, and reading a paragraph and describing what it meant. He also asked me to remember lists of items after some time had passed.

The results showed a common mixed pattern of normal and abnormal functioning for brain injury patients. In my case, as he reported in his notes, I now was able to actively recall the events of the day prior to the accident, but virtually none of the events of the following weeks. Thereafter, my memory was spotty, though gradually but slowly improving in recent weeks. In particular, I had persisting difficulty in retrieving previously and recently learned information, including names, and I still had difficulty concentrating, along with recurring headaches. Yet on the surface, he found me "alert, oriented, fluent, and articulate". And emotionally I seemed normal—or had "normal affect" as he put it. Plus other test scores seemed normal, such as my ability to remember 5-7 digits in reverse or forward order, sustain focused attention, change subjects readily, speak in a coherent and well-organized way, and understand what I heard. I also gave him a seemingly normal reading and writing sample, and was able to put blocks together according to the patterns on simple diagrams.

However, his tests missed so much, as often happens when brain injury patients are tested, because these tests weren't able to test for more complex reasoning and responding, as is needed in dealing with everyday business matters. They only test relatively simple cognitive awareness and response. As a result, even the doctors weren't aware yet of the extent of my brain injury, and Dr. Higgin's favorable prognosis was overly optimistic. It would take much longer than anyone imagined for me to return to normal.

CHAPTER 4

•

THE BEGINNING OF THE END

A WARNING OF THINGS TO COME

I didn't realize how long it would take my life to return to normal, because now I began to feel increasingly hopeful, as did my mother and father who came to visit frequently. I really loved seeing them, along with my long-time friends who stopped by. It made me feel I had a whole team of continuing supporters.

Then, like an ominous warning of the future, my mother brought what looked like an ordinary get-well card to the rehab hospital soon after I was admitted. It was enclosed in a plain white envelope with my name handwritten outside, and my mother thought the card would help cheer me up—like any message of good wishes from a friend.

When I opened it, I nearly went into shock at first, and then went into the deepest depression. It was a warning from my mother-in-law—I'll call her Shirley Raymond, who wrote me in essence: 'You leave my son's estate alone. Don't you dare give anything away.' Her language on the surface sounded sweet and diplomatic, phrasing her threats in dulcet tones like: "We would appreciate it if..." instead of saying "Don't do this". But I could see through the honey. I saw the sword she was sharpening underneath for attack, especially when she asked me about my prenuptial agreement with Bob and his possessions. Or as she so sweetly put it:

> We have many unanswered questions in regards to Bob's death. We would prefer to not have to bother you about these things and do realize how painful it is for you. It is also very painful for

us. Bob told us about a prenuptial agreement. Would you please send us a copy of this?

When Bob moved out of your home he brought his belongings into an apartment...We understand that since Bob's death, all of these things were brought back to your house...We would appreciate it if you would please consult us before giving away any of his things as we feel Bob would want us to help make decisions. We are so sorry that this has happened to you and all of us, but we feel that we should, and can, all work together on this in an amicable way.

I couldn't believe the demands she was making, such as when she complained that I had given Bob's diamond ring to his brother, when I had given Bob this ring myself when we were together over Christmas. Then, when his brother came to see me in the hospital right after the accident, I had given him the ring as a gift, telling him: "I really think Bob would like you to have this." I thought this because he was Bob's only brother, and the ring was my gift to Bob in the first place. So I felt Shirley's request for the ring and her other demands were not only petty, but wrong. Plus, I thought it was in such bad taste to send such a letter now, while I was still in the rehab hospital recovering from surgery!

Her letter seemed so outrageous, and that's when I realized I was going to have real problems with her, especially since she asked for the prenuptial agreement. All at once, I was certain that this was a prelude for her to try to get her hands on things that belonged to me.

Meanwhile, as I read this and grew depressed, my mother began to sob herself, saying she felt terrible for giving me the letter, and I began shaking and crying hysterically too. After all the physical pain I had experienced, plus the tremendous grief at losing Bob, this letter was so upsetting. I felt devastated and very afraid.

Soon, I began to find I had good reason to be, since this was just the beginning of a tortuous legal web Shirley began, which started with her trying to enforce the prenuptial agreement I signed in which I waived any right to Bob's estate. Then, she sought to get other settlement funds and property from me. I couldn't understand the legal and financial ramifications at the time, but I had this panicky feeling of danger lying ahead, that added to the stress and pain I was already feeling, just trying to physically recover from my injuries and brain damage.

MEMORIES

Over the next few days, the letter weighed on my mind more and more, because it brought back memories of times when Shirley showed how much she disliked me. So I became increasingly worried and disturbed about what she might do next and how difficult she might make the road ahead for me. Until now, the hospital had kept me very busy, with something different scheduled for each hour from physical rehab to occupational therapy or group therapy. But now, her letter and fears about what she might do kept running through my mind. She had already done so many terrible things, I remembered. Now, I felt, things would get even worse.

I was especially worried as I remembered the warnings about Shirley that began when I first met Bob. Besides recalling his warning: "Stay away from my mother, she's no good," I remembered what happened at the rehearsal a week before the wedding. We were planning to have the wedding ceremony in a little Catholic church, and I wanted my mother to light one candle, the Raymond family to light another, and Bob and I would light a third. I wanted to do this, because the Church sees lighting the candles as a symbolic way of joining the two families, and I thought this candle lighting would be a nice symbol of our new togetherness.

When Bob told Shirley about my idea, she was so angry we were marrying in the Catholic church, outside her own faith, she claimed she couldn't walk up the stairs of the church because of the limp she still had from polio as a child. But there were no stairs at this church, and she had previously climbed a couple of hundred stairs at a wine tasting at a Napa Valley winery a few days before the rehearsal.

Her lie seemed like one more indication of how angry she was at me because Bob converted to Catholicism, and because she lost control of him, once Bob stood up to her and married who he wanted.

So I had premonitions that Shirley would try to hurt me, and eventually she could because of the prenuptial agreement I signed. When I signed it, I thought I was doing it for Bob, because he wanted to show me he was marrying me for love, not money, because at the time, I was the one who had more property and money. He wanted to show me he was different from my first husband, who had married me for money, and sexually and mentally abused me. This way, he said, I could be sure if anything happened in our relationship that he would give up any claims to my estate. Though I didn't want the prenuptial myself because I trusted Bob completely and felt the agreement showed a lack of trust, I finally went along with him. Unfortunately the agreement was written the same way for both of us, so I similarly agreed to waive any claim to his estate. It wasn't very much when he died, besides the Rolex watch I gave him as a wedding gift, he just owned some sentimental things from his grandfather. He had so little because he put most of his current earnings into everyday expenses, like the glamourous vacations we took. While there was little in the estate, when I waived any right to it, I also waived any say over who would be the administrator of his estate. And that's what gave Shirley the ability to control the estate, and later sue me on its behalf.

Thus, her letter with its reference to the prenuptial really frightened me. It was like a premonition of things to come, though I didn't know what. I just knew it meant bad news.

As a result, even before I got out of the hospital, I decided to speak with my attorney who immediately advised me not to have any more contact or correspondence with anyone from the Raymond family. So I immediately severed ties with everyone in the family. From now on, any contact would be through my attorney. It was the beginning of a growing legal-insurance nightmare.

OUT IN THE REAL WORLD: DOCTORS AND FRIENDS

Meanwhile, while this legal-insurance nightmare began brewing, my life after I got out of the rehab hospital in April was one of seeing doctors daily for the next several months and then of seeing them several times a week for the next several years. I spent hours each day seeing them as an outpatient, since I couldn't simply go home and live alone in an ordinary independent way, due to the effects of the head injury and the halo. I couldn't even take a normal shower because of the halo. Instead, the hospital had to send someone over to rebuild the shower so I could shower from the waist down. Also, I had to learn a special way to wash my head. I had to bend over, put the whole halo apparatus in the tub, and have someone else wash my hair.

Then, too, I had to have my house modified in certain ways, and I needed daily help from family members and others who came over to help. Even sleeping involved many changes. For example, the hospital sent over a hospital bed, which I put in the family room. It was motorized so it could be placed in a raised position so I could sleep sitting up, since I couldn't lie down due to the big screws in the back of the halo. I also had to have someone come over each day to help me take care of and clean the pins in my head and the vest I was wearing. So my mother or the next door neighbor came over daily to help.

This pin care was very important, because as the nurses at the hospital instructed, I had to have the pins cleaned everyday with a solvent, so they wouldn't get dirty and cause an infection, which can create permanent damage. For instance, I recalled that when I was in the rehab hospital, I saw a man who didn't clean his, and he had scars on his forehead the size of a quarter.

It was very hard to do all these things, and without the busy hospital schedule that kept me from thinking, the agony of what happened hit me over the next few weeks. Usually, I woke up pretty groggy in the morning, because I had to take Halcion, a sedative, to help me sleep sitting up with the halo. Then, I normally went out on the deck and tried to stay out of the sun, because if the halo got too hot, it would make the screws in my head hot, and the pain was excruciating.

While sitting there, now that life was quiet again, I was alone with my thoughts, which were so bleak and painful. As a result, I would sit there crying all day, while still in a state of blankness, because I didn't want to believe Bob was dead. It was so hard to accept. So I kept pushing that realization away each time it came back, like a persistent ghost.

Day after day went on like this, and usually, the height of my day was when my mother or the neighbor came over to care for the pins, because I couldn't do anything else but just sit there.

The worst day was when I had to go to an orthopedic specialist once a week, so he could tighten the screws. It was an incredibly painful experience, because when he tightened the screws, I heard each one going into the bone in my head, and the pain shot through my head like an explosion. Plus the pressure of the tightening was so great, it felt like a vise clamped around my head and closing down with each turn of the pliers.

Afterwards, I couldn't even look at any bright light for awhile, because it was so intensely painful, causing excruciating headaches. So I had to put on sunglasses to shade out the light. I also couldn't listen to most sounds either. Everything sounded so loud, it was like a big rumbling noise all around me. And when the phone rang, the sound pierced through me like a gun blast.

Thus, when the tightening was over, I immediately returned home, and once inside, I turned off the lights, phone, and answering machine. Then, I had to sit down and unwind for several hours, just to recover from the trauma of this weekly torture.

At least, despite the sadness, pain and doctors over the next few months, my friends and family rallied around. They provided me with a supportive anchor, against the growing storm from my mother-in-law and lawyers.

They did so much. For example, I couldn't cook meals at first, so my Mom brought some food over, and a few friends often stopped by to cook me dinner. I felt they were really there for me, and that helped me start to come around.

I remember the first meal I cooked at the beginning of May. Just as I had learned to do in cooking class in rehab, I put post-it notes all over the kitchen to tell me what to do, because without them, I didn't know what to turn on when, and I didn't know what ingredients to put in next. So I would forget and get confused.

After I finally cooked the meal with the help of these notes, I called one of my girlfriends, excited that I had done it, and she said kiddingly, "I should own stock in post-it notes." I laughed—perhaps for the first time since the accident. I felt like things might be finally turning around.

Most of the time, though, I felt a lot of frustration and anger, so my formerly happy-go-lucky personality changed — a change that lasted for the next few years until the final settlement in 1993. I became quite irritable, which I almost never used to be, and I had lots of headaches. After my doctor gave me an antidepressant and a medication for the headaches, this led me to gain weight, which was very frustrating. Before the accident, I had gotten in shape by working out in an aerobics class after battling to keep my weight down all my life, so I was the trimmest and fittest I had ever been before the crash, which is why, my doctors told me, I probably survived. But now it was frustrating to see all of this trimness and fitness go.

Also, in these first few months after I got out of the rehab hospital, I didn't feel like going anywhere, because I was very tired most of the time. So mostly, family members and friends came over to see me.

That's when I became more and more aware of how my mental abilities had declined. This occurred because as we talked, I began discovering how I had forgotten some things, but not others. Also, I found I was still having problems with my memory and my speech. I didn't recognize this at first, because I had not started to speak much before. Now as I spoke more, people began to point out the lapses.

For example, a very close friend came over and we had what I thought was a perfectly normal conversation. But later, he told me that many times while I was talking to him normally, I would suddenly stop halfway through a sentence and start another sentence. As a result, he couldn't follow what I was saying, though he said nothing, at the time, because he didn't want to hurt my feelings. Now I think it was probably good he didn't tell me, because I wouldn't have understood. I probably would have just gotten upset and frustrated.

At least, through this terrible time, my friends continued to stick by me and came to see me regularly—every few days or so. I don't think I could have made it without their support, although it was scary for them, as well as for my family, because the doctors were now telling them: "We don't know if she's going to get better." And my mother was scared she would have to take care of me the rest of my life.

Yet, while I had trouble remembering and speaking coherently, at least I understood what people told me, though usually I wouldn't remember what they said later. But I really appreciated it when they shared their good news with me. It made me feel happy for them, and I felt I was still a participant in their lives. That's why what they told me didn't make me feel regret for where I was now; though ironically, my friends sometimes hesitated to tell me things, fearing they would trigger regretful memories. This happened, for example, when my best friend, who had been the maid of honor at my wedding, got engaged soon after the accident. When she came to the house to visit, she was afraid to tell me about her engagement, thinking I might resent it or feel bad. When she finally told me, I was thrilled for her and told her so.

Some of my friends also helped by doing many things for me which I couldn't do myself. For instance, one friend had a house-cleaning business, and after she stopped by and saw that my house was filthy, because I couldn't clean it myself, she came over one Sunday and cleaned the whole house for me. Other friends did errands for me or drove me to my endless doctor appointments. So they were there when I needed them, and their support really helped me feel better and want to struggle even harder to get well.

KEEPING A DIARY

I also began to keep a diary, which helped me pay more attention to what I was experiencing now, as well as work through the memories of the past that continued to haunt me, and think about the "What if?" and "Why didn't I?" questions that still bothered me. Keeping the diary also helped me better focus and clarify my thoughts, which contributed to the healing process, too.

I started keeping the diary in the beginning of May, about three months after the accident. Looking back now, it expressed the continual ups and downs that commonly affect brain injury patients— one day you note a little progress; then you feel discouraged; then you try to work hard to progress again; feel discouraged some more; then go on trying and hoping. For example, here's what I wrote that first week in May.

May 1, 1989:

I keep thinking about what I was doing the same time last year. Everything seemed so perfect then. I wish I could have those times back, though I know I can't.

May 2, 1989:

I know it's going to be a long day—an appointment with orthopedist Jim Brooks, the screw tightener, my weekly nightmare. It hurts so much. Then, I'll be seeing Dr. Cox, who did the neck surgery. He wants to check on the pain and weakness I experienced in my arms last week. I don't mind talking to him. But I don't want to talk to anyone else after seeing the screw tightener. So I'll just turn the answering machine on instead.

May 3, 1989:

Once again, I woke up hoping that today would be a new day—that all this suffering would be over. But unfortunately, once again, I wasn't right. How much longer should or can I endure this? The pain in my head is indescribable and always with me. I don't feel like eating, which may be good for my waist line, but not for my health. The halo has only been on about two weeks—at least 2 months more to go. Can I stand it?

May 4, 1989:

I woke up with a headache this morning, feeling pain in my ears, over my eyes, on the side of my head. Then, I went to the eye doctor to see his prognosis. At least, my friends are rallying around me. Dave called from California to express his sympathy, and several other friends sent a beautiful flower arrangement. It was so nice of them; it gives me hope.

May 5, 1989:

Today I finally made my first excursion out of the house to Natalie's restaurant. Another old friend Tony came by and took me. As we were eating, suddenly Bob's and my wedding song came on the radio, and I broke out crying. But I told Tony to keep on talking, and I managed to compose myself. Other than that, it was fun going out to the restaurant, and afterwards we returned home and watched a video, MIDNIGHT RUN. One of the first high spots, through all the pain.

May 6, 1989:

Two old friends came over today—Libby and Marilyn. It's nice to have such good friends. But my eyes have been really sensitive to the light today, and the pain in my neck hurts so much. I can't wait to fall asleep to escape the pain.

May 7, 1989:

Today would have been Bob's and my first anniversary. It's so emotional and painful to think of, but after so many good friends came by and called, that helped to make me feel okay, even lucky. What a lot of good friends I have. Lois, Susan, and Nicole stopped by at 5 for a glass of wine. Then Ron, Rocky, Lennie, and Kris made a great dinner—garlic chicken with asparagus and chocolate cheesecake. It's almost starting to feel like old times again. Seeing or speaking to all of my dearest friends makes me feel I'm a fortunate person after all. The pain is actually becoming liveable, and I'm looking forward to tomorrow.

May 8, 1989:

Today I had to go see the "maintenance man", Jim Brooks, who tightens the screws in my skull. I returned home with my head pounding, but at least I'm feeling more positive that it will get better. I just think every day is one day less that I will have this pain.

* * * * * * *

So by early May, things seemed to be finally turning around. But that's before the problems with the lawyers, insurance companies, and my mother-in-law began—the coming storm that hit me totally unprepared.

CHAPTER 5

•

THE ULTIMATE BETRAYAL

DISCOVERY AND GUILT

The first big blow came on the afternoon of May 10th when I learned that the accident was caused by Bob. It came as a tremendous shock, for now, besides just trying to recover from my injuries, I felt an overwhelming sense of guilt that I was at fault, too, even though I wasn't driving.

I felt terrible, because I realized if we had been going at a lower rate of speed, the accident might not have happened, and Bob would have survived. Even though my mother and attorney tried to break the news to me very gently when they called, I still took it hard. It wasn't easy to accept, knowing that none of this had to happen.

I blamed myself for not telling Bob to slow down. If I had told him, he would be alive today. I felt so guilty because I could have changed things. It took a long time, before I could finally let go of that guilt and tell myself: "You've got to stop running yourself into the ground with guilt over this and get on with your life." Back then, I felt so weighted down with everything, including my own injuries, I couldn't let go.

Then, on top of feeling guilty, I began to step into a legal quagmire that would engulf my life for the next five years. After the earlier warnings from my mother-in-law, the first real threat came from the report of Donald F. Avila, a tire expert at Scientific Tire Systems in Ohio, who discussed whether the tire which blew out was to blame for the accident. If it was, this meant the manufacturer was at fault, and I could feel less responsible, because then an outsider, not me or Bob, was to blame. Additionally, the manufacturer would be responsible for all the damages from the accident.

Unfortunately, Avila reported the situation was just the opposite. There appeared to be no way to blame the manufacturer, because Bob was simply going too fast. Avila put his explanation in the scientific language of detailed computations of tire size, strength, wheel weight dimensions, and tear measurements. Basically he firmly concluded that the tire was cut by something on the road that caused it to lose air, and then it exploded because of Bob's high speed. Or as he somberly put it:

> It is our opinion that the tire does not contain any defects in workmanship or materials... Operating the tire at high speeds, with an ever increasing loss of air, allowed the tire to break apart into its present condition... There are no signs whatsoever of any manufacturing irregularities.

His conclusion hit me like a heavy hammer. So Bob was clearly to blame, and perhaps indirectly, I was, too, for not telling Bob to slow down.

LITTLE BY LITTLE

Still, while I felt wracked by guilt and struggled with trying to put these feelings aside, at least my physical and mental condition gradually improved, as I recorded in my diaries over the next few days.

Thursday, May 11, 1989:

It was pouring rain today—a reminder that I still have far to go, since the rain contributes to the aches and pains. So my head is aching, and the shoulder I broke is bothering me. The pain is making me remember the accident again, too. I keep remembering how Bob was driving fast. He always drove that way, and perhaps I could have or should have stopped him. But I didn't. Yet I can't change the past now. I can't change what's over, though it's upsetting to think about.

PREPARING FOR BATTLE

Meanwhile, as I got better physically and mentally, the coming legal storm was building, as I started reporting what happened to the lawyers and insurance companies, and my mother-in-law's questions about the accident became more insistent.

Her questions to me started on May 11th when my Florida attorney and long-time family friend, Mark Bidner, who had been handling some of my personal and business dealings, asked me about the accident and my injuries. Though I didn't have the ability to think about these questions until now, some of my lawyers had already laid the legal groundwork several months before by writing for reports, documents, and bills to show what happened and the costs. It was as if they were operating in a parallel legal world of activities, while I was living in a mostly shrunken world of medical procedures, as the visits to doctors took over most of my life.

Bidner began the legal process about a week after the accident in mid-February when he referred my parents to the Miami law firm of Kaplan and Freedman. He recommended that this firm do most of the work on the accident, since they specialized in personal injury cases, while he continued handling my personal and business affairs.

Paul Freedman, who became the lead attorney on my personal injury claim, started working on the case by collecting various reports of what happened, such as the Traffic Accident Report by the police. Additionally, he was the one who hired tire expert Don Avila to learn if there was anything wrong with the tires. He filed papers to get back my totaled Mercedes to check out if there was anything mechanically wrong with the car. And he worked out arrangements with the agency that insured the car, Liberty Mutual, to share the expenses of having experts examine and reconstruct what happened. This way, he and the insurers could appropriately assign blame and settle these losses. So far, it seemed like just another routine case.

Then, as February, March and April wore on, still more records and authorizations were needed, such as a photocopy of the auto insurance policy, the records of the Mercedes Benz dealer, and additional repair slips and authorizations for medical information. Then, at the end of March and early April, my health carrier Blue Cross and Blue Shield began seeking records too, while Freedman began collecting reports and bills from the many hospitals and doctors I was visiting. Plus now he wanted a copy of Bob's death certificate and the funeral bill.

I was still largely in a fog over these details, since I was concentrating on starting my outpatient rehab program. But Freedman and the insurers went on sending out their many record requests, and I went along with them, unable to do much else at the time. I had to assume Freedman knew what he was doing, since certainly I did not.

By early May, his efforts seemed promising. Some of the records started coming in, and Freedman reported his first success—a small reimbursement from Liberty Mutual for about $6000 for my medical expenses right after the accident in Florida.

WEEKS OF UPS AND DOWNS

Meanwhile, I continued to focus on getting better, and in the next weeks, I mostly experienced progress, despite some bad days and frustrations. A key reason was the continuing strong support of my family and friends. They helped motivate me to get better. By mid-May, I even felt well enough to help plan the memorial service for Bob later that month. As I wrote in my diaries that May:

Friday, May 12, 1989

Larry and Marilyn came over today with a quiche, and Lois made a great dinner. I'm so lucky to have such friends. I saw my psychologist Dr. Golub today, too, who really has helped. We discussed Bob's service, and I feel ready to start planning for it now. As I told Dr. Golub, before I wouldn't have been strong enough to go out in a boat in my halo. But now I had built my strength up, so I could.

Saturday, May 13, 1989

I woke up to the rain, and boy did I feel it in the sharp pain in my left side of my head and ears. It always seems to hurt so much more when it rains.

I'm going to start concentrating on improving my writing and reading. I can see now how I have certain shortfalls in my brain, and I've got to start learning how to do things I used to know how to do again. I've got to start working on my speech, too. I want to get on the waiting list for the Northeast Rehabilitation Hospital speech therapist, so I can start as soon as possible.

At least I'm getting back my sense of enjoyment of life again. I'm beginning to enjoy my time alone, and that's some progress.

Monday, May 15, 1989

Today, I'm feeling much better. I rode my bike for six miles, did floor exercises, and could even lift small weights, although I paid the price for this afterwards. I felt a pain going down both of my arms into the shoulder sockets, and I felt a pain in the right side of my chest when I breathe. But I still feel generally better with more energy. After I came home from visiting my mother for the usual vest and pin care, I turned on the radio to listen to music for the first time since the accident. I never tried to listen to it before, although I used to listen to it all the time before the accident. Now when I listened after all of these months, I really enjoyed it. Another sign of progress.

Tuesday, May 16, 1989

Though today's weather was terrible and I still have some shoulder pains, I'm still feeling fairly good. I started working on the memorial service for Bob. I decided to use a passage from a book called How to Survive the Loss of a Love *by Melba Colgrove, Harold H. Bloomfield, and Peter McWilliams. My neighbor Nicole gave it to me right after the accident, and when I read it over and over, it really helped me deal with my grief by showing me I could learn from the grieving experience and move on. That's why I want to use this at the ceremony, because it has been so meaningful for me.*

I also put up a wedding picture on the wall. It was a picture of Bob and his 5-year-old nephew Scott, which was taken a few days before the wedding at the rehearsal dinner. It showed Scott sitting in Bob's lap comparing their identical ties. Bob was very close to his nephew, and that was always a very touching photo for me. So it was a big step putting up that picture. It's like I can finally start facing those memories again.

Friday, May 19, 1989

I thought the pain in my arms was just due to exercising. But my arms are still bothering me, and I'm feeling a tingling numbness in my left hand and forearm. I hope that isn't anything serious that will alarm the doctors when I see them.

But otherwise, it was a nice day and my spirits are up. I'm looking forward to getting Mom her birthday gift this morning. And after we go see the doctors, my friend Karen is coming over.

****

Yet, while I felt generally better over the next week, as the day of saying a final good-bye to Bob approached, I found myself again thinking more and more about what I lost, making it harder to deal with the physical pain, despite some bright spots. As I wrote in my diary:

Saturday, May 20, 1989

Another gorgeous day. I have to keep reminding myself to look on the bright side. I enjoyed having Mom over for coffee on her birthday. Yet other things have made this a very difficult time for me. I've started making calls to make arrangements for the disposition of Bob's ashes. Also, my left hand felt very numb, and when I got hot in the house, the pins in my head started to burn from the sweat. But I've got to hang in there and remind myself this pain will soon be over, since I'll be seeing the doctors on Thursday. Hopefully I'll only have to be in this awful halo for six more weeks. It's hard to imagine what it's like to take a shower and feel the water against my face and back. I'm looking forward to the day when I can feel this again.

MORE DOCTORS AGAIN

Finally, on May 22nd, it was time to see the doctors for a follow-up to learn how well I was doing. Nervously, I headed off to the Northeast Rehabilitation Hospital in Salem, New Hampshire to find out. At the hospital I met with a physiatrist, a doctor specializing in physical therapy, Dr. David Jaeger, and then saw my neurosurgeon Dr. Edward Cox, who I had first seen a month ago in mid-April, before I was well enough to start keeping my diary. I went to see them again to check on my progress in physical therapy, get X-rays, and learn when they could take my halo off. Though I was concerned about the feeling of numbness in my right leg and left hand, otherwise I was still hopeful.

Dr. Jaeger was encouraging, saying I had improved significantly since my previous visit. Among other things, he noted in his report that I had: "significant improvement of headaches" despite complaints of "intermittent blurred vision," continued "pain in the shoulders" and "intermittent numbness in the upper extremities." Also he scheduled me for speech therapy and a neuropsychology evaluation the following week; noted I would have a psychology follow-up to deal with my continuing anxiety about Bob's death; and recommended "a short program of physical therapy" to work on reducing the discomfort in my shoulders.

Meanwhile my other doctor, Dr. Cox offered encouraging news that the halo would come off soon. In July, three months after my surgery, he said, he would take some X-rays of my neck injury area to make sure everything had healed properly as expected. Then, if the X-rays showed the fusion took place, he would remove the halo.

I was ecstatic to hear him say this. Finally, I felt, I could see the light beyond all my numbness, pain, and suffering. Although Dr. Cox said he wasn't completely certain the halo could be removed, the good possibility that it might be gave me hope for the future. I even felt I could apply my will power and determination to make those planned arrangements come true.

As a result, as my mother drove me home from the rehab hospital, I tried to put all my memories of Bob in the past again. And the warm May sunshine helped me feel a hopeful sense of renewal for the months ahead.

SAYING GOOD-BYE TO BOB

Later that night, however, I felt sad having to go over the past again, when the deacon who married me and Bob, Ron Gagne, came over to help me set up Bob's funeral service. He wanted my input to help him plan a mass at a local church and make arrangements for handling the ashes after the service. It was depressing as we talked to think about how my uncle would pick up Bob's ashes at the funeral home and to make plans for scattering them on Cape Cod the following week.

Making the planning for Bob's memorial service even more upsetting was my mother-in-law's unusual request. She wanted to obtain some of Bob's ashes, which I feared meant that she wanted to maintain her hold over Bob, even beyond the grave. As I wrote in my diary over the next few days:

Thursday Morning, May 25, 1989

The service for Bob is tonight, so I'll rest all day, since I need everything I can for his service. A strange thing happened. My lawyer Mark Bidner called to tell me that Mrs. Raymond would like some of Bob's ashes. I couldn't believe that she would ask for this. After all, the plan is to take them out to sea and release them there, and I invited Mrs. Raymond to be on the boat, too. However, according to Mark, Mrs. Raymond said she heard rumors that the boat was too small for her and her husband and that they weren't welcome. But that isn't true. I invited her, and I told Mark to tell her that. In any case, I don't think it is right for her to ask for ashes. I think all of Bob's ashes should be released at sea as he would want.

Thursday Night, May 25, 1989

Now that the service is over, I feel really relieved. It went so well. There were so many people there—about 75 of them, including friends from high school, business associates, neighbors, and family members. That turnout was a real tribute to Bob, as was the beautiful service led by Ron, the deacon who married us. It was so moving when Ron talked about the undying love Bob and I had for each other, and how we lived 30 years in the three years we were together.

Amazingly, two hours before the funeral service, I found some pictures of a trip Bob and I took together to Tortola, an island in the Caribbean—one of the happiest trips we ever took. The pictures suddenly fell out on the floor when I reached into the closet for a pocketbook to wear for the service. I hadn't used the bag in over a year, and when I picked the pictures up I saw they were from this trip. They showed us sport fishing in Anegeda, another small island, and sailing in Tortola. Finding them at that moment was like another reminder of how special Bob had been, since they fell out just before the service. An incredible coincidence.

Later, after I returned from the service with my friend Libby, who'll be spending the night, I felt extremely tired. But I feel really pleased I could actually make the arrangements for the event. It makes me a feel a little more like my old self again. And so to bed.

****

The next few days were better, too. I was cheered by the good weather and my supportive friends. I was able to get out and do more, too, even though I still felt some continuing pain and numbness. As I wrote in my diary:

Saturday, May 27, 1989

 Today, was a nice day. I can finally see the light at the end of the tunnel. I opened the windows, and turned on the radio. Later, after I did a load of wash and ran some pool cleaner through the pool, I sat on the deck, thinking of all the good times Bob and I had shared here—gardening, puttering around, swimming in the pool. We shared a lot of good memories and wonderful plans. It's strange how I feel both happy and sad to think about them. Happy to remember, sad to think those times are gone for good.

Sunday, May 28, 1989

 Another nice day. Ron, the deacon who married Bob and me, and his wife, dropped by and drove me to the scattering of Bob's ashes on the Cape. Though I thought the Raymonds might still come, they weren't there. A half dozen of Bob's closest friends came, and after we boarded the 38' motorboat, which a good friend of Bob's donated for the occasion, we motored out in silence across the bay until we were about 100 feet from shore.

 Then, as we quietly drifted, I threw a wreath of red roses overboard and then I recited a poem in his memory. It was a passage that meant a lot to me, taken from the book How to Survive the Loss of a Love. It expressed exactly what I was feeling in the words: "And through all the tears and the sadness and the pain, comes the one thought that can make me internally smile again: 'I have loved.'" It was hard to get through the passage, though, because I was so broken up. I kept dissolving in tears, overcome by emotion, and I don't think anyone really understood what I was saying.

 When we finished saying our good-byes, we motored back to shore. After lunch, I had a long talk with Mom and Dad about the good times I had with Bob, which were hard for me to put out of my mind.

Tuesday, May 30, 1989

 The last two days have been so beautiful. Yesterday, I spent time sitting on the deck thinking about Bob, and afterwards had dinner with my next door neighbors, Scott and Sally, who Bob and I had gotten to know. I feel like I'm starting to get back into the swing of things, and hope to get to know these neighbors better.

 Today, I rode my bike, and afterward put some real estate up for sale for the first time by listing my condo in Florida with a broker. However, one thing has started to bother me. Thinking back about the accident, I remembered that the car had an airbag. But it didn't work that day, and I wondered why. "Was something wrong with it? What good are these airbags if they don't work?" I had used that instead of a seatbelt, and I wonder if that might be a problem. I'll have to talk to my lawyer Mark about that.

Also, I wonder why my right foot and left arm are still numb. I'll have to talk to the doctors about this. But otherwise, I feel I'm making real progress. I even washed my hair today. It's still an ordeal with the halo on. But I feel a lot more physical strength when I wash it, and the halo doesn't hurt as much.

Wednesday, May 31, 1989

I had another breakthrough today. Uncle Paul brought an easel over, and I drew my first picture. It was a charcoal still life of my family room.

I also feel encouraged by my talk today with Dr. Cox about the continuing numbness in my right foot and knee. He told me the problem wasn't normal, but he felt it would help if I was more active. "Get your blood circulating more and try not to sit," he told me. "The extra activity should help you have more feeling."

DAYS OF DEPRESSION

Yet, while I seemed to be making progress, in June, I became deeply depressed again, because recovery again seemed so far away. The process was taking so long, even with the signs of healing. Also, after the ceremonies to say good-bye to Bob, his loss seemed even harder to accept.

Now, too, my lawyers—Mark Bidner, Paul Freedman, and his partner Joel Kaplan—now hinted at legal complications, though I didn't fully understand them at the time. Freedman had been trying to collect damages for my injuries by writing for various documents since early March—traffic records, medical reports, photographs of injuries, and insurance policies. Also, he had some recent success in collecting some funds from one of my insurance claims— about $50,000 in damage to my Mercedes.

However, after investigating, Freedman and the lawyers representing Mrs. Raymond and Bob's estate had come to agree with the traffic homicide investigator that the main cause of the accident was that Bob was going too fast—about 80 miles an hour—so he lost control of the car when the tire blew out. Thus, he was responsible for the accident. Legally, this meant, Freedman told me, that these other lawyers could no longer represent both me and Bob's estate or family, since Freedman would now be suing the estate for damages on my behalf.

Though I didn't realize it at the time, this decision about legal fault had very serious repercussions. Not only did it contribute to the growing rift between me and my mother-in-law, but it led her eventually to claim that Bob wasn't responsible for the accident, on the grounds that I was driving. Once she did, that derailed my own claims for settlement, while I had to argue that Bob was the one driving, not me.

In turn, this battle created a problem in paying for all of my treatment. Freedman expected that I would soon collect a large accident settlement from both Bob's insurance company and my insurance company. So in early June, he worked out a lien agreement with my rehab clinic—the New Medico Community Re-Entry Services in Lynn, Massachusetts—to cover about $650 a day in services. The fee negotiation seemed like a simple matter at the time. Yet when my own settlement ended up in limbo due to my battle with my mother-in-law, New Medico eventually turned into an angry creditor, like many others, in the months ahead.

At the time, though, not understanding the potential problems brewing, I went along with Freedman when he asked me to sign papers from time to time authorizing him to proceed as he thought best in gathering information and working out financial and medical agreements. In fact, I was glad to turn over the legal details and worries over to him, since I understood so little, and I wanted to focus primarily on recovering from my injuries. As I wrote in my diary for this period:

Friday, June 2, 1989

Everything suddenly seems so bleak. The weather wasn't very good yesterday, and my shoulder was bothering me again. So was the numbness in my hands, and I felt it in my foot and knee as well. I've been putting on the pounds, too, with all this sitting around.

Then, when I went to New Medico to make arrangements to go into rehab, that was very depressing. They told me it would be 30 days before I could start, because they were currently booked up. Also, they wanted a delay, so my lawyer could resolve the payment agreement, so the hospital could get paid by my insurance company. But whatever the reason for the delay, it makes me feel like I have to go on hold until I can start the program.

After I came home, I saw my psychologist Dr. Carol Golub. We talked about what happened, and about how sad I am about losing Bob and my independence. Later, my friend Lois Maher came over and tried to cheer me up. It was good to see her again, since we had become such good friends working together in real estate. When we talked about some of the projects we had worked on together and what other projects we might work on in the future, that helped me feel more hopeful about the future. But even so, I still feel so depressed and discouraged. Will I ever be back to normal? Will I ever be able to put my life back together again?

Saturday, June 3, 1989

I woke up in a good mood, but when Mom showed up unannounced while I was exercising because I didn't answer the phone, I felt more depressed than ever. Just seeing Mom made me feel even more keenly how much I had lost my independence and privacy, because people have been constantly worried about me and checking up on me. They don't trust me to be able to take care of myself properly.

Also, seeing her reminded me that a year ago today was the last day of my honeymoon with Bob, and less than a year later he was buried. It's a part of me that's gone forever, and suddenly, I began wishing it was me that was buried instead of Bob.

Tuesday, June 6, 1989

Though I had a couple of good days, now I feel so depressed again. On June 4, my friend Robbi Ernst from San Francisco, who had helped me plan our wedding in the Napa Valley, sent me an invitation to a murder mystery vacation in England. I felt so cheered that this was something to look forward to and dream about, especially since a few other good friends are going.

But today feels like a real setback. My lawyer Paul Freedman called to explain that he was working out arrangements with New Medico to pay for the treatments for the head injury. He told me the agreement would set up some kind of lien on my property. Then, when I worried about this, he assured me that once the insurance settlement came through, the lien would be removed. So that would take care of everything, he reassured me. But it was depressing to think about the financial details, and Mom and Dad said they didn't want to talk about this with me, saying it was too much for me to deal with right now. So we just told Freedman to go ahead and do what he suggested.

Then, to top things off, MasterCard called because my bill was overdue, since I haven't been able to take care of the bills. Their call came like sudden bolt out of the blue, because my father has been paying the bills to keep the mortgage holders from foreclosing on my house and condo in Florida and the 20 acres of land I own on a lake in New Hampshire. And he had already paid off some of the biggest creditors. But he wasn't able to take care of everything.

So now after four months, the creditors are starting to call, and I feel like changing my phone number, because these calls are so upsetting. Why can't the creditors just be patient and understand? I'm feeling so depressed over the lack of control in my life and the loss of my husband. And now on top of everything, I feel the bill collectors are closing in, which is making me even more depressed.

Thursday, June 8, 1989

Two more difficult, depressing days. On Wednesday I tried doing some exercises—aerobics and riding my stationery bike, and I broke down crying because everything is getting to be too much. Fortunately, my friend Susan Olsen, who I met four years ago at a health club, called while I was crying, and she really helped me snap out of it.

Then, today, I went through a picture-taking session for Joel Kaplan, one of my lawyers, who works with Freedman. I went to the photographer's office so he could take photos of me showing my various scars—a vertical scar on my abdomen from the splenectomy, a horizontal one on my back where the doctor removed a rib for the neck fusion, a scar in the back of my neck, and the scars on my forehead. Kaplan wanted the photos to show my injuries and how I'm doing for insurance purposes, and as he explained, the worse they looked the better. But even so, I felt terrible posing there in my ugly halo, looking like a fat overweight slob because of all the weight I gained. So I sure wish the pictures didn't have to be taken, and I never want to see them again.

Today I also went for my halo check at Orthotic Consultants with my orthotic doctor, who specializes in designing and fitting prosthetic devices, and when he checked, he found that all four of the screws were loose. So he had to adjust them—meaning another session of bone-crunching tightening. After he finished, I discovered my eyesight had gotten worse. Though the doctor told me my sight will get better, it was discouraging to hear that one more thing was wrong. But at least, just four more weeks, I hope, before this ugly contraption comes off. If only I can continue to hold out that long.

Friday, June 9, 1989

I woke up again depressed. If only I could join Bob in Heaven soon. I've been praying more and more for that.

The halo check yesterday has really gotten me down. My head is aching so much again. I feel it over my ears, around the back of my ears. And the rain has made the pain even worse. So I cancelled the dinner I planned with Mom and Dad, and my brother and sister-in-law Paul and Cindy. I just wanted to be alone.

Now I feel like sleeping forever and ever—to join Bob—or to wake up when the halo is gone. Only one month and six and a half hours left. I pray to God the pain and the sadness will stop.

****

It's amazing to think that's what I wrote back then. Now as I write, six years later, I find it hard to imagine how I got through this period. Though I kept a journal to try to sort out my thoughts, the days seemed to blend together—each day filled with continuing pain and numbness, though I had many friends and family members around me who helped me get through each day. It was so hard, just dragging through day to day, hoping each one would somehow be better. As a result, I mainly looked forward to going to sleep at the end of each day and counting off one more day until the hated halo came off.

Still, somehow, like a small insistent voice inside me, I kept wanting to do my best to retrain myself to think normally again and be as independent as I could be. Perhaps more than anything, this strong inner will kept me going, and over the next few days, I felt a sense of renewed commitment. As I wrote in my diary:

Saturday, June 10, 1989

As I woke up, Mom and Dad stopped by to drop off their two Maltese dogs, Cagney and Tiffany, on their way out of town. Fortunately, the dogs could mostly take care of themselves, and I liked having them around.

Around noon, I spoke to my good friend Susan Olsen, which cheered me up, and I rode my bike for an hour or so for exercise—and to help get over the continuing numbness in my right leg and arm. I'm getting so tired of this. At least, just 27 days till the halo is, hopefully, off.

Monday, June 12, 1989

Today I finally started in the New Medico program, after my application for delayed payment was approved a few days ago. Cindy drove me over, and after I filled out and signed all sorts of paperwork, the New Medico speech therapist, gave me a comprehension test to take. I had to read a short paragraph, wait a few minutes, and describe its contents to test my ability to recall things. Afterwards, I met with the therapist to discuss the results. They were encouraging, since she told me that I've already started making many adjustments to make up for the deficits due to my injury. For example, she said she was impressed with the way I was writing everything down and was trying to remember phone numbers without having to look them up. A good sign.

My ride home that afternoon, however, turned out to be a total fiasco. I had to ride in a bus for the handicapped, and because of the heavy weight of the halo, I was thrown all over the bus. When I got to the halfway house for the New Medico treatment program, there was no hospital bed and no one was available to help me with my pin care, though Dr. Carper, the head of New Medico, had promised he would send someone over to help. So I called my mother to pick me up and take me home, because I felt so abandoned and alone again. Also, I knew I didn't want to stay in the New Medico program one more minute.

Wednesday, June 14, 1989

Though Dr. Carper called a few times yesterday to say he would send someone to help and urged my mother to have me return to see him, I didn't want to talk to him. I felt he had let me down in not having someone at the halfway house to handle the pin and vest care as he had promised.

Today I woke up with a more positive attitude. I decided I had to stop depending on other people like Dr. Carper for help and do more things for myself. I had to take control of me again. So I set two priorities: 1) Be as independent as possible, and 2) Work on cognitive retraining in speech therapy, so I can think more clearly again.

Then, feeling a sense of new purpose, I cleaned the kitchen and sat down to plan a meal and wrote up a shopping list. After that I made plans to go shopping for the first time the next day. Now my mother won't have to do the shopping anymore, although I will still need her to drive me there. When I told her about my plans, she sounded like she couldn't believe I can be independent. But I'm going to show her I can. I want to do that now more than ever.

Friday, June 16, 1989

I'm still feeling that determination to help myself, since nobody else can really do so. As a result, I've been feeling much better for the last few days.

Today was a big day—I went back to the Northeast Rehabilitation Hospital in New Hampshire, where I was an inpatient when I first got the halo. This time I went back for speech therapy. My friends Nicole and Marilyn drove me there, and when I met with the speech therapist, Renee LaBelle, I really enjoyed the experience. She gave me a variety of word finding games, such as doing simple crossword puzzles. Also, she suggested that I should write down the things I want to do and note the good ideas that come to me, so I don't forget.

Another first today was when I did my aerobics. It was the first day my leg and arms didn't get numb.

Sunday, June 18, 1989

On Saturday, my back was really sore from exercising to my aerobics tape, which showed me I'm more out of shape than I thought. But I didn't let that get me down, and these past few days have been pretty good.

On Sunday, I made my first real dinner for my parents. Making it helped me feel even more confident, another thing I could do. I made some chile, since Dad said he wanted this, and chile turned out to be the ideal choice, because I could put all the ingredients together in a single pot. This was much easier for me than trying to do three things in different pots at the same time. Dad even wanted to take some of the chili back home with him, he thought it was so good.

Then today, I not only spent an hour doing aerobics to Jane Fonda's tape, but I rode 10 miles on my bike. I'm feeling much stronger now. Finally, the numbness in my hands and legs is completely gone. I feel like I'm really taking charge of my life, and that's making all the difference. Now I feel even surer I will be ready to have this halo off in three weeks. July 7th. I can hardly wait.

****

Meanwhile, as I was becoming more upbeat, in early June Freedman assured me that all was going well legally, too. He was still writing letters to collect still more documents supporting my claim—even records of several traffic violations by Bob the previous year—and getting even more medical reports from my growing number of doctors and hospitals. So everything seemed to be proceeding smoothly.

Within a few weeks, this would all start coming apart. Soon questions began to arise over whether I was actually covered as a passenger, and Freedman, expressed this worry in a letter to Mark Bidner, who was still handling my personal and business affairs. Freedman thought I might only be covered if I was a passenger in a commercial vehicle, not a private car.

Meanwhile, another insurance company, Traveler's which insured Bob, was trying to opt out of providing coverage. As I learned later, the company's claims representative Susan Lyle, sent a letter to the agent at another insurance company stating that Travelers wasn't liable because of some new Uninsured or Underinsured Motorist statutes, which provided lower limits of liability.

It was the beginning of a growing insurance and legal challenge, though I didn't realize how serious the problem was at the time. Instead, for now, I felt a sense of renewal and confidence that everything would work out, and I was determined to work hard and do whatever necessary to get better. As I wrote in my diary those last weeks of June:

Wednesday, June 21, 1989

Only 16 days left till my halo's removed, and its another gorgeous day.

Yesterday, after I rode my bike and arranged for the pool guy to clean up the pool, I went to Northeast Rehab to see the speech therapist for another 60 minute session to evaluate my abilities. I feel like we made real headway, and I'm looking forward to seeing her again.

Saturday, June 24, 1989

Had another "screwing" Thursday, as I call it. It was even funny, when I went to see Jim, my orthotic consultant, for my regular weekly screw tightening, and he told me about a man with a halo who got stuck behind his refrigerator. When the man's wife came home from work, she found him trapped behind it, looking very embarrassed and very cold. The man felt even worse when his wife had to ask a neighbor over to help her move the refrigerator, because she couldn't move it herself.

Afterwards, my headache, which I've had since the screws were tightened a week ago, was a little worse than usual. But at least, I reminded myself, only two weeks to go. Just keep on pushing—then all the agony will be over.

I finally got the pool cleaned on Thursday, too. It had started to look like a pond, with a grey film of algae growing all over the water. But after the pool guy brushed the pool with his wire pad and put chemicals in it, the film disappeared and the pool looked fine.

Then, Friday, I woke up with bad headache again—even worse than Thursday. But today, Saturday, I felt much better. I even made some turkey soup and lentil pilaf which were pretty good, and I found I was able to whip up a dinner much faster than before. I didn't have to put up post-its to tell myself what to do. Another sign I'm getting better.

Since I was able to do this all on my own, now I only have to have help with the pin care and with people driving me around to see my doctors. I told Mom and Dad when they called from Florida, and they were very pleased to hear this. They also said they were having a great time, and I was glad they finally could enjoy themselves. I feel like my accident was so hard on them, because they were always so worried about me. Now I'm glad they can finally let go of this tragedy.

Then, Charlie called from Naples to report on how things were going with the business he has been running for me since the accident. He wanted to tell me he was flying in for a visit. He sounded so reassuring, saying everything was fine and that he hoped I could return to Naples soon. It felt really good to hear from him. After knowing him for 30 years, I was reassured to know he was taking care of my business. I felt relieved having someone I had known so long there watching over things, someone I can trust.

Monday, June 26, 1989

A nice quiet Sunday yesterday. I even woke up without a headache. Then I laid out in the sun by the pool, soaking the sun up on my face and front. It made me feel like a person again.

Today, I went to see Dr. Jaeger at Northeast Rehab for a general check-up. Karen came by around 2 p.m. to drive me over. I told Dr. Jaeger everything seemed to be going fine, except for the recurring headaches, and he recommended a new prescription. Instead of taking 20 Advils each day, he advised me to try the anti-depressant, Elavil, since it seemed to help other head injury patients at the hospital with recurring headaches. I'll do anything to get rid of these headaches, I told him. He also referred me to a neuropsychologist at Northeast Rehab, Dr. Higgins, and told me to have more neuropsychological testing, which I said I would. I left feeling it was a good meeting.

****

Thus, by the end of June, 4½ months after the accident, everything seemed to be hopeful. Besides my diary accounts, the doctor's reports were largely positive, though they noted some areas that still needed work. For example, Dr. Jaeger not only reported that I told him I was feeling better and was following his pin care instructions, but he said my physical exam looked good, too. "There's good to normal strength of the upper and lower extremities," he noted.

The report of speech therapist, Renee LaBella, who tested me with a number of tests, was equally encouraging. These tests included the Ross Test of Higher Cognitive Processes and the Woodcock-Johnson Psycho-Educational Battery. Though she reported various deficits, which I recognized myself, she felt my mental state was "alert and oriented," and I was eager to "transcend all obstacles and recover quickly" even though she felt the possibilities for further education, employment, or resuming my business still uncertain. She liked my "delightful sense of humor," too.

Though I didn't see her report until much later, it was interesting to see how she carefully broke down each area of functioning, describing in detail what I was able to do compared to what would be considered normal—just as she would do with any brain injury patient. For example, in my case, she described five different areas of functioning, making notes like the following:

Auditory Comprehension...Patient demonstrates difficulty with embedded sentences, material of increased complexity, length, abstract qualities...Has trouble with logical and grammatical sentence comprehension.

Verbal Expression...Patient has mild word retrieval deficits in conversation. However, she sometimes uses circumlocutionary speech as a skillful tool to compensate for word finding difficulties.

Oral-Facial Exam...Voice...Speech Production...These seem to be normal. The frequency, intensity, and vocal quality seem to be on a normal level for the patient's age and sex.

Reading...This seems to be good through short, concrete paragraphs. Then, comprehension is moderately reduced as the material increases in length and/or complexity.

Writing...She has good syntax and word usage for paragraphs. She has a somewhat lowered ability to organize material...Her encoding skills are mildly reduced, which is reflected in misspellings or her lowered accuracy in her ability to make letters.

Overall, LaBella felt the future prognosis good, feeling there was a good chance that I could eventually return to work and successful independent living, even though she listed a number of problems in her Summary Impressions and Prognosis. These included "mild problems with auditory comprehension and verbal expression, particularly in comprehending complex or lengthy material; some mild word retrieval deficits; some trouble in comprehending reading material that is lengthy or complex; a lowered ability for attention

and concentration; long-term memory problems for events both
prior to the accident and following it; and a reduced ability to freely
recall what was said in written paragraphs and in conversations—
both right after reading or hearing information or after some delay." Overall, she felt the outlook was good because of a number of
positive factors, including my age, "a lack of severe deficits," my
"high level of functioning prior to the accident," my "high degree
of motivation," my "progress to date," and my "family support."

I felt it was an encouraging beginning, and I signed up for 60
minute speech and language therapy sessions three times a week,
which continued for the next two months through August. Yet, even
with all of Renee's optimism, I still felt frustrated that the process
would take much longer than I expected. Nevertheless, I was determined to follow through. As I noted in my diary that day:

Tuesday, June 27, 1989

*After I got up and shook off my morning headache with an Advil, Lois arrived to take me
to the rehab hospital for my speech therapy. She was so helpful. But it bothered me to realize that
Renee, my speech therapist, saw deficits in my concentration and in other areas. So though
everything is starting to look up, speech therapy is going to take a lot longer than I ever
anticipated.*

*But I enjoyed all the interesting word games and exercises Renee gave me, and besides
enjoying them, I found them intriguing. They've got me thinking about how and why doing them
can help one overcome a head injury. I also know I've got to keep working with these exercises to
get back to work and be independent again. So I'm going to give them my all!*

Saturday, July 1, 1989

*For the first time in three weeks, no headache. The Elavil must finally be working. I feel
renewed. I actually exercised on my bike again. After lunch, Marilyn came over with her
husband Larry, and they took me out for a picnic. We had a wonderful time taking pictures. I
wore the shirt they gave me which had a picture of a patient lying in a hospital bed, and
underneath there was the caption:"We had to remove your brain for a couple of days, so just try
to relax." After I put on the shirt, Marilyn strung a string of Christmas lights through the bars
of the halo and took pictures. It was a lot of laughs, in an odd sort of way—like making fun of
what was really a very sad situation. But it took my mind off the sadness of it all. And as we
drank a bottle of our favorite Opus One wine, we kidded about how we were lighting up the room*

in celebrating Independence Day early—since I thought and hoped the halo would be off in a week, if the X-rays showed the fusion had taken. I couldn't be sure yet, but this celebration was a way of helping to reinforce my hope.

****

Now hoping I had only one more week before the halo came off helped the next few days pass more quickly and easily. Mostly I spent them seeing old friends, exercising, and relaxing in the sun. When I saw my friends, I realized how much I appreciated having this supportive network of friends there for me after the accident. I'm not sure I would have been as determined to work on getting better or would have been convinced I could do it, if they weren't there. As I noted in my diary over the next few days:

Monday, July 3

Yesterday, Paul and Cindy took me to have dinner with Mom and Dad in New Hampshire. Afterwards, we spent time visiting other friends nearby. Another fun long day that helped me feel I'm really getting better.

Then, today was one more beautiful day without a headache. After another friend, Irene Pappas, stopped by, we sat in the living room chatting about old times. We also discussed plans to celebrate the Greek Easter the week after the traditional Easter holidays by cooking a whole lamb over an open pit in the backyard, since Irene loves to cook Greek food—a tradition passed down by her Greek husband.

Later in the afternoon, I took Irene into the spare room where I kept many of my wedding gifts from when Bob and I got married. We had stored them there while we got ready to move to Florida, but had never used them. So they were still in the spare room, and I hadn't looked at them after I returned to my home in Massachusetts after the accident. But now, going into that room and showing my gifts, I felt a little shaky and many memories flooded back. But now the memories seemed less painful and further away. So the pain of Bob's loss has been getting easier with time.

Tuesday, July 4

Today was Independence Day, and in just three days, if the halo is removed, I can celebrate my own Independence Day. I hope!

To help celebrate, Paul and Libby stopped by with a sample of the wedding cake they were planning to get for their own wedding in about three weeks. We toasted the day with Rasberry Daiquiris, and passed around pieces of cake. In the evening, we lit off a half dozen Roman candles and sparklers. They lit up the backyard with red, white, and blue streaks of light, and crackled like short claps of thunder in the sky. Thus, all and all, it was a really glorious Fourth of July, and I felt grateful to Paul and Libby for making it happen. I really love them both.

Thursday, July 6

Yesterday, Mom and Dad returned from New Hampshire, and Mom came over to help with my pin care and comb my hair. Just two days until it's all over, I hope! My headache wasn't even that bad. After I woke up with one, the Advil quickly chased it away.

Later that day it was great seeing Lois, who stopped by on her way to New Hampshire from Luxembourg. Strangely, as she came in the door, I suddenly started to cry because I realized how much she means to me. Then, as she described her experiences, I felt I wanted to go to Luxembourg, too. After we talked about her trip, I updated her on my ordeals for the last few months, and she was so understanding. It was so good to see her, I felt a little sorry to see her leave.

Still, all the discussion about future travel plans left me upbeat and hopeful about new possibilities. Only one more day!

****

Finally, that day I had been waiting for arrived, and I hoped it would be a new day of freedom, a new beginning. True, there had been a few warning signals about brewing problems, like the questions raised by my mother-in-law about the report that Bob was at fault in driving. Also, I still had a long rehabilitation process to restore my thinking and speech. For now, all I could think about was that I might look and act normally again. All the rest seemed, at least now, very far away. As I noted in my diary:

Friday, July 7, 1989

D-Day at last. The day I have been praying for—the removal of this 9 pound weight on my head. If only it happens.

I was so excited, I could hardly sleep the night before. I was already up when Dad called at 7:00 a.m. to wake me up. After I made breakfast, I could hardly eat, because I was so jittery with anticipation. So I walked a couple of doors down to Dad and Mom's house, and Mom drove me to the hospital.

At 8 a.m. we arrived at the hospital, and we waited in the lobby for Dr. Cox, the neurosurgeon, and John Brooks, the orthotic consultant, to arrive. John was about an hour late, but even so, I didn't let that spoil my good feelings for the day. "What's another hour?" I said. "After three months with this thing, what's just one hour?"

After they arrived, Dr. Cox took a side view X-ray to confirm that the halo was really ready to come off. He wanted to make sure the bones in my neck had fused as he had hoped. I felt on pins and needles as he examined the X-ray, waiting to hear his verdict. When he finally said "That looks good," I breathed a big sigh of relief. At last.

Then, as I sat on a table, Dr. Cox held my head gently. Meanwhile Jim Brooks removed the vest and the bars of the halo, so only the section with the screws remained attached to my head. "Now bend down and see if you can hit your chest with your chin," Dr. Cox told me. "Then lift your head and move it backwards as far as you can go."

As I moved my head as instructed, Dr. Cox took a series of X-rays, to be sure all the bones in my neck were still in proper alignment. Meanwhile, Jim Brooks put the bars and vest of the halo he took off in a large black garbage bag to be thrown out. As he threw out each piece, I felt reassured that I was fine and that the remaining portion of the halo, which was screwed to my head, was finally going to come off.

Once the X-rays were finished, Dr. Cox took them off for developing, and when he returned, he announced: "It looks like fusion took place." The words sounded magical to hear.

Then, Dr. Cox came over and held my head firmly, while Jim Brooks unscrewed each screw. However, Dr. Cox didn't give me any anesthesia for this—no novocaine, nothing, because he didn't believe in pain killers for what he considered a routine procedure. I could feel the sharp wrenching pains race through my head, along with a loud crunching noise in my ears, as Jim loosened the screws. The pain was much worse than when I had this hated contraption put on in the first place, since I had been under general anesthesia and was unconscious then. I wished I could be now, and didn't understand at the time why they didn't put me under. The pain was so great. But they kept going.

Soon I felt my brain moving and shifting, as the liquid around my brain was redistributed. I also felt a tremendous sense of pressure, as my head suddenly felt very, very heavy. That's because I was feeling the weight of my head that I hadn't felt in three months. Now I felt this heaviness bearing down on my neck.

"Don't worry. The heaviness you feel is perfectly normal," Dr. Cox told me when I complained.

Finally, Dr. Cox brought out a soft white collar and put it around my neck. "Now keep this on all the time for the next two to three months," he said. "Then try slowly weaning yourself from *the collar."*

About a half-hour later, as we walked out the door of the hospital and to the car, I felt a great sense of freedom. Finally, this day had come. The halo was off and I felt like I had just been let out of prison.

****

Later that night, I reflected on my first day of freedom and how it was a chance to try new things and see what I could do.

Friday, July 7, 1989 cont.

After I got home, I went straight to my bike and peddled as hard as I could. I felt so full of emotion, I started crying as I peddled. This time, though, my tears were tears of joy, and I worked up a sweat, which I was not able to do in the halo. Afterwards, I showered for the first time in three months. It felt so good to feel the water on my head and body. I realized how much I had missed.

Later, Dad stopped by with a friend Leo, and we all went to Natalie's, one of my favorite Italian restaurants, to celebrate.

Afterwards, on returning home, I reflected on everything that had happened this day. It really felt like a new beginning, like I had finally returned to life feeling renewed and whole, after feeling and looking like an alien for over three months. With that contraption on my head, I felt like a freak because people were constantly staring at me when I went anywhere. But now all that was over!

Around dinner-time, while I was thinking these thoughts, a big hurricane blew up, and it seemed like a sign from heaven reaffirming my thoughts about a new beginning. It blew the door open in the garage, and as I heard it raging against the window, it broke the branches off of the trees outside. It was so strong that after about an hour around 7 p.m., it knocked the power out, and didn't come back for 12 hours.

Later, after the storm had calmed down, it was still hard to sleep. There had been so much excitement, so much that was new, it was hard to stop my mind from turning things over and over. Then, too, though the halo was off, my head throbbed in the back from all the extra weight on my spine, and it was uncomfortable to roll over. Also, each time I tossed or turned, my neck ached, and it was a real struggle to move it into the right position so I could fall asleep again. I had trouble rolling over or otherwise changing position, because after I was immobile for so long, my neck had atrophied, and I had no muscles left in my neck to hold up my head. So to raise or lower my head, I had to lift it up and down with my hands. Also, making it even more difficult to sleep, my cat Fluffy was crawling around and meowing all night, perhaps because he sensed my own restlessness.

Yet, even if getting to sleep was so difficult, I still felt upbeat and hopeful. All I could keep thinking is: "What a day!" and "There is a God, and he answered my prayers."

CHAPTER 6

•

TRYING TO COPE

FEELING FREE AGAIN

The feeling of freedom once the halo came off was exhilarating. I felt that way for the next few days, as I discovered how to move again without carrying nine pounds on my head.

I made dozens of calls to friends and relatives, reporting the news. Ironically, most of them were afraid to call me themselves to ask, fearing they might upset me if the halo wasn't taken off. So I called them.

It was also wonderful to finally sleep in a regular bed in my own house. It was like enjoying a new luxury. Though I still had to sleep in a collar, I felt a wonderful new sense of privacy in my own room. Before I had to use a hospital bed in the downstairs family room to avoid going up and down stairs as much as possible because of the danger of tripping with the halo. I had to spend most of my time downstairs, too, since most of the things I needed to do, apart from washing my hair in the upstairs bathroom, were there.

I also luxuriated in being able to stretch out in bed. Before the halo came off, I had to sleep sitting up in the hospital bed, because lying down put too much pressure on the screws in the back of my head, so it hurt too much to sleep that way. But now, free of the halo, I could sleep upstairs, lie down, and relax in a real bed. I was overjoyed that I finally could.

Yet sleeping in my own bed brought back sad memories too, since it led me to miss Bob even more since he wasn't there. Each time I got into bed, it was another reminder he was gone.

That's why the first time I slept in my bed after the halo was removed, I started crying, after being so happy initially I could sleep there. As I cried, I grabbed the pillow Bob had used and held it for some time as if it was Bob. I fell asleep that night with it next to me, and I slept that way for about a month after that.

So the memories of Bob lingered, while I spent the next few weeks and months trying to get back to normal. This often required learning to do things again that might otherwise seem very routine. After five months of being in and out of hospitals and three months of wearing a halo, everything seemed new again—especially the next few days, as I described in my diary.

Saturday, July 8, 1989

I was up all night and couldn't sleep very late my first morning home, because I found the new bed so strange and because my cat Fluffy kept howling or scratching at the screen window of my bedroom to get in. I repeatedly woke up hearing him, and at 5:15 a.m., after I heard him scratching at the window again, I finally opened the window and let him in. An example of how persistence pays, I guess. Then, I tried to get back to sleep. But soon Mom came by at 8:00 a.m. to drop off the dogs, and I gave up trying to sleep anymore.

Instead, I spent the morning relaxing in the sun. I took off my collar for the first time and lay there, feeling all my cares slip away. Afterwards, I put my collar back on and cleared off the deck, which was a mess from the storm. A little later, my brother and sister-in-law, Paul and Cindy, stopped by. Seeing them was a wonderful reminder of being back and starting to live a normal life again.

Sunday, July 9, 1989

Another nice day of discovering the new things I can do now that I don't have a big weight on my head. Joy and Mark Pierce, good friends who were the bridesmaid and groomsman at my wedding, came over to pick me up in the morning. They arrived in a chauffeured stretch limo, and after a couple of hours, we drove on a narrow winding road along the rocky coastline to Rye Beach in New Hampshire. We stopped by the pool and spent several hours swimming, sunbathing, and having a picnic. Later that afternoon, when we went for a walk on the beach, the smell of the ocean and the feel of the sand under my feet was wonderful. After dinner, as we drove back in the stretch limo, I remember thinking how marvelous this felt. It was like more old times coming back again.

****

Soon, though, after the initial euphoria of being out of the halo, the reality of everyday life set in again, and I started feeling discouraged by new problems and disappointments. As I wrote in my diary that July:

Tuesday, July 11, 1989

It almost seems like things were too good to last. Yesterday, Mom took Dad to the doctor and discovered he would have to go to the hospital, because he severed all the tendons in his knee when he fell down the stairs Saturday night. So now, after I finally got out of a halo on Friday, Dad will be in a cast for four to six weeks. At least it's an incentive for me to get better so I can help Dad.

While I was at the rehab hospital today for speech therapy, Mom took Dad to the hospital. After I returned home from my regular speech therapy session with Renee, I went to Mom's house to visit. When I arrived early that evening, I saw Mom sitting in the living room looking really worried and tried to cheer her up. While I was there, my brother Paul stopped by after visiting Dad and reported Dad was still pretty groggy. As Paul spoke, I couldn't help thinking: "What a year! So many things have gone wrong. What more can happen?" I felt like I had really been hit with the trials of Job! And I ended up with a headache again. It wasn't as bad as when I wore the halo, but it was still an unwelcome reminder of the past.

Wednesday, July 12, 1989

Today, I went over to see Dad. He was in a small semi-private room with two room-mates—one an elderly man about 80, the other a man about 60, who only spoke Polish. As I walked hesitantly over to Dad, uncertain how he was feeling, he pulled himself up and smiled groggily, saying he was glad to see me. So I pulled up a chair to talk. But soon he said he was very tired, since the elderly man kept wandering around the room all night, keeping him up. Also, he told me that despite some pain pills the nurses gave him, he had been in a lot of pain, and the big cast around his leg was heavy and uncomfortable.

"I know," I told him, without having to say anything about the halo. Then I helped him get out of bed for the first time. He leaned on my shoulders as I helped him get up and take a short walk on his crutches.

Afterwards, I went to see Renee LaBelle for speech therapy and had a really good session with Dr. Golub, my psychologist. We talked about dealing with my continuing feelings of guilt over Bob's death and the many things I wished I had told Bob before he died.

"So what about the future?" Dr. Golub asked me. I told her how I feel like I have a new life now, and was determined to make this one very different. I had spent so much time working hard

before. "But now," I told her, "I'd like to slow down a little and take the time to 'smell the roses.'"
Also, I told her: "I'd like to help other people with head injuries deal with their own grief and
difficulties in recovery. I want to somehow make sense of what happened to me, and I feel like
helping others who have experienced what I did will help."

THE HARD WORK OF RECOVERY

Yet, as much as I wanted to make these changes, I still had a long
way to go to make this happen. Besides healing physically, I had a
lot of work to recover mentally and emotionally, too. Though Renee
reported I had made some "minimal" gains in all stated target areas," I still had a lot of work to improve in areas where I had once
excelled—such as reading comprehension, deductive reasoning, and
recalling what I had just read. Unfortunately, Renee explained, I
could only comprehend material from moderately complex paragraphs with 65% accuracy, and I had to use various strategies to
understand, such as reread, summarize, and paraphrase material. I
had even lower reading comprehension for complex and lengthy
materials.

At least, Renee felt my deductive reasoning skills were almost
normal, except when it came to doing several tasks at once, where
my accuracy was only about 60% without additional cues. But even
here, I used various compensatory strategies to do better, as do many
brain injury patients, such as using cues to pay more attention to
pertinent information and ignore irrelevant information.

Finally, Renee reported on my recall skills for information after
she presented me with a series of paragraphs to read, finding that
around 60%, too. And here I also used still other compensating
strategies to achieve these results, such as reading the information
slowly...and rereading it as necessary.

In short, five months after the accident, I was functioning at
around 60-65% accuracy in most areas—much lower than my level
before the accident. Thus, I knew I would have to really work hard
to get back to my original level of performance, if that was even
possible. "It'll take a strong commitment, repeated practice, and
concentrated energy for several years," Renee told me.

However, I wanted to try and was determined to do this, I told her. Thus, Renee established three short-term goals for me—to increase my reading comprehension, deductive reasoning skills, and immediate recall for paragraphs by 10%, so I would function at around a 70-75% level. Then, once I achieved this, I could work towards the next level—and the initial accomplishment would help to spur me on.

"Well, I'm definitely committed," I told her, and I was. Even if I had to put in hours and hours of hard work each day, I was willing to push myself very hard to relearn everything. Yet, while I was determined, I felt frustrated too, realizing how much I had lost and how far I had to go. When I managed my real estate business and Mail Boxes franchise, I found my ability to think, analyze and plan had helped me rise quickly to the top. Now the harsh language of mathematics and statistics was chilling. I could see I had lost about a third of my abilities. It seemed I had so far to go to regain what I lost.

Writing in my diary over the next week helped me express this mixture of determination to become normal again combined with my feelings of frustration over the difficulty of getting there.

Saturday, July 15, 1989

I finally had a chance to step back into my old life again. In the afternoon, Mark and his wife Joy picked me up to go to the Abenaqui Country Club in Rye Beach, New Hampshire. We went to the pool and beach there about a week before, but now they were taking me to a gala dance at the Club's very exclusive Colonial Lodge. After a quick stop for dinner on the way, we drove in along a road that wound through the golf course to the lodge. Then we made our grand entrance. We walked through the high white columns in front, which made the lodge look like a colonial-style mansion, and entered the huge ballroom. A pop music band was starting to play, and as I looked around, I saw people sitting at tables in evening dresses and dark suits and ties.

At first, as the band played, I sat at the table between Joy and Mark watching the dancers and feeling very isolated and alone. As I saw happy couples dance by, memories of dancing with Bob flashed by, and I felt a sudden twinge of sadness. Then, I brushed those feelings aside.

Meanwhile, Joy and Mark kept persuading me to dance, and several times, Mark stretched out his hand to invite me to dance with him. But I just shook my head. It had been so long since I had gone dancing, though I had always loved doing this. Now, though, I felt like a wallflower wanting to dance, but I was afraid. I worried I might lose my balance because of my head injury and feel foolish. But finally, their persistence wore me down, and I stepped out on the dance floor with Mark, while the band played a Beatle's song. It felt exhilarating to be dancing again, the first time since the wedding, and as we whirled around, I felt better and better. It was like another ghost had been let out of the closet.

Then, Mark and Joy guided me around the dance floor to meet other people they knew. As we passed small groups of people standing or sitting at tables talking, Mark guided me over to several groups to introduce me. It felt good mixing with people again. But my big problem was remembering everyone's names. So many people, so many names. I used to be bad on names, but now I'm worse, much worse.

Tuesday, July 18, 1989

Another speech class today, as well as a neuropsych exam with Dr. Higgins, my neuro-psychologist.

I especially liked my speech class, and I'm really enjoying the exercises that Renee, my speech therapist, gives me. For example, we had one today about Mary going to the office to meet someone, and two hours later she met with someone else. I had to fill in the time she was going to meet with each person—9 a.m. for the first one, 11 a.m. for the second one two hours later.

Then Renee gave me a problem about a garden. There were carrots planted on the north-east corner, artichokes on the west-end, bean sprouts on the southeast side, and so on. I had to determine where the different plants should go. I remember how I learned to do this kind of problem in 1st and 2nd grade, and it was so easy to solve then. But now I have to think about these problems for awhile before I can figure them out. It's like learning how to think again.

Still, while I enjoy these problems, I'm starting to find all this therapy on top of learning how to live normally again very tiring. I realized that while I was waiting for Mom to pick me up at Northeast Rehab about 3 p.m. after my neuropsych exam, when I saw Dr. Higgins, one of the doctors who had just examined me, looking at me strangely. I wondered why, then I realized I had been staring blankly at the wall for about 5 minutes. A moment later, he came over and asked me:"Did you have a long day?," as if he sensed how I was feeling. I was embarrassed he had noticed. So I just nodded a quiet"yes" and thanked him for his concern.

Around 6 p.m., after Mom dropped me off at home, my neck felt so sore. Maybe I had done too much and strained it, I worried. Then, I took a nice hot shower, fell into bed, and slept for about 12 hours, until 7:30 the next morning. I haven't been that tired in a long time.

MOVING ON: THE UPS AND DOWNS OF RECOVERY

Yet even though I was feeling tired and burned out at times, I did more and more over the following days, and the more I did, the more in charge I felt of my life. At the same time, I experienced continuing ups and downs, in the way I felt, a common part of the recovery process for brain injury patients. It's like a recurring pattern. Patients feel better, get charged up, and do more, until they encounter a set back. Then, after feeling down for awhile, they find the power to charge themselves up again and move on. That's how it was for me.

Mostly, though, for the next week, I felt really good, although I still had to overcome a few more stumbling blocks in my medical progress to move on, and I was still blissfully unaware of the legal storm that was brewing. As I wrote in my diary at the end of July:

Thursday, July 20, 1989

Today, I woke up after sleeping another 12 hours. Guess I really needed it. This afternoon I got my first permanent for my hair since the accident—another step towards getting back to normal. I waited to get this, because it took so long for the hair to grow back on the back of my head where the doctors shaved everything off. But my hairdresser Ralph did a great job at hiding my scars. My hair doesn't cover the scars entirely. But at least, there is now hair on the back of my head, and it makes so much difference having it there. It makes me feel like there is truly a new life for me.

After seeing Ralph, I went to visit Mom and Dad, and that was encouraging, too, since Dad was out of the hospital and walking without his crutches. Both Dad and I compared our new signs of recovery. Dad showed me that he could now walk without crutches, and he walked up and down the stairs to demonstrate. Then, I showed off my new neckline, since I was able to go for the whole afternoon without having to wear my collar.

Saturday, July 22, 1989

I finally got out to go to the grocery store. I called Mom and asked to go to the store with her. I hoped this would be still another hurdle I could overcome. But once we were inside the Purity Market, I found that everything looked blurry, and I couldn't walk a straight line. I went zigzagging down the aisle like a drunk, and I suddenly felt very frightened. It was an experience I never had before—not being able to walk, and I felt so dizzy, I was almost ready to pass out before I finished shopping. To steady myself, I grabbed onto the grocery cart, headed to the check out line, and held tightly onto the cart as I waited in line. Then, I staggered to the car and I felt relieved to open the door and sit down in the car where my mother was waiting. After my mother drove me home, I laid down, feeling totally exhausted and upset, because I had been doing so well for the last few weeks, and this trip to the store seemed like such a set back.

Tuesday, July 25, 1989

More doctors again. Yesterday, I saw Dr. Golub, the psychologist, and felt really glad to see her to express the pent-up feelings of guilt, anger, frustration, and loneliness I've been feeling over the past weeks. I told her that I often wonder if my life will ever get back to normal. Everything has been taking so extremely long. And now, after once loving to be with people, I feel so insecure about meeting people, because I'm not sure if I will remember their names or know what to say.

As I told her, I'm not the same as I was before. I'm a new me. I feel like I've been waking up a different person each day, because everyday, I feel like I'm someone new. I'm not even sure exactly who I'll be or how I'll feel from day to day.

Then, today, I saw Dr. Cox, the neurosurgeon, who checked the movement of my neck. He asked me to move my neck in all directions—left, right, up, and down. Unfortunately, though, he wasn't too happy with the amount of movement, since he felt my neck was still too stiff and rigid. He explained I wasn't able to turn it enough, even though I was trying so hard to do so.

After that, even more bad news. Dr. Cox warned me I could have possible seizures, and had about a 50% chance of having them, because of the type of head injury I had. Oddly, he explained, such seizures usually don't start until several years after the accident due to possible brain swelling after the initial trauma, so he couldn't tell if I would have them or not in the future. But in case I did, he wanted me to be aware of this possibility, so I could be better prepared if the seizures occurred.

Finally, he told me to see an opthomalic neurosurgeon to find out why my vision was blurry. "Keep a diary on your dizziness and your inability to walk straight," he said.

It was so depressing to hear these things that when I got home, I just wanted to go to bed and did. I realized, because of the possibility of seizures, how much the head injury was affecting every aspect of my life and would continue to do so. It was like being in a prison I could never leave.

Thursday, July 27, 1989

I've been feeling very depressed since I saw Dr. Cox, both yesterday and today. Making things even worse, he told me I shouldn't drive yet. I hate feeling dependent on others. I wish I could simply get in the car and go somewhere myself. But again, everything is taking longer than

I thought. To try and speed things up, I tried moving my neck more than Dr. Cox recommended. But it wouldn't move any further, no matter how hard I tried to push it. So I kept getting more and more frustrated, the more I tried.

I also feel like all this trauma has been making me get older faster. I noticed a few more gray hairs a few days ago, and today Cindy drove me to Ralph's, the hairdresser, to cover them up. He had to use two bottles of hair coloring because there was so much gray. Sure, there were some before the accident. But I feel the accident has made them worse.

STONES IN THE ROAD

Then the legal morass began to hit, since my mother-in-law Shirley was now taking steps to formally accuse me of being responsible for Bob's death, claiming I was really driving, not Bob. So besides blaming myself for not asking Bob to slow down, I now had to face Shirley's false accusations blaming me for something I didn't do. These accusations really hit me hard. As I wrote in my diary:

Friday, July 28, 1989

This morning, when I went to visit my father, he told me the worst news I could imagine. He said my mother-in-law was planning to sue me for wrongful death, because she had learned that Bob had lived and suffered for about 2 hours after the car accident. She also believed that I was the one who was driving, not Bob.

The shock was incredible. First, I felt terrible to learn that Bob had suffered so. I got up and rushed outside to get some air, because I started to hyperventilate, just thinking about him experiencing so much agony. Then, as I stood on the walk shaking and sobbing, my father came over to comfort me and took me back inside.

After I calmed down from thinking about Bob's pain, the shock of what Shirley was planning to do really hit me. I could hardly believe what I heard. Sue me! Claim I was a driver, when Bob always drove! I had always disliked Shirley and called her "Salem," as did many of my friends, since I thought of her as something of a witch. But now this. I couldn't believe she would stoop so low. It took me two hours to calm down and feel I could function again.

After lunch, when I went to the rehab hospital for speech therapy with Renee, the news weighed on my mind and I couldn't concentrate. Instead, I began talking to Renee about how Bob suffered so terribly before he died, and broke down in tears again.

Following the session, when my mother drove me home, I wanted to be left alone, so I could more deeply grieve for my lost husband. I had been so busy till now seeing doctor after doctor, day after day, I didn't feel I had any time to really grieve for Bob's death, and through grieving, feel a sense of completion and letting go. I didn't have time to think about him during the day, only at night for a few hours before going to bed. But now that I finally have the time to grieve, Mrs. Raymond is talking of filing a wrongful death suit against me. So I feel I can't even grieve in peace, because now I have to deal with that. So now there will be lawyer after lawyer besides doctors. What can't everyone leave me alone?

Finally, I took a pill the doctor gave me at the rehab hospital to relax me, and went to sleep. I needed to escape and forget.

Monday, July 31, 1989

A few days ago, when I started cleaning out closets, I felt I was finally in charge of my life again. I felt like I was going to throw things out, start a new life, be a new me. But yesterday, while cleaning the closets, I felt so sad. As I went through the old clothes and pictures, it brought back so many memories. Like the T-shirt I dyed for Halloween when I dressed Bob in a tutu. Seeing the T-shirt brought back such funny memories of him waltzing around at the party like he was doing pirouettes. Now I cherish these memories so much, though they are filled with such sadness, too.

Then, this morning, when I saw my psychologist, Dr. Golub, I was glad I could pour out my feelings after learning that Mrs. Raymond might file a wrongful death suit against me. I told Dr. Golub that I thought she was planning to do this because she is so filled with guilt about the death of her son, that she wants to make someone pay. And she feels it should be me. Dr. Golub agreed with my theory.

But I don't know if I can handle what happens if Mrs. Raymond actually files this suit. I feel like I did when I went through my first divorce. It was so painful because of all the feelings of hatred, betrayal, hopelessness, and anger. And now I probably will have to deal with this totally unjustified suit.

Tuesday, August 1, 1989

Today, when I went to speech therapy with Renee, I felt so foggy. I have so much on my mind. I can see so clearly what my mother-in-law is trying to do, but that's making everything else so confusing. Also, thinking about the suit has got me thinking about Bob and missing him again so deeply, that I feel really mixed up. A few weeks ago, I felt I was in charge of my life again. But now I'm doubting myself and feel more depressed than ever. Once more I feel like I don't care if I live or not; I've been wishing I could die to be with Bob, once again.

At least I finished the neuropsychological exam today. So that's one thing I accomplished successfully.

****

Unfortunately, when the results came back from the comprehensive exam I had taken a few days earlier, they contributed to my feeling that everything was falling apart. Dr. Higgins' report highlighted how much I had lost and how far I still had to go in getting back my mental functioning. He had given me about a dozen tests over a two week period—for finger and grip strength, for complex figure drawing, memory, putting objects in categories, sorting cards, intelligence, and for other measures. They had names like scientific recipes: The Finger Oscillation Test, the Grip Strength Test, the Trail Making Test, Rey Osterreith Complex Figure Drawing, the Stroop Color-Word Interference Test, and the Wisconsin Card Sorting Test. Plus there were some common standards like the Wechsler Adult Intelligence Scale and Weschler Memory Scale.

His report was detailed and precise. For example, he noted that I had a pretty good grip and speed with my right hand, but not so good with my left hand, suggesting "a right hemisphere deficit." But I did fairly well in copying complex figures on the Osterreith Complex Figure Design test and now had an average level of scoring on the Wechsler Adult Intelligence Scale—99 for performance, 94 on verbal, and 96 overall on the whole scale—a big difference from the 138 score I used to have. Though I knew my ability had declined, it was discouraging to see this in such stark clinical terms, or as he put it, he observed "a marked decline from the patient's premorbid level of functioning," and he pointed out that I had the most difficulties on the verbal subtest, because of "considerable difficulty with information comprehension and similarities."

Seeing his explanation was especially depressing, because of the way he expressed it in jargon of science, such as observing that I had "deficits" in many "posterior functions," notably "those associated with the left temporal regions." It was like seeing myself examined under a microscope and having a scientist clinically describe every broken piece or part. I wanted to be a whole person and feel whole again, and here my whole life was being reduced to medical reports, graphs, and charts.

When Dr. Higgins gave me a personality test—the Minnesota Multiphasic Personality Inventory—that highlighted how emotionally fragile I was at the time, something I already knew. He wanted to document just how fragile more precisely. In this case, Dr. Higgings reported that the major problem was my feelings of depression and loss, combined with my feelings of growing pressure due to family conflicts. That was his gentle way of describing the brewing legal storm with Mrs. Raymond. Then, he concluded that overall, I was "experiencing difficulty with control of her emotions" and "would probably benefit from ongoing professional psychotherapy."

Or as he finally recommended:

> She should undergo a course of treatment designed to remediate her cognitive difficulties and to address her memory problems. She would also be likely to benefit from a course of psychotherapy designed to remediate her depression to help her come to grips with some of the her family issues and to help her with the grieving process.

I already knew most of these findings from my own experience. His report helped to summarize and provide an official medical imprimatur of how much I had lost. What was so discouraging was to be reminded again of how far I had to go to get back to where I had been, despite my months of work in rehabilitation. I felt like Sisyphus pushing the boulder up a hill and continually falling back only to keep pressing ahead.

Then, on top of all that, I had still more depressing news when I met with my accountant about my desperate financial plight. As I described what happened in my diary for the next week:

Wednesday, August 2, 1989

After I did my aerobics for the morning, Mom stopped by and drove me to see Steve Goldberg, my accountant. I was already feeling depressed before we got there, and his news made me feel even worse. "You're almost on the brink of a business and personal bankruptcy," he told me. Then he explained that if my mother-in-law who was threatening a wrongful death suit actually sued me, she could send me over the edge.

He also urged me to call my creditors and try to work things out, since many of them were already starting to call repeatedly about when they would be paid. If I could work out an agreement, Steve thought, I could at least hold my creditors off from suing me. He thought that might be a positive bit of news. But after hearing his financial report, I felt like going right to bed. Between my mother-in-law, my beloved husband gone, and the long struggle with my health—everything is becoming too much to handle. I'm starting to feel like I don't care or want to care about anything anymore. I'd like to just go to sleep and not wake up, so everything is gone.

Thursday, August 3, 1989

I wish I knew how to pull myself out of this depression. I was crying all last night, before I finally got to sleep. The exercising doesn't even help anymore. I feel overwhelmed by all these memories, thinking about what my mother-in-law may do, and facing the brink of bankruptcy.

After returning from speech therapy at the rehab hospital, I finally let it all out. I went into my room, threw myself down on the bed, and cried very hard, maybe for an hour. Finally, after I felt a sense of release from crying, I spent the rest of the afternoon doing aerobics. I still felt depressed, but at least the hysterical crying was over. I felt drained and cried out.

****

Yet, despite the bad news and more setbacks, I kept trying. It's like that was the only thing I knew to keep doing. Otherwise I would give up and want to die.

One way I kept trying was trying to learn how to drive again, and this became one important breakthrough. Though it was scary to get behind the wheel of a car once more, I pushed myself to succeed and felt a great sense of accomplishment when I could finally do it. So here and there, I experienced bits of sunlight through the gloom. As I wrote in my diary in early and mid-August:

Sunday, August 6

Today, I tried driving for the first time. I started out by driving on the private road where we live. And that felt fine. But when I pulled out on a two-lane winding country road, another car came the other way, and I panicked. I was only driving about 20 miles an hour, but suddenly I wasn't sure if I could judge the distance between myself and the other car. So I pulled my car over to the side of the road. I was so afraid of another crash—and the fear was even stronger, because it brought back vivid memories of the crash with Bob.

In the afternoon, however, I made myself get back in the car, and I drove to the grocery store—*another first, since it meant driving on city streets. It was terrifying, but I did it. It was scary all the way, since I felt terrified every time I got to a corner or a car passed me in any direction. Also, all that turning and looking at intersections to see if any cars were coming hurt my weak neck. But at last I made it, and I feel good I did.*

Friday, August 11, 1989

Yesterday and today, I saw more doctors, and had a mix of bad and good experiences. I felt some optimism when I saw Dr. Breed, the opthamologist, yesterday, and after he checked my eyes, he said I was coming along fine and didn't need optical glasses.

But the plastic surgeon, Dr. Sevinor was less encouraging. "You'll always have those two scars above your eyebrows," he told me. "And you'll always have those scars on your abdomen from the splenectomy, on your neck from the fusion, and down the middle of your back where they removed a rib." I wondered about plastic surgery, but he explained: "There's no plastic surgery to help them, though the scars on your neck aren't so bad, because you can cover them up with your hair." It was a dispiriting prognosis, because I have always had such pride in my looks. But now, it's like a permanent sentence to look less than my best.

Then, today, I met with Dr. Higgins about further neuropsych exam results. The good news was he said I scored the highest he has ever seen on adaptability. But the bad news was that I scored the lowest for verbal memory. I suspected this would be the case, since I've been having so much trouble remembering anything. Still it was sad to hear him tell me the official results, but at least he offered a little hope of adapting based on my current level of skills. So I'll be meeting him next week, so he can help me choose a new vocation based on what I can do.

Finally, Dr. Higgins told me I have feelings of depression, anxiety, and paranoia because of Mrs. Raymond, which wasn't much of a surprise. I could have told him I would score that way without taking the test.

****

The next days were better, however, and I felt more optimistic once again, because I was able to do more things and be with more people. Even with the threat of a lawsuit hanging over my head and the grim prognosis from my accountant, the weekly rehab sessions seemed to be finally helping. Life seemed to be returning to almost normal, and I felt good about the world again. As I wrote in my diary expressing these more hopeful feelings:

Sunday, August 13, 1989

Yesterday, I woke up to Fluffy and Bogie, the Maltese dog my brother and sister-in-law Paul and Cindy left at the house, bouncing on my bed. After dressing, I decided to bake. I thought this would be good for my therapy. I started off making some banana bread, though I forgot the vanilla and vinegar. But afterwards when I made some wheat bread, I didn't forget a thing, and it came out tasting very good. So I feel like this was one more accomplishment.

Today, I drove to Lovell Lake in New Hampshire with Bogie. I was able to drive the whole way myself, after practicing on the back country roads in Topsfield several times before. But my neck was a little sore when I got there, because of having to continually turn it to check behind me.

After I arrived, Lois Hart picked me up to take me a dinner party where a half dozen old friends were waiting, and it was like the good old days. It was good to see everyone I grew up with and saw at the lake each summer for over 30 years.

We sat around having a wonderful dinner at Rick and Cindy's talking about what everyone was doing, and Rick mentioned how lively I seemed now, compared to when he saw me in the hospital.

Afterwards, I came home feeling how great it was to do the everyday things I used to take for granted. As I fell asleep watching a movie about Iranian hostages, I felt I was finally starting to feel free again.

Monday, August 14, 1989

Another round of visiting with other friends from the lake. This time, when I went to visit Larry and Marilyn, they stared at me with surprise and gave me a big hug, with big smiles on their faces. They couldn't believe how much better I looked, since they had seen me right after the accident. Then, after Jim and Lois stopped by, we had a big feast with the leftovers, which Larry and Marilyn picked up from the baptism service they just had for their baby girl.

Later that afternoon, I headed for Ipswich, Massachusetts, where I had a great dinner at my brother Paul's, which included his wife Cindy, Mom and Dad. But there was one sour note. As we were eating, Paul looked me in the eye and said, "Why don't you get back to work and stop all this rehab? They're just taking your money."

I was in shock to hear him say this. Lately, I had been hearing many other people wonder why I didn't go back to work, too. But I felt my family would be more sympathetic and supportive. But now I realized that many of them don't understand. They don't realize how much I need the rehab and the speech therapy to be normal again. But they don't see that. They don't understand.

Wednesday, August 16, 1989

Two days of more rehab work. It was depressing to go back yesterday after hearing Paul say "You don't need it." However, after I arrived, I saw the nurse I had months before when I had my halo on, and it felt good to be there, knowing this rehab was helping me get better. When I saw the nurse, she told me she was getting married next spring, and at first, she didn't recognize me, because I looked so different with my halo off. I recalled how she used to help me comb and braid my hair when I wore the halo, and I felt good thinking how she had been one of the few bright spots back then. Seeing her now helped me feel this experience was even further in the past. I didn't even recall her name.

Afterwards, I had a good speech class, which helped me put Paul's comments in perspective, too. I know I need this treatment, whatever he might think.

Then, today, I met with the head injury doctor, Dr. Whitlock. I went to see him since I discovered a strange lump on my head a few days ago. It was unnerving, because I was starting to think that everything's getting better. But seeing him was another reminder to wait and see, and take each day a day at a time, as they say in recovery programs. I just have to keep my hopes up.

Still, it's hard to keep hoping sometimes, like today. When Dr. Whitlock tested me, he noticed my balance was off when he asked me to walk in a straight line and then stand on one foot with my eyes closed. I couldn't stand without falling. Dr. Whitlock was also concerned that my left eyesight was weak, though my right eyesight was normal. But hearing this wasn't a surprise, since I've been seeing double from time to time. Will I ever finally get better? Dr. Whitlock scheduled an appointment for a Cat Scan and arranged for me to see a neuro-opthamologist to decide what to do next. I can only hope.

Thursday, August 17, 1989

Today was another breakthrough, however. I went for a massage for the first time in over a year. I couldn't get the full treatment, since my massage therapist, Nancy, couldn't turn my neck or press where my rib had been removed. But otherwise, it felt great—I haven't had a massage in so long.

Later that afternoon, though, was something of a bittersweet occasion, when I got together with a few friends on what would have been Bob's birthday. After Joy stopped by, we sat by the pool, talking about what a good person Bob was, and the many wonderful times Bob and I had together. Then, after Mark, her husband, joined us for dinner, I brought in some of my homemade wheat bread. It was much easier to make this time. After dinner, I brought out a bottle of wine that had been in Bob's wine cellar as a remembrance of his birthday and a remembrance that his spirit was still with me.

Friday, August 18, 1989

Today I went for my Cat Scan, which was a little scary. I not only was nervous, hoping nothing would show up, but I felt uncomfortable going back to the X-ray department, since I spent so many hours in X-ray departments, operating rooms, and other hospital rooms. As I walked in, the room looked bleak and forbidding, with its stark white walls, X-Ray machines, and huge MRI or Magnetic Resonance Imaging machine, for taking cross-section images of different parts of the body. The Cat Scan machine itself was especially forbidding—a long white metal cylinder that looked cold and desolate, like a big white coffin. Dr. Whitlock and his assistant asked me to get inside and lie down. Then, they put blocks on either side of my head to prevent me from moving. It was like lying down in a coffin, and I felt claustrophobic. After they pressed a button, they released some current into my head every few seconds for the next 45 minutes. Each time they did, I heard a tapping and felt a tingling sensation. Afterwards, Dr. Whitlock told me he would have the test results in a few days and report back to me.

****

After that, the next few days were mostly good ones, full of a growing round of social events, and I started thinking about returning to Florida. I hoped, by going back, to resume my old life running my business. I realized I wasn't ready yet, but more and more I hoped I could. As I wrote in my diary at the end of August:

Sunday, August 20, 1989

Yesterday afternoon, I met with some people I hadn't seen since I moved to Florida. It was at an informal get-together put on by some old friends from high school days—Mary Jane, my best friend from high school, and Peter, her husband. Yet, while it was good to see everyone again, I felt strangely out of place and self-conscience, because I found it so hard to remember many words when I tried to think of them. Also, I found I can't carry on more than one conversation at once, although such conversations are common in these big gatherings. As a result, I'm not comfortable around a lot of people anymore. At least, not yet. So I felt relieved and relaxed when I came home after the get-together, watched TV, and went to bed.

Today at church, what a surprise! At the 11:30 church service, while I was praying, Father Driscol, the church priest, came over to me and tapped me on the shoulder to say hello. He recognized me because of my collar. Then, he asked me how I was doing, since he hadn't seen me since he stopped by about three months earlier to visit me at the house soon after I got out of the hospital.

Afterwards, I went to a surprise wedding shower for the fiance of an old friend, Phyllis Herbert, who was marrying an old high school buddy. This time I felt better being with a large group of people, since these were people I already knew, and I easily remembered their names since I had known them so long. So my experience was so different from yesterday, when I met so many new people it was hard to remember all their names. Also, it was comfortable to sit and chat informally as Phyllis opened her gifts—nothing too intellectual. Now I'm looking forward to the wedding, too.

Tuesday, August 22, 1989

Yesterday was a good beginning to the week, since I had a good rehab session. My work with weights three to five times a week seems to be paying off. Dr. Jaeger, my overall rehab doctor, who coordinated all my different doctors and therapies, told me my left side was much stronger and I was doing very well. Then, for the first time, my speech therapist Renee gave me a book to read.

Afterwards, as I waited in the hall to see still another doctor, I saw Sam, another neck injury patient, who was there to have a halo removed. As I spoke to him, this brought back memories of the days when I was in a halo myself, and it reminded me how far I had come.

Later that afternoon when I started talking to my psychologist Dr. Golub about going back to Florida full-time, she urged me not to go. She said I wasn't ready. She thought I still had too many psychological issues and emotional problems to deal with to think about work yet. It was so frustrating to hear her say this, because for several months, I had been looking towards returning as a goal for when I got better. I still didn't want to believe that I couldn't handle being on my own yet.

Today, though, speech therapy was fun. I had a chance to become a little kid again, as I watched apples jump about and fall down on a computer screen, while I tried to collect them and put them in a basket.

Wednesday, August 23, 1989

Today, I had a long talk with my mother about the way things were going before the accident and why I wanted to go to Florida then to become more independent and still hope to go back now for the same reason. It was the first time we really talked about these things.

I told her I wanted to get away from Massachusetts, because I felt my father was always around trying to control me, and he never had any words of encouragement for the work I was doing. He never once said I did a good job, even though many other people I worked with—like my co-workers and the bankers I dealt with—complimented me on my dedication, knowledge and ability. My Dad's approval had always been important to me, so his lack of any show of approval helped to make my self-esteem feel really low. So I felt a need to prove myself now.

Unfortunately, Mom thought I was acting destructively by trying to take on too much at once, as I had last year, when I started a new business, planned my own wedding to Bob, and arranged to move to Florida all in the same year. "But you have so many good friends in Massachusetts," she kept telling me. And I do. But I feel all the ties are holding me back—even now, because I want to make it on my own, in spite of my setback and serious difficulties. More than ever, I want to make my Mail Boxes franchise in Florida a great success. All by myself.

However, even after our discussion, I don't think Mom understood. So to get rid of my feelings of frustration, I started cleaning the house—and I felt like I was cleaning out the frustrations and cobwebs in my mind, as I cleaned.

Thursday, August 24, 1989

I'm feeling more strongly than ever that I want to go back to Florida, if only I can. I spent the morning thinking about what I would take with me if I go, if only my neurosurgeon Dr. Cox, gives me the go ahead next week.

That evening I met my old friend from high school, Joe Fowler, who was handling my Mail Boxes franchise sales in my absence, for dinner at a restaurant near my house. He had closed one sale I had started before the accident and sold a second franchise afterwards, so I considered him a really good friend. At dinner, we made a pact to help each other. He told me how he had lost his fiancee a few years ago in college, when she died in his arms. Then, he suggested that since I have such a terrible memory due to the accident, he could help me remember. "Anytime you call anyone about your business," he told me, "call me immediately afterwards, tell me what you said, and I'll remember it for you." And he really meant it, too, not just as a joke. Now that's what I consider being a good friend. Anyway, I told him I would try—if I remembered to call, of course!

Sunday, August 27, 1989

I feel like I'm getting back in the social swing of things again. After another session of rehab Friday, I went to a birthday party for some old friends with Mom and Dad. It was great seeing these friends, some I hadn't seen since the accident.

Then, Saturday, I spent a whole day cooking to get ready for friends who are coming on Sunday. I did more than I've been able to do in a long-time. First, I helped Mom and Dad put the ribs on a barbecue. Then, I put together a cheese dip, mixed and baked the banana bread, and made some dilled potatoes. I was so proud of what I could do.

But unfortunately, the one disaster was the chocolate mousse, since I used bittersweet instead of semi-sweet chocolate. Also, the mousse boiled over, so it spilled all over the floor. It was frustrating to feel I was doing so well one minute, and then discover that doing all these things at once isn't as easy as it used to be. So the mousse turned out to be one thing too much. It was like that last little straw that brings down the camel. I guess I have to be a little more aware of when things are reaching that boiling point in the future!

Then, after I finished getting everything ready and cleaned up the kitchen, another old friend, Nicole, who helped with my pin care, came by, and we sat in the sun and relaxed.

Finally, the big event. Around noon, everyone started arriving—and it felt so good to be with so many old friends again—Paul and Libby, Nicole, Lennie, and Kris. They were all around continually when I really needed help after the accident—calling, picking me up to go places, bringing me things, and even helping with my daily pin care, like Nicole. So I felt really appreciative when I saw them again.

We sat around the pool, enjoying dips and drinks, and talking about past times. When I mentioned that Mrs. Raymond might sue me, we talked about how she had done many destructive things to everyone. For instance, she refused to rent her house to Lennie and Kris, because they were not married. We also made fun of her and Mr. Raymond for not divorcing even though they were so unhappy together. After talking about her, I felt much better. I wasn't going to let thinking about her spoil today for anything.

Afterward, we lounged in the sun for a couple of hours, and in the early evening, we had the big buffet I had spent all yesterday preparing—ribs, potatoes, home made bread, tomato salad. Everyone left the dinner feeling stuffed, and later, I was glad that Lennie and Kris stayed over. As we talked about the accident, I thought about how short life can be and how one never knows what will happen. "That's why," I told them, "you really have to value the people in your life and let them know you appreciate them when you can, because you don't know how short life will be." "That's exactly right," they both agreed.

CHAPTER 7

•

THE GATHERING STORM

LEGAL DEVELOPMENTS AND PSYCHOLOGICAL WARNINGS

As I began getting back into the social swing, my lawyers were still collecting documents for my accident claim—and getting growing hints of legal problems ahead. While my old family friend and lawyer Mark Bidner who handled my personal and business dealings started the process, the lawyers he referred me to, Paul Freedman and his associate Joel Kaplan, had continued to handle my claim.

Through July and August, Freedman kept trying to get additional documents showing my treatment by various doctors and medical centers. He also advised them to send their growing number of bills to my insurance company, Blue Cross and Blue Shield of Massachusetts.

All fairly routine. But complications were looming.

One was that Mrs. Raymond's attorney, Linda Goldman, told Freedman that she wanted to be reimbursed for her funeral expenses and that she was opening up an estate for Bob. In response, Freedman, asked Mark Bidner to check into the possibility of my filing a claim against the estate, on the grounds that Bob was driving. Therefore, Freedman believed, Bob's estate and any insurer for that estate would be liable for any damages, besides whatever I got from my own insurance.

Then, I later learned, if Freedman collected anything, Blue Cross wanted to be reimbursed. As Blue Cross advised Freedman, the company was putting a lien on any benefits Freedman collected for me, so they could get back whatever they had already paid out or might still pay out in medical bills. Still routine perhaps. But that exchange reminded me of sharks circling, deciding who was going to do the kill, and how to share the results later.

Then in late August—on August 25th—came some really disturbing news when my attorney Joseph Zaks, who was looking into my prenuptial agreement with Bob, expressed some concerns about this to Mark Bidner. In the agreement, Bob and I had released each other from claims on each other's estates. So now the big question was whether this meant that I had no right to manage his estate after his death and that his mother, Mrs. Raymond, could take over instead. Zaks wanted to try to keep this from happening, and he wrote to Bidner warning that Mrs. Raymond's attorney Linda Goldman was about to file a petition to handle Bob's estate and appoint Mrs. Raymond the administrator.

At once I knew this was bad news. I had been telling Freedman and my other lawyers for the last few months, ever since I got home from the hospital and began to understand a little of what was going on, not to let Mrs. Raymond take charge of the estate. Now if I couldn't handle it myself, what then? I told Bidner, who was handling the estate matters, to try to have an impartial third party appointed as the administrator. It didn't look hopeful, Bidner reported, since Goldman was acting as if Mrs. Raymond's appointment was a fait accompli. In fact, she had written to Zaks inviting me to file my own claim against the estate if I wished.

"But can't we challenge that?" I begged Bidner. But he didn't think a challenge was worth the effort, not understanding the danger of having Mrs. Raymond in control of the estate. Rather, he advised me not to put a lot of effort into challenging the situation, because I had waived any claim to Bob's estate because of the prenuptial agreement. Thus, he tried to reassure me, saying there was nothing Mrs. Raymond could do to hurt me even if she was the administrator. After all, he argued, Mrs. Raymond would be bound by law to distribute the proceeds of the estate according to Bob's will and other legal restrictions.

Eventually, Bidner convinced me. So on his advice, I did not have him file any formal opposition to the appointment. In retrospect, I wish I had trusted my gut feelings of danger, because once Mrs. Raymond became the administratrix, she gained the power to file a suit against me on behalf of Bob's estate for wrongfully causing his death, even though that wasn't true. Once she did, this set the stage for disaster—years of litigation and all the financial problems that ensued.

At the time, I was barely aware of these possible complications. I was just gradually getting my life back together, spending much of my time seeing old friends, visiting various types of doctors for treatment and therapy, and mentally and emotionally still struggling to cope with all my losses. So I had little ability to deal with these legal matters.

In fact, Dr. Golub's progress report at the end of August showed how very difficult it was. As I knew myself and her report made very clear, I was still very very depressed about Bob's death and my own physical well-being and ability to work or lead a normal life again. Also, I was anxious about my welfare and lacked self-confidence because I still couldn't function at my previous level. I still had "ongoing trouble with short-term memory and other functions" and was "unsure how much cognitive damage will be permanent" making it difficult to plan for what to do with the rest of my life. Plus, she noted, I still felt very upset at having to be dependent on my family and others due to my injuries, because I had worked so hard to separate myself from my father's business interests and prove myself on my own merits as an independent business woman.

But here I was like a child again, dependent on my parents to get around from day to day. I also felt like my business enterprises and investments were suffering without my involvement, but I still couldn't deal with them personally and had to rely on my father and other business associates to manage them for me. On top of all that, I was afraid I might lose a substantial amount of the financial assets I had worked so hard to accumulate. My ability to earn in the future was very much in doubt.

It's the kind of bind which often affects brain injury patients, or as Dr. Golub expressed it in concluding her report: "Ms. Quinn feels in a bind between the help she needs and appreciates, and the loss of her hard-earned independence."

Thus, as much as I might look normal on the surface, I continued to have severe bouts of depression. I frequently had suicidal thoughts though I didn't act on them because of my religious beliefs, and I spent many sleepless nights, agonizing over the trauma I felt and worrying about my uncertain future.

To deal with all this, Dr. Golub felt I would need to stay in therapy for at least another year. So, in this depressed and anxious state, I had little ability or interest to deal with the growing legal mess. In fact, I preferred not to deal with it, because hearing my lawyers describe the latest problem made me feel even more anxious and depressed. I just wanted to let go of the past and move on with my life.

GETTING AWAY TO FLORIDA

I thought going back to Florida as soon as I could might be the answer. By the end of August, I decided to do that, starting with a short business trip. I had heard from my old friend, Joe Fowler, who was taking care of my business in my absence that a new franchisee had recently bought a franchise from him as part of my area franchises. I thought this would be a good time to go to see how the new franchise was doing. Also, I could see how my original Mail Boxes franchise in Naples was faring under Charlie, another long-time family friend, who had taken over as the manager of this store while I was gone. He had flown down from Boston to take care of things, and because I knew him so long I trusted him to do so. Then, too, I longed to go since this would be a respite from all the doctors, even Dr. Golub, who was so helpful and supportive. And I wanted this chance to finally strike out on my own. As I wrote in my diary just before I left:

Tuesday, August 29, 1989

Yesterday, I saw Dr. Golub, and it was good to talk about my feelings of guilt. Also, I felt better sharing my feelings of hurt because my family doesn't understand. As I told Dr. Golub, they expect me to be fine and start working again now that the halo is off and the wounds have healed. But they don't see the other mental and emotional problems I feel. For example, when I told Mom I wanted to get away and relax for awhile, she retorted, "Why? You haven't worked in six months. What do you need to relax for?" She didn't understand. At least I feel I can better cope with this lack of communication after my meeting with Dr. Golub.

Today, I saw the last of the doctors, although I want to keep seeing Renee, my speech therapist, for awhile for cognitive retraining. What a relief to be finished with all these doctors. I feel almost healed. Even my opthomologist said he expected a full recovery. And Dr. Cox, my neurosurgeon, said he was happy about my progress and I could fly without any problem. "Just take it slow," he said. "No twelve hour days." I was so happy, I went to see Mom and celebrated with a glass of wine, before heading home to pack.

Today has been the first time, I've been really happy. I feel like I'm flying so high, I can't touch the ground with my feet. Wow! What a feeling! It's been so long since I felt this way.

Wednesday, August 30, 1989

Today, off to Florida. I woke up at 4:30 a.m. to feel Fluffy jumping on the bed and meowing to wake me up. Then, I got up excitedly to pack. Afterwards, I headed for the airport and got there an hour before the 11:15 a.m. flight—a big change for me, since I always used to rush at the last minute to catch a flight. But I wanted to arrive early, since I was so excited and a little apprehensive about making the flight, since this is the first time I was finally on my own again. Then, on the plane, I kept thinking about the meeting with the new franchisee, and what I would say and do, hoping I could do it.

Unfortunately, because I kept thinking about these plans and it was hard for me to focus on more than one thing at a time because of the head injury, I forgot about having to change planes in Orlando to board the connecting flight to Naples. So I missed my connection and watched helplessly as the plane pulled away. It was the first time I ever missed a flight, and after I got on a connecting flight—a small commuter airline, I thought how strange it was to forget and have to find another plane. I felt like a kid learning all over again.

When I arrived at the Naples airport and Charlie met me at the gate, I felt so dumb, because of missing the connection. But it was good to be back in Florida again, and getting there was one more thing I could do on my own.

LEARNING THE LIMITATIONS IN FLORIDA

Yet, as I soon discovered, there was much I couldn't do on my own—namely running my own business. Though one of my reasons for going to Florida had been to find out what was happening with the store Joe Fowler sold to the new franchisee after the accident, I discovered I couldn't fully understand what was going on. Instead, I had to depend heavily on Joe's advice, along with the support I got from the Mail Boxes' corporate office, because I couldn't understand the books or how to set up and administer the system. Before, I had known the system inside out. But now, experiencing these difficulties brought me face to face with my limitations. They showed me how much I needed to continue the rehabilitation process. Then, too, being in Florida brought back more sad memories of Bob. As I noted in my diary about my trip:

Thursday, August 31, 1989

I woke up today eager to start looking at new sites for the new store. Yet I was still nervous about doing these things, since it's back to work for the first time. "Will I be able to do it?" I wondered.

At 9:15 a.m., Craig Timmons, my real estate broker who leases spaces for stores, arrived to pick me up, and he took me to look at a proposed site. It looked like a good site because it already had a big grocery store as a major anchor tenant and a high volume of passing traffic on the road. I felt it was a real accomplishment to get out in the field again, even if I did have to depend on someone to drive me around.

Friday, September 1, 1989

Today was encouraging, too. I showed the prospective franchise buyer, Jim Husson, around, pointing out several sites, including some strip malls and several shopping centers with major anchor tenants. I pointed out that these big anchor stores would be good draws for the franchise, and I felt good because I think I did a good job when I showed him around and gave him reasons to buy, although I was a little embarrassed, because Jim had to drive. But even so, I was able to show him several possible sites, and I was able to do it much as I had many times before, when I showed commercial leasing spaces in Boston.

However, after I returned home, it was difficult when I went into the garage and started going through the boxes of possessions, which Bob and I had shipped to Florida to start our new life. I felt very sad seeing all those momentos again, especially the engagement gifts. Seeing them hit hard, and I started to get depressed. Then, I thought of the words Bob always said to me: "Don't worry. Be happy," and I felt much better. After that, I plunged into going through the boxes to put them away in the house, since they were left in the garage while I was in the hospital. I knew I had to go through these things sooner or later, so I decided it might as well be now.

Sunday, September 3, 1989

Two more successful days. Yesterday, I finally spoke with several real estate brokers about showing my villa which I had put up for sale. Before I was very uncertain about selling it, because I felt like I was letting go a part of my past with Bob. But now I felt ready to let that go, too. So I urged the brokers to put out feelers for potential buyers, and if anyone was interested in buying, I would consider their offers.

Then, today, I relaxed on the beach with Charlie. It was comforting talking about old times and friends from high school and what they were doing with their lives. As we soaked in the sun, I felt a sense of accomplishment I had done so much.

Monday, September 4, 1989

Still another accomplishment today—visiting with my prospective franchisee, Jim Husson a second time. Joe Fowler, who was handling the franchise sales while I couldn't, had gotten him interested in buying a Mail Boxes franchise, but I still had to meet him to answer some last questions and close the deal. Afterwards, with lots of help and coaching on what to do from Joe, I somehow got through the sale to Jim and closed it.

Later, at the Mail Boxes store, I spent about an hour calling up the company's corporate offices for more explicit instructions on what to do to run the store on a day to day basis. I had to learn most of this all over again. While the site visits had been relatively easy to do, anything that involved concentration or detailed paperwork was very difficult. I had to think through and agonize very carefully over things that came automatically before, and sometimes I felt very confused. But at least I could call up Joe and yell "Help!," and he would tell me what to do.

Also, I spent a lot of time on the phone with my attorney Mark Bidner, going over how he was handling the lease for the space Husson was renting for his new store.

Tuesday, September 5, 1989

Today, besides running errands and getting things at the supermarket and pharmacy, I got my nails done for the first time in months. After I got home, Craig, my broker, called to say he was waiting to hear from a potential buyer for the villa, though I'm having second thoughts. I'm still not sure I really want to sell it. I had to put it on the market because of my financial problems. Still, I guess, as much as I love the place, I'll have to go through with the sale. I just don't have the money to do otherwise.

I got a lot accomplished today, too. Besides speaking to the various people involved in the franchise sale: Husson, the prospective buyer, and the Mail Boxes Etc. lawyer, I worked out arrangements with the Post Office to set up a subcontract station in the store.

Afterwards, I felt I did really well, which helps my self-esteem. When I first arrived back *in Florida, I discovered so many things I couldn't do or needed a great deal of help doing. So it was great to see what I can do now, though it's hard for the people here to realize this. They don't realize how much I lost and how hard I have had to work to gain back what I now have.*

Later, I had dinner with Fred and Bette, the real estate brokers and family friends who sold me the villa where Bob and I were going to live. I discovered they were at my hospital room to see me after the accident. I didn't recognize them at the time, and they told me about all the confusion at the hospital back then. When they asked the doctors and nurses to explain what had happened, no one knew exactly what occurred and who was alive or dead. It was a sad reminder to think about that now, but I felt good to learn how concerned they were about me and to feel their strong friendship and caring now.

Wednesday, September 6, 1989

After several days of hard work, today was a chance to relax. I lay by the pool for about three hours in the morning—from 9 to 12 noon, then spent the afternoon watching TV. But again I can't seem to get away from old memories. While I was watching Lifestyles of the Rich and Famous, the program showed the Mandarin Hotel in San Francisco, and featured the exact suite where Bob and I had stayed the week before the wedding. As I watched, I burst out crying, thinking about Bob and how much I miss him.

Thursday, September 7, 1989

Unfortunately, it was time to go home today. I really didn't want to go. After packing, I lay in the sun for a few hours, thinking about how much I enjoyed being in Florida. Though I realize how much further I still have to go to get back to normal, at least I feel free and independent here.

BACK TO MASSACHUSETTS

The next day, I was back in Massachusetts, and over the next few days, it was a whirl of seeing old friends again. Several were getting married—so my days were filled going to weddings. But afterwards, I felt oddly sad and depressed, because all the beautiful wedding excitement reminded me of my own wedding and loss. As a result, I felt very discouraged when I went to my speech therapy lesson and found it more difficult than ever to concentrate and think. As I wrote in my diary for the next couple of weeks in September:

Friday, September 8, 1989

I arrived in Massachusetts late last night and got up early to repack and go to another wedding in New York. This time, my old friend Glen from high school is getting married to his long time fiancee Phyllis, from New York. After two of his friends picked me up and we arrived in the late afternoon, I went to the rehearsal dinner. It seemed like all my old friends from high school in Massachusetts had flown or driven in for the wedding, and it was great talking with them and laughing at old jokes. I felt like my old self again. It was the first time I didn't talk about the accident, and no one seemed to be aware that I was any different.

Sunday, September 10, 1989

Yesterday, I woke up with a big hangover—thanks to all the Grand Marnier at the wedding, I guess. But I was fine by the afternoon to go to the wedding. It was a beautiful occasion, held in a large marble church with about 100 guests. However, during the wedding ceremony— the first I had attended since my own, I felt like I wanted to disappear and die. I missed Bob so terribly. I ran through the hall to the bathroom, and I broke down at the sink, crying. A few minutes later, a woman I didn't know very well came in and held me in her arms until I calmed down. Then, we went back inside.

After the reception, I joined a small group in the hotel room of the parents of the bride and groom. We talked until 2 a.m,, when security arrived and told us we were keeping the other guests up.

In the morning, I joined a dozen other people from the wedding for breakfast at a coffee shop near my hotel. However, when I went to pay, my credit card didn't go through at the front desk. I was surprised and very embarrassed when the clerk told me this. At least he was calm and relaxed when he reassured me that these problems with declined credit cards happen from time to time and told me:"Just get another card, and it will be fine." So I went back to my room and got my American Express card from my suitcase, and fortunately this was all right. But I still worried about what might be wrong, since this had never happened before. Was something possibly wrong with my credit now?

Around noon, we headed back to Massachusetts, arriving around 5 p.m. I was feeling tired and glad to be home, though glad to have seen everyone again.

Monday, September 11, 1989

Strangely, I woke up feeling depressed. Maybe it's a come-down from all the excitement of the last few days. Or maybe it's because when I spoke with Charlie on the phone, he seemed so depressed. He told me had driven by the accident site yesterday by chance, and he suddenly felt overcome with grief thinking about the accident and how much he missed Bob. I thought it was *very odd that he should become so emotional about this after all this time, particularly since I never thought he was that close to Bob. But his emotional upset was unnerving, and it pulled me back into the past, too.*

Still, I stayed calm and told him to follow up on getting the lease on the new store finalized, since I couldn't do it myself while I was here in Massachusetts.

Wednesday, September 13, 1989

I woke up depressed again, on the verge of tears. I don't know why everything seems so bleak again. One reason may be that I just learned that Mom and Dad aren't getting along again, when Mom told me she has been increasingly angry at Dad for constantly trying to control her and tell her what to do. It's just like he keeps trying to control me.

Then, it was disturbing to discover that Charlie botched up the sale of the new store to Jim Husson. I tried talking to Husson to resolve the problem, but I couldn't understand what the problem was or explain what to do about it. So it looks like we may lose the sale. At first I felt really angry, and then very frustrated and depressed, because I feel so helpless to do anything. Not only am I out of town, but I can't understand or deal with people the way I used to. Eventually I felt so frustrated I started thinking: "The hell with it. Everything is so hopeless, I just don't care."

At least there was one bright spot in the last few days. In one of my speech therapy sessions which I attended three times a week, Renee suggested I should join a head injury support group. She said that a psychologist at the rehab hospital I attended had started one, and I decided to contact him about joining such a group.

Mostly though, today was discouraging. Besides waking up feeling depressed, I had to pick up thank-you cards from the printer to send to the people who had attended Bob's service, and that was hard to do. It was all I could do to keep from crying.

Then, I went to my father's office to run copies of the Mail Boxes franchise sale to Husson, after Charlie called to say it was back on again. While I was there, my Aunt Lydia and Uncle Joe dropped by, and when I saw them I suddenly broke down. I was feeling so overwhelmed from everything else and my vision was becoming so blurry from concentrating on the copying, that when I saw them, I couldn't hold back the tears any longer. Seeing these people I knew and trusted so much was like the trigger that led me to suddenly let all my feelings out. They helped calm me down, and afterwards, took me to a nearby Chinese restaurant for a late lunch.

After we arrived, my Dad met us there, since the restaurant was next to his office building. It was a welcome respite relaxing with everyone over lunch, and I felt much better. But afterwards, I felt very tired, and soon had a splitting headache, probably from all the crying. When am I going to finally feel better?

FEELING BETTER AGAIN

"When?" It was a question I kept asking, and the next few days I actually did feel a little better. But it was hard to know if this would last, or if this was just another up phase in the cycle of ups and downs that many brain injury patients experience. Yet, while this up phase lasted, I felt energized and full of hope again, as I once more tried to do new things, and experienced new accomplishments. As I wrote in my diary over the next few days in mid-September:

Friday, September 15, 1989

At least, I was in better spirits today, though a call that never came has me worried. The Mail Boxes corporate headquarters was supposed to call about having the commission from the Husson sale assigned to them instead of to me, because I couldn't pay them their earnings from the store for several months because of the accident. So why didn't they call? Is anything seriously wrong?

But after worrying for awhile, I managed to put my concerns aside. Instead, I tried to focus on looking good and presentable again. I rode my bike, took a long walk, and had my hair and nails done, which helped me feel better.

Sunday, September 17, 1989

Yesterday, Saturday, I felt better again. In the morning, I tried cooking several things at the same time—some onion bread, muffins, and a hamburger special. I wanted to see if I could handle doing several things at once. As it turned out I could, which felt good.

Then, after the pool guy stopped by to clean the pool, I put on one of my exercise tapes and exercised harder than ever. It was the first time I had done this energetic exercising in a month. I found I had more energy than ever, though I felt a little shaky when I started, since was a little rusty from not exercising for so long.

Today was even better, since Glen, a good friend from high school, who just got married, came by to pick me up, so I could visit with him and Phyllis at the new house they were remodeling. It cheered me to see them on a more personal basis than at their big wedding in New York. I really enjoyed touring their quaint New England style house, and seeing the modern touches they were adding, like new hardwood floors and carpeting.

Another highlight was meeting a man who had also suffered a head injury. After I told him about the head injury support group I was thinking of joining, he asked me to call him later if I did.

Monday, September 18, 1989

Today, I slept late and relaxed, since the past two weeks have been so hectic. Between traveling by air to Florida, driving to New York for the wedding, and going to all the parties here, it has been exhausting. I realize I can't take all this excitement the way I used to.

In fact, today has been a time to reflect and come to certain realizations about myself. I've been so consumed with getting better and overcoming the physical injuries and the mental losses, I realize I'm not even sure who I am anymore. So it's time to try to find myself again. I have to take some time to get to know me and love myself again. It's been so long since I've had a relationship with someone and have had anyone to share my love with. So I'm going to have to love the new me, since I'm a new person since the head injury. Then maybe someday, I'll find someone to share my love with me again.

Wednesday, September 20, 1989

Two more good days. Thursday, I really enjoyed my speech therapy class, because I started to see a slight improvement. I found I could concentrate better and for longer periods of time. So it was more fun than ever, because finally I saw this improvement after feeling stuck for so long. Even with a slight headache, blurry vision, and dizziness in the afternoon, I still felt good.

But I guess I better get these problems checked, since Dr. Cox, my neurosurgeon, warned me I might experience some seizures after I was getting better, due to possible brain swelling months after the initial trauma. So I'll have to talk to the head injury specialist, Dr. Whitlock, and see what he says I should do.

Then, this morning, I managed to negotiate the final arrangements for the Mail Boxes franchise lease for Jim Husson. At last, the sale finally went through. A small victory! After so much struggle. I wasn't always sure if I could handle this or not, but I did all right. One more accomplishment to feel good about. So I was in a much better mood today than for long time, because I'm seeing even more improvement. Before, each little improvement seemed so slight. But finalizing this sale feels like a big coup. So maybe with some vocational counseling, I can go back to work on a regular basis soon. In a few days, I'll start the vocational counseling program.

THE BEGINNING OF THE END

Thus, by mid-September, about seven months after the accident, everything was finally looking up. But everything soon came crashing down when I discovered someone I knew and trusted had betrayed me. The first intimations of serious trouble came September 21st—and over the next few days things rapidly fell apart. In days,

I went from feeling I was about to return to normal from my injury to feeling totally devastated and uncertain about what to do now. As I described what happened in my diary:

Thursday, September 21, 1989

Today started terribly and ended worse. I forgot to set the alarm, and woke up late and depressed, because I had barely enough time to get ready to go to my speech therapy with Renee at the rehab hospital. After dressing, though, I decided not to go. I was too upset by rushing to get ready.

Then, I had an afternoon conference call with my attorney handling the franchise sale for Jim Husson, which was supposed to be finalized. Husson had worked out some compromises with his own attorney, and his attorney and Husson called to ask me to agree to the new terms they worked out for the lease. But it was hard going, trying to read all of that technical language. Once I could once whiz through it. But not now. All these business details are still too much for me. So I struggled through reading the lease and discussing it as best I could, and I came away with a huge headache afterwards. But after talking to Husson and his attorney, I decided the compromises sounded reasonable and agreed. We finally had a deal. So at least that was one high point.

But later that day when I looked through the mail, I got the surprise of my life—the beginning of the end. The statement said that $4600 was due to American Express for purchases made for the Mailboxes store in Peabody, Massachusetts for May, June, and July. I couldn't believe it, since I certainly hadn't made any of these purchases.

To find out what had happened, I called Charlie, who was managing the Peabody store from the store in Naples. Since he was in Florida, he had put a friend, Debbie Bayrd, in charge of the Peabody store. At first, Charlie sounded very embarrassed and hemmed and hawed, trying to find an excuse about why these purchases might be on the statement. Then finally, he came clean and admitted that he had made the purchases himself, and that he and Debbie had been taking money from the accounts for several months.

I was shocked as he went on explaining what he had done. I realized he had taken these funds without my knowledge or authorization. He had embezzled from me and apparently, he had told Debbie how to embezzle from the company, too, telling her step by step by phone what to do at the Peabody store, while he did the same thing in Florida. But why? How could he do this? He said he had some personal needs that got out of hand, and he charged these purchases to the American Express account for the store. "I had to float some extra funds to cover some expenses," he said.

Incredible! I dropped the phone in shock on hearing that, and after I hung up, I crawled into bed and put the covers over my head. I felt like I had been hit over the head with a 2x4 board and was in a daze. How could Charlie do this? He had been a trusted family friend for over 30 years. He knew my mother, my father. I saw him come by the house many times when I was a child. Our families spent weekends at each other's house. One Sunday our family went to his house; the next weekend, he and his family came to spend the day at ours.

That's why when I was barely functioning after the accident, I turned everything in my business over to him, because I trusted him so much. And now I realized what he was doing. He had put Debbie in as manager at the Peabody store and taught her how to embezzle.

I suddenly felt very desperate as what he said sunk in. I think this is going to be the beginning of the fall of everything. And since Charlie was a long-time trusted friend that makes it even worse.

Friday, September 22, 1989

Today, was my 35th birthday. It was supposed to be a happy, joyous occasion, especially since I've been getting back on my feet physically. But instead, I felt in a real funk. I could barely get up in the morning, and didn't get up until very late, because I still can't believe what Charlie did. But he did it. He did!

I couldn't even get away from thinking about what he did when I left the house. When I went to the Peabody store to check up on how things were going, I got a phone call from American Express. They were going to be sending out an accountant on Monday to go over the books and find out what was going on. What a great "Happy Birthday" present! I left the store reeling.

After a brief respite for dinner with my parents and brother Paul and his wife Cindy, I called my lawyer, Mark Bidner, as soon as I got home to tell him what Charlie had done. I told him how Charlie had cashed the money orders and used them for himself. Mark said I wasn't responsible. But I don't know. Maybe I am. Or maybe I will have to make the funds good anyway to keep the good faith of the American Express company. Unfortunately, I can't do anything now about what happened. What's done is done, and there's no way to stop the damage now. So I'll have to deal with whatever happens next as best I can. But how? I don't know what to do, if anything, or whether I can do anything at all.

And now it seems so ironic to think back on everything I once had. The accident itself took so much. Now, with one fell swoop, it feels like whatever I have left after the accident is about to all be taken away. I keep thinking about all those years of hard work and effort. I spent about 15 years from 20 to 34, working in my father's real estate business. By 34 I had a $2 million estate, a nice house north of Boston, 20 acres on a lake in New Hampshire, a beautiful condo on the East Coast of Florida, and a wonderful new villa in Naples I just purchased. So I had everything. Everything.

Then, starting with the accident, piece by piece everything has been torn away. And now, after working so hard to rebuild my life, I feel like it's all going to come crashing down even more. And the one person I trusted with my business did all that.

Sunday, September 24, 1989

It was so hard to get up today. I woke up so depressed. Finally, I pulled myself out of bed around 10 a.m. and went to church. Incredibly, the service was all about evil people stealing from employees. It was like a message aimed right at me.

Monday, September 25, 1989

Today was another grim day of finding out exactly what Charlie did and how I stand financially as a result. I met with my accountant Steve Goldberg, and he told me that the first thing we would have to do is sell some of the stock I owned to try to recoup what funds we could to pay American Express and other unpaid bills. Then, he sent me to the bank to open up another Mail Boxes account in my name only, so I could use this as an operating account to pay ongoing expenses without Charlie's signature.

Finally, I returned to Steve's office, and we tried to figure out a strategy to deal with the whole mess. "This is incredible, incredible," Steve kept saying again and again, and in the end he told me to go back to Florida as soon as possible to salvage what was left of the business there. He was at a total loss as to what to do about the Peabody store where the embezzlement had occurred, and said we might have to close it.

I left feeling even more discouraged about how bad everything was. The whole sorry situation seemed so impossible to resolve. I wanted to go home and die.

Tuesday, September 26, 1989

Today went by like I was in a complete fog. When I saw Renee, she said she was very worried about me, because I didn't show up for our speech therapy appointment last Thursday and didn't call. Then, I poured out what had happened. She tried to comfort me by telling me about all the progress I had made in my thinking abilities, and she urged me to believe that everything would work out okay. But I still felt so terrible. When she tried to go on with the lesson, I found it too hard to concentrate. Even though she kept urging me to relax, saying "It will all work out. It will all work out," all I could think about was finding out the full extent of what Charlie did. The news of his embezzlement was so devastating—the last thing I wanted to do was think about word games in speech therapy with Renee.

After the session, I was supposed to go over a lease with another client. But I couldn't do it. I recalled how difficult it had been to go over the lease for the Husson sale when I was actually feeling good. I understood what I read while reading the lease, but afterwards, couldn't remember anything I had read. And now I was so upset, I didn't see how I could look at any lease at all. So finally I asked Joe Fowler and Mark Bidner to go over it for me, and they did.

Wednesday, September 27, 1989

Another day of even more bad news. I met with my accountant Steve Goldberg again, and he told me that the business was deeply in the hole because of what Charlie had done. He also explained that there was little we could do to get any of the money back, because Charlie had already spent it. So about the only thing I could do was to press charges against Charlie and try to protect the Florida area franchise from being ripped off, too.

After Steve finished telling me the prognosis, I realized I have to go back to Florida myself to sort out the mess. I feel so far away and helpless here, and there's no one in Florida that I trust anymore. So it looks like it's up to me, if I'm going to be able to salvage anything.

Thursday, September 28, 1989

I saw Renee at rehab today to tell her my plans to return to Florida, and she urged me not to do that. "Don't go," she warned. "You need to keep working with your speech therapy to get back to normal, because you aren't functioning at a high enough level yet. You could lose what you have gained in these months of work."

Afterwards, I left more confused than ever about what to do. Go back to Florida? Stay here? I was totally unsure. Later that day, when I went to see a vocational counselor, Sue Cunningham, for coffee, I had to fight back the tears as I told her what happened. I was so upset, I shook all over, and she reached over to hold my hand to steady me. She tried to be reassuring, telling me, "It'll all work out. Don't worry. But you should stay here to finish your speech therapy and vocational counseling." So gradually, she calmed me down.

But I couldn't take her advice. I explained that I had to return to Florida to run the store myself to try to save it until things were under control. Though she urged me again and again to take a vacation and put the crisis out of my head, I said I couldn't.

Sure, I thought, it would be nice to be able to get away and put all my problems in the past. But who could enjoy a vacation under such circumstances? Who could concentrate on having fun? Driving home, I felt so drained, I was ready to collapse. But as much as I might want to get away and put everything that had happened far out of my mind, I knew I couldn't. I had to go back to Florida. I didn't feel there was any other option. I had to go back to save what I could of the store. I had put so much into it. I couldn't lose it now.

Friday, September 29, 1989

Today, when I met with my psychologist, Dr. Golub, I told her my decision to go back to Florida to straighten things up. Like Renee and Sue, she urged me not to go. "You have so much left to work on," she said. "You are still dealing with your grief and pain from the accident and losing Bob."

Yes, I agreed I was. I also felt she had helped me so much, and I didn't want to interrupt the sessions. But I told her that I had to go, and that I hoped I could resume the sessions after I got back, hopefully soon. But for now, I had to go. I knew I had to go.

PART III:

REACHING BOTTOM

CHAPTER 8

•

DISCOVERING THE WORST

DEALING WITH DISASTER

After I discovered that Charlie had embezzled from me and virtually bankrupted my business, I felt devastated. On top of everything else, this was a crushing blow. I had felt I was finally able to overcome the worst of my medical problems and at last I hoped and thought I was ready to start running my business again. Now I felt my whole world collapsing again, like a ship sinking at sea, after I learned my business might cease to exist because of Charlie's actions. As I wrote in my diary after hearing the news:

Saturday, September 30, 1989

I haven't cried like this since I don't know when. God, I really wish I was dead... I just want to go away and be by myself.

But I'm still going to try to fight this. I won't let someone do this to me. I feel if you keep telling yourself you can't do it, you won't. So no matter how terrible I feel, I've got to press on.

But can I? When I spoke to my lawyer Paul Freedman last night, I told him how hard I've been trying to get back to normal. And now this. I don't know how much more I can take. Now I have to go back to Florida to deal with it. Why? Maybe I'll make an even bigger fool of myself in front of the customers. But I've got to try to meet this head on.

Sunday, October 1, 1989

I spent the day packing today to go back to Florida. As I packed, I kept thinking about how the worst thing I ever did was to buy the Mail Boxes franchise there. It not only took me away from Bob for months, while he stayed in Massachusetts to work out a way to manage his business from Florida. But it nearly wrecked our marriage because of the distance between us.

Then, when Bob finally agreed to move to Florida with me, we had the accident and I lost him forever.

After packing, I collapsed in a fog. What am I doing? How long am I going to be doing it? I don't know what I'll be doing anymore or for how long. All I know is I just repacked everything I brought up to Massachusetts three weeks ago.

Still, I feel I have to go to Florida to try to save the business. Maybe my health is more important, as my doctors and psychologist tried to tell me. And I agree I'm making a big mistake not finishing my speech therapy, as Renee warned me at our last session. But I feel like I'm in a bind. I can't let the business go down the tubes. There's no one else to go to Florida to sort all this out. Just me, though I'm not sure I can do it. I feel so tired and exhausted with everything. At least, my brother Paul seems to feel I can handle it. "Just do what's necessary to get things up and running again," he told me. I'm not sure I'm mentally prepared. But I'm determined to try to do what I can.

I still feel like somehow God is punishing me for some reason which I don't understand now. But I feel I have to take some action to prove myself. It's like a test I somehow have to get through successfully. Then I'll be all right. So I've got to go to Florida and take that test. I've got to move on.

Monday, October 2, 1989

Today, Mom drove me to the airport.

I was still feeling terribly confused and devastated as we drove there at 6 a.m., and the flight made me feel more so. I felt so nervous and scared about what I would find at the Mail Boxes store. Plus I felt unsure of my ability to go on without continuing my rehab program, as all the doctors, nurses, and counselors have suggested.

When I got to the gate, I had to fly coach—the first time ever since I met Bob, because I never had to think about cost before. I always went First Class. So just taking the flight helped to remind me of how much I lost   Bob, my ability to think properly, and now my business. I couldn't even eat the dinner the stewardess brought me, I felt so upset.

Finally, mercifully, the flight landed at the Ft. Myers airport in Florida, and Craig, a friend and local residential real-estate broker, picked me up at the gate. Craig had worked at the store part-time after the accident and became a friend.

As we drove home, he began telling me about the villa and what was still there. I wanted to know this, since Charlie had a key to get in. That's why, before picking me up, Craig got the key from Charlie's assistant Debbie, who was in charge of the store when Charlie went to Boston. Then, Craig went to check the villa, though he didn't tell either Debbie or Charlie he would do this, so they wouldn't get suspicious and maybe try to invent excuses for what they had taken. As Craig spoke, it became clear that some things were missing, like the radio, VCR, and a clock radio; though I won't know exactly what's gone until I get there. Even then I may not be able to account for it all.

I guess I'll also have to decide what to do about Craig, after I sort out things at the store. If it's still open, should I keep him on? I feel bad if I have to let him go, since he's been so helpful and seems so sincere. But even so, I'm not sure I can trust him. After all, he was working very closely with Charlie. What did he know? What should he have known?

PICKING UP THE PIECES

Over the next week, I discovered just how bad everything was when I went to the store to learn what happened. Not only was the store in a physical shambles, but the records were in disarray. Sorting things out was like going through the ruins of a fire—the deeper I dug, the more wreckage I pulled out. And it was even harder to do this, because it was hard for me to think logically due to the accident. Plus I felt so depressed, angry, and alone, realizing that so many of my problems were due to the betrayal of someone who had once been a trusted friend. Just knowing Charlie did this to me made everything so much worse. As I wrote in my diary:

Tuesday, October 3, 1989

I finally went to the store today and it was an absolute pigpen. Yuck! What a mess! I hardly know what I'm doing here, and I almost feel ready to say I don't care anymore and walk away from it all. But I kept on working and cleaned up the store, moving boxes, sweeping, and mopping up.

Then, I went through the files, books, checking account, and other store records to try to reconstruct what was spent for what. In the process, it seemed clearer and clearer what Charlie had done. I found the business checking account he used to buy furniture, groceries, and pay the rent. He even charged the store for getting his hair done and for repairing a friend's car—all on the company checking account. It was worse than I had even imagined.

Afterwards, when I returned home to the villa, I started unpacking the garage to put away everything left in boxes from before the accident. All of our things were still there in dozens of cartons, since we had just moved to Florida and the moving company dropped off everything the day of the accident. It was so sad to open up the boxes, since each time I opened one, this brought back the memories of what Bob and I had brought to Florida to start our new life here. The wedding gifts were especially hard to look at—the silver champagne bucket, a beautiful Chinese plant holder and Chinese vases, some crystal glasses. Now without Bob with me, they seemed like such a waste. I finally stopped unpacking about half way through the boxes, unable to go on anymore.

Wednesday, October 4, 1989

Today I had lots to do to find out what the status of the business is—and to see what might be saved.

I spoke to my lawyer, Mark Bidner; accountant Steve Goldberg; and then tried to get in touch with Jim Husson, the new franchisee, to make sure everything went through properly with the sale of a franchise location to him. Then, I called USPS—the United States Postal Service—to work out the contract details to have a postal office at the store. Also, I met with the new bookkeeper to find out how much money was still left in the business. It was hard to collect my thoughts to do all these things, yet somehow, I pushed myself to get through the calls and meetings.

It's incredible. There are so many things to do. I feel under such pressure. And in the middle of all this, my mother called and wondered why I hadn't hooked up my cable TV yet so I could sit back and relax. She has no idea of what I'm up against. I don't think anyone really does. They just see the problems at the store as one more business hurdle to deal with, and think I should be able to respond accordingly. They don't see the problems I still have with thinking, or realize the deep emotional hurt I feel over everything that has happened, from losing Bob to Charlie to maybe losing the store.

Friday, October 6, 1989

Yesterday, I had to get up early to get the packages for the Post Office ready to go, as well as finish up the other packages for the AM Express. Then, I met with Husson to finish up the postal contract and finalize the paperwork for his franchise.

Meanwhile, as I was doing these things, I kept thinking, "What's the point? It's all going to collapse anyway, isn't it?" I felt so down and discouraged, it was hard trying to act like I was excited about the Mail Boxes store. Still, I tried not to let my real feelings show—my usual modus operandi these days. Just let everyone think you're happy and keep going.

But it's so difficult to keep doing that. I try to think about other things, but my mind keeps coming back to Charlie. I still can't believe how he could take all that money, since he was a trusted friend for so long. Then, when I was at the lowest point in my life from the accident, he kicked me down even lower. I don't know if I'll ever be able to get over this. I feel a lot less trusting of anyone, and feel like I want to retreat and hibernate for the rest of my life. I won't have to worry about whether I can trust anyone again if I do.

Today, when I looked at the checkbook, I saw that things are much worse than I imagined. Charlie helped himself to funds again and again—about $25,000—and he never paid the landlord or vendors. So now I'm doubly in debt, and he has totally destroyed me. I felt so disgusted and hurt that after I closed up the store, I went home and cried all afternoon from anger, shock, and disbelief.

But at least one nice thing happened to dispel some of the gloom and my total disillusionment with human nature. John Anderson, who runs a nearby office business much like Mail Boxes, didn't charge me for the fax and then offered to help anyway he could.

But apart from John, I still feel devastated and don't know which way to turn or who to trust. Just to be sure Charlie can't get inside and do any more harm, I had the locks changed to the villa. Now I'll have to change the store locks, too.

Saturday, October 7, 1989

Today, I went to the store at about 2 p.m., and tried to clean up some more. I swept, threw things out, and went through files, much like I had before, since everything was such a mess. Then, around 5 p.m., Andy, another Mail Boxes owner from the East Coast of Florida, came over to help run the store for me because I couldn't, and he helped me clean up as well.

After we finished around 6 p.m., we went to Plums, an Italian Restaurant in town, which features meals that are cooked as you watch. It was the first time in months that I really relaxed and had a good time. I also felt a sense of relief, as we talked about Andy possibly becoming a partner to handle the business, since I can't run it myself now.

Monday, October 9, 1989

Yesterday, Sunday, I finally had a chance to get some of the Florida sun and unwind. In the morning, I sat out in the sun, soaking it up. For awhile, at least, I forgot about Mail Boxes, Etc. Then it rained so hard, I decided to go to the store and finish cleaning up. I drove back using my parents' car, which they had left at their second home in Florida. I finished picking up the last things still on the floor and vacuumed, till the store looked clean and presentable again.

I also changed the locks on the door before I left for the day. Around 2 p.m., Ron, the locksmith, came over to do this. I'm glad I did, because later that night, when Debbie, Charlie's assistant at the store, tried to get in, she couldn't. When Charlie called me to ask why the key wouldn't open the lock and I explained, they were both very upset. But when I asked Charlie if he wanted to explain what I discovered missing at the store, he didn't want to talk about it. And, in truth, I really didn't want to see or talk to Charlie or Debbie either, once I saw how bad things were at the store. I'm still in shock just thinking about what they did.

Then, today was a chance to relax again, since the store was closed due to the Columbus day holiday. In the evening, around 7:30 p.m, Andy showed up to visit and I invited him to stay for dinner. Afterwards, we watched a few late night movies on the tube—Hanoi Hilton and Bye, Bye, Birdie.

Tuesday, October 10, 1989

Today, I finally opened the store with Andy's help. Though he would have to spend seven or eight hours a day over the next few weeks to help keep it open, he was glad to do so to get the store back on track. This way, he told me, I could see how we worked together, since he hoped to become a partner with me in the area franchise, since he only owned one store.

Before opening, I put up a sign to explain that the store was now under new management. Afterwards, as people came in the store, if they had questions, I briefly explained what happened. If people were new, it was very easy. They were very pleasant and said it was nice to have me as the new owner. But it was different with the regulars. Some were fine with the change and treated it as an ordinary change in the course of business. But others were disappointed that Charlie wasn't there, because he had a real gift of gab and they enjoyed talking with him. Also, they didn't have any idea yet about what Charlie had done, and I didn't think it appropriate to tell them yet about the embezzlement. So I tried as best as I could to make up a reasonable excuse to explain why Charlie wasn't there anymore, so they would feel better about the change and continue to come back.

Unfortunately, soon after we opened, the calls started coming from creditors wondering when they were going to be paid by Charlie. He had been assuring them for about 3 to 6 months that they would have their money in a matter of days. Thus, when I told them that Charlie was no longer in charge and had run off with the money, they wanted to know when I would take care of their payment. So I had to persuade them to be patient and try to understand. I'm not sure if they did, though at least all of them agreed to wait. And at least Charlie will one day have his day in court and with God, because of what he did!

Wednesday, October 11, 1989

Today was another busy day. I barely had time to think or write. I kept finding out about more and more of the checks Charlie wrote on the company account. And the more I kept finding these checks, the worse I felt. I still feel terrible, now. It's so depressing to think that one person could do all that he did.

GETTING THINGS GOING AGAIN

Yet, in spite of what happened, I somehow kept going, doing what needed to be done. Though I found it very difficult to understand and remember many things, and felt so desperately depressed, I knew I had to go on as best I could, learning as I went. Otherwise, the only alternative was total despair. Also, as it became necessary, I began to find others to do what I couldn't myself, such as by hiring new people to work with me and Andy at the store. As I wrote in my diary in those very dark days:

Thursday, October 12, 1989

Today was something of a breakthrough. For the first time, Husson came over to observe my store to better understand how to run his own store. If only he knew how frazzled and confused I felt. But, of course, I didn't let that show. I just acted like everything was fine, so he could use what we were doing as a model to help him succeed. Thus, for a couple of hours, Husson watched us pack boxes, weigh them, write up sales receipts, put mail in mail boxes, run the cash register, meter the mail, make keys, and deal with other day to day store operations.

While he was there, a woman stopped in asking about the "Employees wanted" sign I had put in the window, and Andy and I interviewed her. She seemed eager to learn, and I got the impression she is very organized and reliable. So I decided to hire her and she starts tomorrow. It's a little scary to think of what I have to do to show her the ropes, because I have a hard time believing I'll remember everything I need to teach her. Also, I know I'll have to let Andy explain how to pay the vendors, since it's a complicated procedure where the books have to reflect what is rung up on the cash register, and I don't remember the details. But I'll try my best to teach her what I can.

In the evening, I spoke to Steve Goldberg, who told me that Charlie was in Boston and was supposed to come to his office with his attorney. They were supposed to explain what Charlie had done and go over the discrepancies I found in the books at the store. But as I suspected, Charlie didn't show up. I'm certain he's going to take off...And I think he should after what he did. I know I wouldn't want to face someone if I had used them the way he used me so badly. Then, again, I'm glad he didn't show, because I think I might explode if I saw him or talked to him in a three-way conversation with Steve—and that might make dealing with him even worse.

TRYING TO COPE

Meanwhile, as I tried to create order out of chaos at the store and in my own head, back in Boston, my friends, family, and business associates tried to help as they could. But since they were so far away, I felt so alone and helpless, and sometimes everything seemed too much to handle. Then, somehow, I would find a chance to relax, regroup, and go on. As I wrote in my diary over the next week:

Friday, October 13, 1989

Today, was a very depressing chaotic day. I tried calling the many vendors who were owed money and tried to reassure them I would try to find the funds to pay them—though God knows how. After awhile the phone calls blurred together like a fog. I can't remember half the vendors I spoke with or what I said. I felt like a tape went off in my head each time I spoke to one of them; and when I called another, I played the same tape again.

Unfortunately, more bad news when Mom called. At first, I was glad to hear she was arriving in a few days to spend the winter in Florida with my father as usual. But then she told me that Fluffy was having serious problems with leukemia. It was the first time I realized that Fluffy was so sick, and my mother said that she couldn't bring Fluffy with her, because the vet wouldn't give Fluffy the papers to fly due to the leukemia. So now my mother wanted to know what I wanted to do about Fluffy. I didn't know what to tell her. It was as if she was asking my permission to have Fluffy put away, and I couldn't bring myself to do that. I didn't want to think about one more death.

On top of this, when I called Mary Anne Foures, the first psychologist I saw at the Naples Hospital after the accident, and asked to make an appointment, her secretary said I couldn't come in because my previous bill hadn't been paid. Not paid? Hearing that I felt like a criminal, and I broke down uncontrollably and kept crying and crying. Apparently, the Blue Cross benefits for psychological counseling had run out; and because of my situation, I couldn't pay her what I owed her or for any more services.

Finally, I pulled myself together to do some aerobics. But soon after I started, I broke down crying again. I kept crying for maybe an hour, and only stopped after Susan, an old friend from Iowa, called and helped pull me out of my deep depression. But even though I felt a little better, I didn't feel up to going out to dinner with Craig, the real estate broker who helped out at the store, and his girlfriend Lisa. I felt too depressed, so I called to cancel. I just wanted to be alone.

Then, as I sat at home reflecting on everything and calmed down again, Dad called. It was comforting to hear from him. But when he asked me how many vendors were claiming I owed them money and how would I pay them, I broke up on the phone again. It was too much to think about and deal with it now.

Saturday, October 14, 1989

At least the day started well with some good news from Massachusetts. My brother Paul called in the morning to say he had been taking care of the Peabody store and things seemed to be running smoothly. He was even able to get back the money orders from Charlie before Charlie wrote any more of them to himself. As Paul explained, he called Charlie and asked him to drop the money orders off at the store, and when the temporary help he had hired checked the numbers, all of the money orders were there. Thank God for that!

But I was pretty tired most of the day, because I was up till 1 a.m. the night before working with Nicole, who I had recently hired for the Florida store, to tell her what to do. She seemed to quickly understand everything, and I thought she would work out well. But I guess we'll have to see. You never know.

After all, I thought things were going to work out with Andy running the store for me. I even thought our arrangement would turn into a partnership. But now I'm not sure that's going to work out, because Andy wants too much too soon. As soon as I mentioned the possibility of a partnership, he wanted a 50-50 arrangement without putting up any money himself—he thinks he should get that for just helping me out. I said I'd have to think about the partnership for awhile, but I don't think so. I don't think I can trust him now.

Then, in the early afternoon, I headed to the beach. After I threw out a blanket, I collapsed on it and fell asleep for about an hour. When I woke up at 3:30 p.m., it was nice to discover I actually got some color in my face and on my arms and chest. It has been so long since I have been able to relax in the sun and get tan—my first time in months.

Later, at home after I made dinner, I brought the pool lounge chairs out from the garage and sat by the pool. As I sat there drinking a rasberry spritzer, I felt wonderfully relaxed for those few moments. Afterwards, several friends from Massachusetts called—Mark, Joy, and Libby, and it was nice to talk to them. Finally, after another hour of aerobics, I settled down on the couch and watched Beverly Hills Cops II by myself and really enjoyed it. Afterwards, I kept thinking that I finally had one good day by myself—the first one in 8 months, and the first one since the accident.

Sunday, October 15, 1989

Today was another good day. After the past week of dealing with such a mess at the store, it was good to spend much of the day doing absolutely nothing—just lounging by the pool for several hours in the morning until 1 p.m. Then, in the afternoon, it was nice to talk by phone with some friends I hadn't spoken to in a while—Cindy, Gary, Glen, Phylis and Dan. They were having a get together in Massachusetts and called so I could talk to all of them at the same time. It was nice to know they were still thinking about me.

Later that afternoon, I started thinking about how I need to prepare and organize a lot more—and avoid any interruptions that keep me from doing this. I realized that my mind tends to jump around more than it used to, and it's hard to remember and find things. So I have to learn to compensate by being more organized. Then, hopefully, being this way will help me know where things are after I put them away.

Monday, October 16, 1989

Though I had a good relaxing weekend and good intentions of how to become more organized, today brought a big dose of reality again after the store opened. It was totally chaotic, crazy, and tiresome. People kept coming in and out to send packages, write money orders, check their mailboxes, and the like. Meanwhile, I had to keep checking what Nicole was doing to make sure she did things right. Plus there were more calls from vendors about the money they were owed. At least a lot of them were understanding and said they believed in me, trusted me, and knew that I wouldn't screw them. And I won't. I will pay each and every one of them. But some were so shrill and demanding; they kept saying over and over they wanted to be paid now or else. I tried to calm them down and promised to pay. What else could I do?

At least Nicole is working out well. She seems to remember things fairly well and acts like she wants to please and be helpful. But I'm not sure about Andy and his intentions, particularly since he stopped helping out at the store and went back to his own store on the East Coast of Florida, until we can negotiate how much of the area franchise he will own. He wasn't willing to continue working with me for awhile to see what he would have to do to continue running the store, though I asked him to stay. I felt this trial period would give me a better idea of what might be a fair partnership arrangement. But he wanted me to make a commitment now. But how could I, without having a better feeling for how things would work out?

In fact, after Charlie, I'm not sure of anyone's intentions anymore. Just about the one thing I am sure of is that the store's records are so chaotic, it's going to take me a long time to square everything away. But can I? On the one hand, I'm very determined to do so, since knowing everything is such a mess makes me want to straighten things up even more. But on the other hand, it's so hard getting things back together again. When I came home at the end of the day, I had a splitting headache, and my vision was blurry again. Am I really up to running my business like this? I go home and I feel so alone.

Friday, October 20, 1989

The past few days and today have been mostly a blur. I've been so busy at the store trying to manage what seems more and more like a leaky ship with an uncertain crew. So I couldn't do much besides taking care of the store. I didn't have time to do my usual aerobic exercises, eat a good meal, or even write in this diary for awhile. It's so hard to take care of myself, because taking care of the store takes so much out of me.

And today I discovered even more things that have gone wrong for the past week. For example, I learned that Nicole has been logging all the packages for a week to the wrong zone. The UPS guy noticed the mistake when he was in the store today, and he sounded very upset when he explained this meant that the packages couldn't be traced and that the bill from UPS would be incorrect. Then, Nicole got upset because she felt so bad about messing up the UPS log.

Also, it was confusing because I had to train Efrin the new guy I hired to work part-time. At least it was quiet in the morning when he started working, so I had about two hours to train him, since he never did this kind of work before. Normally, I would never have hired someone so inexperienced. But when he came into the store looking for work, I needed someone so desperately, I agreed to try him out. I wished I had more time to train him, though, because after it got busy in the afternoon, he was pretty much on his own. So I left it up to Nicole to show him more of the ropes.

Finally, the day mercifully ended at 6 p.m.. After I closed the store, I went next door to talk to Judy, the woman who owns the dry cleaning store there, and I started crying. Even though I only knew her to say hello and make some passing small talk, I felt so depressed, I had to talk to someone. As I told her, I feel I can't take the pressure anymore.

Then, to make matters worse, when I left to go home, Mom's car wouldn't start. So I left it at the store, and after I told Judy what had happened, we went out to dinner and I stayed overnight at her house.

Saturday, October 21, 1989

In the morning, I went back to the store early before it opened to cash out from the day before. This way I could reconcile the amount taken in with the amount in the drawer to start with. I felt too pressured to do it last night as usual, though I didn't feel much better today after three hours of sleep last night. At least I got the reconciliation done by the time Nicole and Efrin arrived to handle the front desk.

Unfortunately, soon there were problems because Efrin didn't pay attention when I tried to tell him what we had to do to get the store ready to open for the day. Then Nicole and Efrin started shouting at each other, because Nicole accused Efrin of not weighing and logging the packages properly.

So it looks like Efrin isn't going to make the grade. He makes so many mistakes. Several times, he didn't ring up things correctly on the cash register. And when Nicole told him to do something, sometimes he didn't hear her. Also, when things are slow in the store due to a lack of customers, he stands at the counter and waits, instead of trying to do something useful, such as logging the UPS boxes and stacking them properly or metering the mail. Plus, he couldn't wait to get out the door at 1:00 when his shift was over.

At least Nicole seems a bright light in the darkness. Since my car still wasn't working, she drove me home, and on the way we stopped for some hamburgers and coke at a McDonald's.

Then, back at home, I began agonizing over whether I'm doing the wrong or right thing in staying in Florida. I feel so frustrated, angry, and depressed by the time I get out of work, I feel devastated. From 3 p.m. on, I usually have to fight back the tears. Then, when I get home, I start crying and can't stop. Day after day, it's been the same—by the end of the day, a headache, blurred vision, and I'm crying. My depression keeps getting worse and worse. I feel like I'm spiraling downward and downward, and I keep wondering if it will ever stop. Will things ever turn around? How much worse can things get? And why? Why me? What have I done to deserve this? I keep asking God, "What have I done? What have I done?"

THE SPIRAL DOWN

But could I turn things around? That's what I kept asking myself, as things seemed to be getting worse day by day. It felt like a runaway train I couldn't stop, even after I went to Boston to visit with my doctors and therapists for a day. As I wrote in my diary over the next few days:

Sunday, October 22, 1989

I flew home today to go to the rehab hospital for a medical checkup to see how I was doing, and it turned out to be one of the saddest days of my life. When I arrived at 3 a.m., Mom picked me up at the airport, and when I got home and saw Fluffy, I collapsed in tears. He looked like a walking skeleton. He wasn't eating and had lost half of his weight. He couldn't even purr. I put him on the bed by my side when I went to sleep, and when I woke up, he was lying there like he was almost dead.

After that, I couldn't get up myself. I sat there for the entire day in a kind of trance petting Fluffy and telling him how much I loved him. A couple of times I got out of bed to bring him some water, and he drank a little. But he couldn't eat anything. It was so sad. I cried and cried.

Finally, I managed to get up and go to Mom's for dinner. I felt torn, leaving Fluffy there like that, but he was too weak to move him to take him with me. I even cried during dinner.

Monday, October 23, 1989

Today was filled with doctors and appointments.

The first appointment was with the vet, since Fluffy was so sick. Mom called the vet in the morning to make the arrangements, since I couldn't do it, and when she came over to pick Fluffy up, he could barely stand. I had taken him downstairs to the family room, and when he tried to get up, his back legs kept giving out and he fell down again. It broke my heart to see him like this. Then, Mom took him to the vet, and I begged off going with her, since I felt so badly about going there.

Meanwhile, as Mom took care of Fluffy, I drove to the rehab hospital to see the doctors, who wanted to see my progress.

First I went to see Dr. Jaeger, who had been my overall doctor at the rehab hospital, overseeing what the other doctors and nurses were doing and deciding what specialties I needed. He began by asking me some questions about whether I was still having headaches or was feeling any dizziness or numbness in my arms or legs. Unfortunately, I had to tell him "yes" to all his questions.

Then, after I told Dr. Jaeger how I had been coping—or more accurately barely coping— in Florida, he gave me the standard neurological tests to test my level of functioning. First he used the finger grip strength test, in which I grabbed his fingers with each hand and squeezed as hard as I could to show how strongly I could hold his fingers. This way he could see if there was a weakness in my grip strength. And there was. As Dr. Jaeger told me, my left hand wasn't as strong as it should be, because the head injury had weakened the left side of my body. As he explained, the right side of my brain was damaged, and the right side controls the left side.

Then, Dr. Jaeger asked me to show him how well I could balance by walking with one foot directly in front of the other—just like cops do when they stop a driver they suspect of drinking too much to see if he can walk a straight line. But I couldn't do it. I kept teetering back and forth as I walked, having trouble keeping my balance due to the head injury.

Next, he asked me to stand still for a minute with my eyes closed—and I couldn't do this either. Lastly, he checked the reaction in all of my joints by hitting my elbows, knees, ankles, and wrists with a rubber mallet. At least, my joints seemed fine, since these purely physical reactions weren't seriously affected by the brain injury. I was just a little slower on my left side due to the brain injury on my right.

Then, Dr. Jaeger sent me to see Dr. Whitlock, the head injury doctor. Dr. Whitlock started the session by testing my memory to see how well I remembered. In one test, he said a series of ten words, waited 5 minutes, and asked me to recall what I had just heard. It was disappointing to hear the results—I only remembered about 70%—much less than the photographic memory I once had.

At the end of the tests, Dr. Whitlock asked me generally if I had any headaches, seizures, or dizziness. Finally, he listened to me talk freely for awhile, to observe my speech and see if it was normal. Unfortunately, it was still hard for me to retrieve words and my memory was still impaired. Thus, since I was still not functioning normally, he told me to come back in three months for further testing. He sent me back to Dr. Jaeger to schedule appointments with both of them.

After I did, I felt frustrated, wondering "Are these doctor appointments ever going to end?" It was sad, too, to confirm what I already knew. I wasn't my old self. I also felt like I was still tied to the hospital and the doctors like a prisoner on a rope. Though I was out of rehab and had gone back to Florida to run my business, now I would have to return to Boston for testing every three months, until the doctors thought I was normal and didn't need to be tested anymore. They thought the checkups would have to continue until at least the following July—nine more months of doctors. I wanted to cry.

Later, when I returned from the rehab hospital, Mom explained that it was all over for Fluffy. The vet said there was no hope for him, and so he had to put Fluffy away, so he wouldn't suffer anymore. I cried and cried at losing Fluffy, though I felt relieved his suffering was over.

Tuesday, October 24, 1989

I flew back to Florida this morning, and when I got back to the house and opened the door, a deep sense of emptiness overcame me. The house felt so empty—like it has nothing for me. It was like entering someone else's house on the market. I felt so alone, like an earthquake had passed through my life taking everything—Bob, Fluffy. I miss them so much.

And here I am in Florida again. I don't really know what I'm doing anymore. I feel like I'm only going through the motions, working and working from day to day—but for what? Yet that seems to be the only thing left for me to do, since I've lost so much else.

At least, Nicole seems to be doing well at the store. Or at least, she says so, and she'll be picking me up to take me there tomorrow. So we'll see how well she did. And maybe getting back to work will do me good. It will help me forget everything, because I miss Bob and Fluffy so much.

Thursday, October 26, 1989

Two more rough days of trying to catch up at the store and getting more behind. With Efrin off and only Nicole at the store the day I was in Boston, so many things piled up—packages to be sent, records to check. But at least Nicole seems to have done what she was able to *do right—one slight bright spot, when there are so few.*

Then, this afternoon, Mom and Dad flew in from Massachusetts and stopped by the store. Thankfully, Dad rented a car for me, which he said I could use. At last I have some wheels for awhile. He rented the car, because I had a hard time driving the car he and Mom own, since it's an older model with small windows, and I had trouble turning my neck to see the cars around me. But the rental car was a newer model with more glass all around, so it was easier to see through the windows, because I didn't have to turn and twist my neck as much to see.

Unfortunately, some more bad news when I met with Leanne, the temporary accountant and bookkeeper I hired, about the books. I had hired her to get the payroll records back in order after an old friend referred her. She reviewed the records to see if they were in the proper shape for tax purposes, but they were all messed up, because Charlie never paid the Federal Taxes this past year. And Leanne didn't know how to fix them.

I don't know how much longer I can take all this bad news. It's one thing after another. I'll keep praying a little longer for something to break. But I keep asking myself—"Why? Why? And is anything I'm doing or praying for doing any good?" But if I stop believing and stop trying to turn things around, what's left? So I feel like I have to keep going on.

REACHING BOTTOM

Over the next few days, however, I kept wondering if I really could keep going. More and more, I felt like everything was closing in on me, pushing me to the edge. It was like being in a pressure cooker, about to burst. Nothing seemed to be working. Everything seemed to be falling apart. No one seemed to understand. Even the people I had brought into the store to help me manage weren't there when I needed them. Plus I felt increasingly out of touch with my parents. And now the MBE corporation was raising questions about what my business owed and asking whether I could successfully continue my business and pay the company what I owed them in back royalties which Charlie never paid. So, increasingly, my life felt like a bomb about to explode. As I wrote in my diary that next week:

Friday, October 27, 1989

But can I keep going? Today was the most frustrating day in my life since the accident.

On top of everything else, when I finished work for the day, I felt so tired, I locked myself out of the store. It happened because I had forgotten to make extra keys, and I gave the only key to Nicole after I locked the store for the night. Then, when I tried to get back in because I forgot something, I couldn't since I didn't have the key and I realized this after searching through my pocketbook for about 10 minutes to find it. After that, I felt so frustrated, I headed right home. Then, when I got there, I stared at the wall for 40 minutes. I felt so hopeless and lost, as I sat there, my mind a total blank, like the wall.

What finally pulled me out of this funk is I had to go meet Mom and Dad for dinner. After I went to their house, they drove to the restaurant. But on the way and at dinner, I was so blue I didn't feel much like talking. Instead, I just listened blankly and stared ahead as they talked to me, which really upset them. They kept saying: "What's wrong with you?...Don't you have anything to say?...Why are you just sitting there saying nothing?" But I didn't know what to do or say, because I felt so drained from working in the store, and I could barely see because my vision was so blurry. I felt bad, knowing they were upset by the way I acted. But I didn't have the energy to think or talk and felt powerless to respond.

On the drive back from the restaurant, I tried to explain how I felt. I told them how badly I was doing, and how strongly I felt I should be getting speech therapy in rehab. But again, they didn't understand, and acted like it was just a matter of simple will power to get better.

My mother said: "Well, you know, the rehab will just keep taking your money. You should be back on your feet already by now."

I didn't feel there was anything more I could say. I cried silently to myself in the back of the car and felt even worse, feeling there was no one with whom I could share my feelings. Instead, I had to deal with everything I was experiencing all by myself. It felt like I was going into an emotional underground—like a deep dark tunnel in the earth, where everything was very dark and scary.

Sunday, October 29, 1989

Yesterday, when I was at the store checking records and bills, I discovered one more thing that Charlie did—he used one of my credit cards. But now I'm already feeling numb about each new revelation about Charlie—so this is just one more wrong to add to the list.

At least Nicole is turning into a friend which helps. After we finished writing up the postal orders, we went out to lunch, and later she came over to have dinner and stay overnight. It was nice after we had dinner and watched a movie to sit by the pool and talk. It was the first time I could talk so freely with someone. Nicole even told me how her father molested her when she was a child. But she was able to put it out of her mind and have ordinary relationships with guys. I felt encouraged to hear about someone overcoming a great hardship. It gives me hope for myself.

Then, today, Nicole took me to her church—a Congregational Church. I had never been in one before, and it was so different from the Catholic masses I was used to attending. Yet, I *really liked it. I found it very uplifting to join the congregation in singing the hymns using the hymnbook in the pew in front of me, even though I was used to the Catholic mass, where the choir does most of the singing and the people who come to worship don't participate as much.*

Afterwards, as we sat reminiscing in the sun, I told Nicole about seeing my mother Friday night and how difficult it was to talk to her or get her to understand. At least Nicole was sympathetic, though she just works for me. It's not like having a family member I can feel close to. So talking to her was another reminder that now I'm my own.

After Nicole left, I thought about what I should do next. I really want to get this case settled with the insurance company for my injury claim so I can start to move on with my life. But then what? Should I stay here in Florida and keep struggling to get the store back on its feet or not?

If only I can start believing in myself and my ability to be independent again.

Monday, October 30, 1989

Today was a crazy day, which started when a driver dropped off 52 huge 2' x 3' boxes for a customer by mistake, since he read the mailing address instead of the shipping address. So the boxes took up most of the store, making it hard to do business for other customers. But fortunately, the customer was able to reach the shipping company, which contacted the driver, who returned and picked up all the boxes just before I closed at 5:45 p.m. Was I ever glad to see them go, and to celebrate, the customer invited me out for a drink. It was good to go out and relax — a little like having my first date in almost a year, although I didn't want it to go any further, especially with a customer.

Then, over to Dad and Mom's for dinner. Unfortunately, the dinner turned into a confrontation again about how Dad was having trouble paying the bills because of me. He complained that he had been paying all of my mortgage payments on the four properties I owned—my house in Topsfield, the villa in Naples, a condo on the East Coast of Florida, and 20 acres of land I had bought to get started in real estate. But now he couldn't afford to keep doing this much longer. Then, Mom chimed in to say she thought that my trips to Boston for evaluations were a waste of time. I felt so frustrated after dinner I wanted to scream, though, of course, I didn't say a thing.

Tuesday, October 31, 1989

After the blow-up last night, things were very strained when I drove Mom and Dad to the airport. We hardly talked to each other on the way, and I felt a great sense of distance from them.

At least work today was very quiet, maybe because everyone was out celebrating for Halloween.

During the day, I called Gary Smith, the MBE officer handling franchise support at corporate headquarters, to explain what had happened with Charlie and the books. I hoped the company would give me more time to work out a payment plan as a result, and it sounded like the corporation would help out and stand behind me from what Gary said. For example, besides giving me more time to pay, he said the company would help me negotiate future leases, since I had so much trouble with Jim Husson's lease. Normally, the area franchisee should do this without involving the corporate office. But Gary said the company would help me do the things I could no longer remember how to do, and then help retrain me in those areas. So Gary seemed understanding, and I feel much better.

Thursday, November 2, 1989

But these last two days were terrible again. Two days ago, I thought things were looking up, but now I feel back at ground zero.

Yesterday was the busiest day in the store, and I was all alone again, because Nicole had the day off and Efrin didn't show up. He didn't even call to say he wasn't coming in. So I had to work on my own with a long line of impatient angry customers who had lots of boxes they were shipping for Christmas. And making everything worse was my pounding headache. By the end of the day, it was all I could do to keep from crying.

Today, when Efrin finally did show up, acting like it was no big deal that he didn't come in Wednesday, I told him he was fired. It was hard to do, since I don't like telling anyone they don't measure up, especially since I feel that way about myself. Thus, when Efrin protested, wondering if I was really serious about firing him, I agreed he could work till the end of the week.

Later, after the store closed, I had to meet with two prospective franchisees from New York, who were interested in buying a franchise—the first time since the accident I had tried to sell one. I did the best I could to answer their questions about running a franchise. I couldn't answer all of their questions, since I didn't remember some specific answers, such as the average number of customers a day and the likely profits in a year. But at least I did better than I thought I would in answering most questions. I actually knew the answers to their more general questions about day to day company operations, though I initially was afraid I might not remember what I once knew.

CRASHING DOWN

But eventually the pressure became too much. Nothing seemed to make sense anymore. Everything seemed so difficult and hopeless. That November 3rd I felt I had reached the absolute bottom, as I wrote in my diary:

Friday, November 3, 1989

Today, I feel like I finally flipped out. Work was a real zoo. It was Nicole's day off and Efrin's last day, and it was obvious Efrin couldn't care less about what he was doing. He wasn't paying attention, put mail in the wrong mail box, weighed and logged the packages wrong, and didn't ring up sales correctly on the register. I constantly had to correct him and remind him to be more careful. Meanwhile, mobs of people were in the store for the Christmas mailing rush. When I closed the door at 5:00 p.m., people were still knocking on the door to get in.

Afterwards, as I finished up the things I hadn't done for the day, like filling out American Express money orders, my desk was piled high with more papers to fill out and I wanted to cry. I almost did, when Leanne, the temporary bookkeeper, showed up to continue reviewing the books.

When Nicole stopped by about 6 p.m., I finally did break down. I started sobbing and sobbing and couldn't stop, as Nicole tried to comfort me.

A few hours later, when I got home, I called Mom and Dad who were back in Boston, and started crying hysterically, telling them I had really flipped out and had finally reached bottom. "I'm just not stable any more," I told them. And I'm not, which is what's so scary. I'm so frightened, I don't know what to do. I keep wanting to cry all the time, and I'm breaking down, crying more and more. All I can think about is how Charlie did all this to me—and maybe what he did is worse than the accident itself. At least I have been recovering from that. But now I feel like he created this never-ending nightmare for me. And I don't know what to do to make it stop.

CHAPTER 9

•

LOSING IT

GOING DOWN

The next few weeks were like a nightmare, I could barely remember later. It was as if I was going through the motions in a fog. I kept going to work at the store and talking to people daily as if nothing was wrong. But internally I was in turmoil.

Over and over, I kept dwelling on what Charlie had done and wondering how he could have done it, since he had been such a long-trusted friend. I kept wondering whether I was up to trying to keep my business alive. I had splitting headaches, blurry vision. Again and again, I questioned whether I could trust anyone I met—in business or socially. And whenever I tried to relax and thought "Maybe I'll finally see the light now!" I repeatedly experienced another blow that would make me feel even shakier. I felt like I was teetering on the edge of a cliff or on a crumbling sliver of ice in a raging sea. Almost anything could push me over the edge. Then, as I tried to pull back and maintain my footing, another gust of wind would push me even closer to falling over.

Meanwhile, on the legal front, a blizzard of paperwork was still going back and forth between my lawyers and the insurance companies to settle my claim. Even though back in September, my attorney Paul Freedman had totaled up my outstanding medical bills to date—about $50,000—and had written letters to my two personal insurers Liberty Mutual and Travelers for coverage, he still needed additional documentation of medical bills from my doctors. So he had to write them still more letters to get this.

Concurrently, another lawyer, Mark Bidner, was trying to figure out my lost income due to the accident, and he asked me to list all my sources of income at the time of accident and what I would have received had the accident not occurred. Meanwhile, my third attorney, Joel Kaplan, was contacting the insurance companies to clarify the coverage they provided and sending them additional bills and reports as requested.

It was a long and tedious process that was still dragging on in November as the lawyers received and sent records to the insurance companies, who paid this bill or that, which Freedman sent on to the doctors or hospitals. Mercifully, the lawyers didn't bother me with most of the details, since I already had more than I could deal with just keeping my business and life in Florida afloat. It was only later that I began to realize what the lawyers had been doing wrong that cost me my business. I couldn't have understood this at the time.

So mainly, except for an occasional request for records of expenses, I was largely unaware of the process. As a result, I wasn't aware of the growing warning signs, starting in November, that the settlement process was about to be derailed—much like my own life. As I wrote in my diary in early November:

Saturday, November 4, 1989

I don't know whether I'm having a nervous breakdown or what. My head feels like it is full of cobwebs. My eyes are blurry. I just don't know. I can't take this anymore. After work yesterday, I was so tired, I didn't dare drive, so I stayed at Nicole's.

This morning, after Nicole drove me to work, I dragged myself into the store. I felt so exhausted, I wasn't sure I could get through the day.

At least there was one bright spot. I called Dave Sandberg at Weaver's, a nearby office supply store, about working for me. I was at Weaver's a year before on a Sunday, and saw him working there. At first I thought he owned the store, because it was usually closed Sundays, and it was closed. But Dave opened the door anyway to let me in and sell me some supplies. I was impressed because he seemed like a hard worker, though I didn't take him seriously when he said 'Give me a call if you need a manager.' But now I remembered his offer and called. Since he said he was ready to move on if he could make more money than now, I set up an interview with him for later that day when things quieted down at the store. After a few minutes of talking to him,

I decided to hire him on the spot. I was so desperate for someone to help, and I felt he might be good for the store, since he had been so dedicated at Weaver's. So I offered him a job starting November 6th. I hope it works out.

A BRIEF RESPITE

Oddly, the next few days were like the lull before a storm. Somehow, despite feeling more and more exhausted, I managed to regain a sense of calm, and as the store got busier with the approaching holiday season, I had little time to think about my problems. Perhaps all that busyness helped calm me and kept me from thinking how burned out I was. Yet, one by one, the difficulties mounted, though I tried to stay positive, hoping things would still be all right. As I wrote in my diary:

Sunday, November 5, 1989

Hopefully, I'm going to try to relax. I went to church at St. Leo's, a Catholic Church in Naples, though it looked so different than the church I used to attend in Massachusetts. My old church was built in the traditional Gothic style, like Notre Dame. Still, it was a relief to spend time in church again after not going for awhile.

After services, I headed off to the beach, and felt like a little kid again. As I splashed around in the surf by the shore, I found myself laughing like I was 10 years old. A little later, as I watched the dolphins swim by, I felt so light and free, almost like a dolphin myself.

I also noticed that I was more aware of everything around me—the beach, the birds, the tiny creatures in the sand. I was more aware of them, because in the last few days, I've been taking more time to slow down and smell the roses. As I listened to the ocean's surf, smelt the salt air, and felt the breeze—everything seemed so new and wonderful again. After listening to the surf for awhile, I put on my head phones and listened to some music, while I lay on the beach.

Later, walking from the beach to my car, I thought how God has really made such a beautiful place, and I felt how much I want to find someone to share it with. My dream now is to walk down the beach, hand in hand, with someone I care about. And for the first time in months, I'm feeling that's possible again. I feel like I'm finally starting to see through the cloud of dust I've been living in. Thank you Lord....

BACK TO WORK

Yet, as much as I wanted to relax, dream, and start hoping again, I soon found I had to put that off for awhile, since it was so busy over the holidays at the store. Over the next couple of weeks, I didn't have enough help at the store and had to work very late. Even though I had recently hired Dave to manage the store and he started working on the 6th, there was still much to do, because of the increasing holiday mail. As a result, I soon found myself working from 7 a.m. till 7 or 8 p.m. at night, not much time for a social life, though it was better since I hired Dave. Before I used to work till about 10 to 11 p.m.

I was so busy, I didn't even have time to write in my diary. The basic problem was I was understaffed. Though the doors didn't open until 9 a.m., I had to get there early to catch up on packing boxes for the UPS and mail pickups later that day, since I didn't have enough people to finish the night before, even with Dave on board to help. And I hesitated to hire anyone else, because I had such a limited budget, since the insurance settlement was still pending. Besides, I had so little time to train anyone, since I was still struggling to catch up with all the current work. It was like a Catch-22. I needed more help; yet I didn't have the time or money to hire the help I needed.

So through mid-November, one day followed another in a blur of work and exhaustion. Then, somehow, like magic, my first boyfriend since the accident came into my life. Oddly, it happened when I was waiting to meet someone else, but I met Bear instead. As I wrote in my diary, my first entry in two weeks:

Wednesday, November 15, 1989

I went to meet a friend at a small quaint restaurant about 2 miles down the road from the store, but I was late getting there, since I was so busy at the store. So my friend wasn't there. But that's how I met Bear. He was sitting at the bar a few stools over, and after I got my drink, he started talking to me. He noticed my Boston accent when I ordered my drink, and he wondered if I was from there. After I said yes, and explained I had just moved to Naples, he told me he was from Miami and began telling me about himself.

I was fascinated by what he told me, and I was attracted to him, since he was very good looking, seemed so strong and healthy, and had an upbeat positive attitude, which I really needed in my life. He had a very powerful build, full of muscles, because he lifted weights. He had even been an Olympic weight lifter for several years until 1980. But unfortunately, that was the year President Jimmy Carter decided to boycott the Moscow Olympics, because the Soviet Union had invaded Afghanistan. So Bear wasn't able to compete that year to be a gold medalist and his dream went up in smoke. He couldn't try again, because after that he was too old, though he still worked out each day to keep in shape, after working at his regular job as an aviation mechanic.

When he told me that missing out on the Olympics was the biggest disappointment of his life, that helped to create a bond between us. It did because after that we talked about disappointments in life, and I told him how I had my own disappointment because of losing my husband. I felt this strong connection growing between us as we talked. I also felt a connection because I had been a real fitness buff before the accident.

In turn, Bear seemed attracted to me, because he was impressed that I was independent and had already accomplished so much in life, including running my own business. And at the time he didn't realize the memory deficits and other problems I had due to the brain injury. Afterwards I gave him my number, and I really hope he'll call. Meeting him has made me realize how lonely I've been and how much I need someone like Bear in my life.

LOVE AND WORK

Meeting Bear was like starting a new chapter in a new book for me, and for awhile, our relationship flowered. He lit up what was both the busiest and the worst time of my life at work. It was so oppressive, because as the holiday season continued, the business became like a deluge, with hundreds of customers clamoring to get packages mailed each day, while I tried to manage with my new and largely untrained help. As I wrote sporadically in my diary over the next couple of weeks:

Friday, November 17, 1989

Yesterday, Bear called at 9 a.m. and asked me to dinner at his place on Friday—which is today. I said "yes" immediately.

It was wonderful to finally have a real date. I got to Bear's apartment at 7 p.m. It was located near the water, and it was a cozy, casual kind of place with bright flowered couches and a work-out bike in the middle of the living room. As Bear opened the door, I told him he looked really sharp in his brightly flowered cotton shirt and jeans, almost like he matched his living-room ensemble. As we walked into the living room, I smelt the nice chicken dinner he was cooking, and I noticed he had the table set with two candles and a big basket of fruit, which I thought very elaborate but charming for a male. I felt so pleased at the way he put himself out to make this a really nice, special dinner.

As we waited for the chicken to finish cooking, he poured me a glass of wine and we sat on the couch talking. As we talked, we hit it off even more than the first night we met. We had so much in common, even some of our injuries. Bear described how he had been seriously injured and in a coma for two days while he was living in Miami, because somebody hit him on the head with a baseball bat as he walked out of a local nightclub late one night. The bat knocked his eye out of the socket. To recover, he spent three weeks in intensive care and altogether about two months in the hospital. He came close to losing his eye, though the doctors managed to save it. Soon after that, his girlfriend was stabbed to death in her apartment, which he had been in the night before. Incredibly, he heard the story on the news, when he saw the front of her house on TV and heard the announcer say her name. It made him feel even worse hearing the news that way.

After hearing these stories, I felt very close to him, because we both had such serious tragedies in our lives. Yet, in spite of what happened, he was still a very friendly, trusting, upbeat person.

So, as we went on sharing our stories, I felt very comfortable with him, like we belonged together. He was reassuring to be with, because he was so warm and seemed to like me so much.

Now, thinking about our evening together, it makes me feel good about myself again. After all this time, I'm finally with someone I like who likes me. Yet it's still very scary to have this relationship, because everything has been happening too fast. We seem to share so much in common, and suddenly had such strong feelings for each other. I'm nervous, because everything is starting to seem like too much too soon.

Saturday, November 19, 1989

This morning soon after I opened the store, I got a big surprise from Bear—a dozen red roses along with a card. I felt good to see them, and a few minutes later he called to make sure I got them. It was wonderful to have someone who is so attentive. Dave and Judy, a temp employee I recently hired, were at the store, too, and when they saw the roses arrive, Judy said it looked like I had met someone. Then both Dave and Judy started teasing me. They both said they were happy for me, but kidded me, too, saying things like:"Oh, this must be serious...You only met a few days ago, and he's already sending roses."

Wednesday, November 22, 1989

I don't know where the time is going. It's getting busier and busier at work. I finally decided I needed to add some staff despite my limited budget. So I hired a couple of new people, who will start next week, right after Thanksgiving when we have the busiest season of the year. But I won't have much time to train them. There's so much to do.

Fortunately, Bear is still around. He has been so thoughtful and caring. We've been seeing each other every day when I finish work, and it has been so wonderful to have someone at the end of the day to look forward to seeing. Like today. After work, I drove over to Bear's place, picked him up, and we went grocery shopping. Afterwards, we went back to his place to cook as usual, because he likes to cook so much.

We've been like glue since we met—inseparable. After work, we've done so much to-gether—a drink at the end of the day, going out to dinner, having dinner at his home or mine. It's hard to remember exactly what we've done when. But each day after work he's been there, eager to do something together, whatever it is. I've felt the same.

Yet at the same time, all this closeness scares me. Is this what I really want? Am I just turning to Bear to hide from the world? I'm starting to feel closed in, although I care for Bear so much.

Thursday, November 23, 1989

Today was the first Thanksgiving in years that I was with someone besides Bob. When I called Mom and Dad and told them, they were delighted I had plans for the holiday. But I was uncertain myself. Seeing someone else has gotten me feeling jittery and afraid.

Still, when Bear arrived, everything seemed outwardly fine. He took me to visit some of his friends for dinner, a really nice couple, Dave and Suzanne. They seemed perfectly matched because they got along so well and even looked like they might be brother and sister. I was especially intrigued because they had several exotic birds from South America in large cages around the living room. Fascinating.

But though I may have seemed perfectly calm to everyone as we talked and had dinner, I was shaking inside, because Bear and I haven't been apart since we met, and I have been feeling overwhelmed by the relationship. I don't want to hurt Bear, but I'm afraid I will, because I'm feeling engulfed. So increasingly I feel like I want to break free and be more independent.

Yet I know Bear is helping me so much now. Not only do we have so much fun, so much to share with each other, but he's helping me feel better about myself. Being with him, I feel I'm almost normal again, although I know I'm different. I can't do all the things I could before the accident. I can't think so fast. Even my tastes have changed, as I discovered tonight when I tried some egg nog. I used to hate egg nog before the accident, but now I really liked it.

So everything's very different, because I'm different. And suddenly I'm feeling very confused about what to do again. I know Bear likes me for me. I know he really cares. And he's impressed by all the things I can do, even if I know I once could do so much more. He didn't have the advantages I did growing up, so when he sees me owning the Mail Boxes store and flying to Bora Bora and all over the world, he's awed by all I have accomplished. Then, when he saw the villa, he was even more awed, because it was so much bigger and well-furnished than his own place.

So everything looks great to him. But if he really understood what I've been going through and how I feel like everything is teetering on the edge, would he really still like me then? Or suppose I was the way I used to be, would I be so drawn to him now? So I have all these questions. That's why when he started talking about wanting to get married and have kids on the way to Dave and Suzanne's, all I could do was nod without saying anything. I'm feeling so pressured, so overwhelmed by it all. But I didn't want to let Bear know. I don't want to hurt him whatever happens, because he's been so good to me, though I don't know what to do now.

In any case, I didn't let Bear know about my uncertainty, and from the moment we arrived, Dave and Suzanne were so nice. They went out of the way to make me feel comfortable. For example, Dave made me a frozen peach daiquiri with fresh peaches just the way I liked it, and both of them showed real interest when they asked me about myself. Also, Suzanne went all out to be the perfect cook and hostess by making the whole meal from scratch—a major undertaking. She did everything, including making the stuffing and cranberry sauce, yams with marshmallows, stuffed celery, pecan and pumpkin pies, homemade bread, the works. It was like she was working as the chef in a four star restaurant.

After dinner, though, I wanted to be by myself for awhile to think things through, so I drove home on my own rather than going back to Bear's. It was the first time since I met Bear I've been alone. On the one hand, he makes me feel so good and warm all over. But on the other hand, I had this strong desire to get away. It's like I'm losing myself in Bear, and I needed a little time alone to get my bearings back again. Then, too, I suddenly started feeling odd wondering if Bob would approve of what I'm doing now. It was like a little stab of guilt reminding me that I'm not ready yet to totally let Bob go. But should I? I just don't know.

NOW THE DELUGE

Meanwhile, as I tried to decide what to do about Bear over the next month, the deluge at work became even greater after Thanksgiving. For the next month until December 24th, the store was going from morning to night, and I had even less time to do anything besides work. I barely had time to sleep before I had to be there the next day.

Some days, I even had to fight off customers who came as early as 8 a.m. They would start knocking to get in, and I would tell them to go away, because I had so much backlog from the day before. But some kept on knocking, angry that I wouldn't let them in.

What made running the store even worse is that I still didn't have enough people or enough well-trained ones to help me. So I kept falling further and further behind in getting everything shipped and out the door. Finally, I went to a temp agency and hired four more people. But again, the store was so busy, there was no time to train the employees properly, and there were so many details that had to be carried out properly to pack and ship a box correctly—from seeing that it was properly labeled and packed to ringing it up on the register properly. So often the new employees missed some of these steps.

Still, as best I could, I tried to supervise the new people and make sure they didn't make mistakes, and Dave helped me do that, too. Even so, the store was so busy, I couldn't do it properly. So there were a lot of mistakes, like boxes sent to the wrong address when a customer came in with lots of boxes we had to address and ship later.

Some of the customers made it even worse. For example, sometimes people would bring in a half dozen gifts to be shipped at the end of the day, expecting us to ship the packages that same day. If someone came in too late, it was impossible to ship it immediately, because we couldn't get the box packed in time to make the day's shipment. Many customers wouldn't understand or accept this and would get angry. Meanwhile, most of the time the line was out the front door, and everyone was impatient and in a rush. So these days were awful.

At least Bear was there at the end of the day, and after I finished work at around 7 to 8 p.m., I would go to see him. I saw him on weekends, too.

Yet, while we were inseparable, and seeing Bear helped me unwind, relax, and get my strength back for the next day, I felt increasingly troubled about our relationship. As much as I liked Bear and felt I needed him to stay on course, I more and more felt he was pushing too far and too fast, since he wanted to get married and have kids and he kept pushing for this. Sometimes at dinner or afterwards, for instance, he would talk about how great it would be when we could do this. Then, I would say "No" or "Not yet," but he didn't want to listen. Instead, he kept saying it would be wonderful, and he kept urging: "Don't worry. Maybe after the Christmas rush is over, we can get married." Meanwhile, I cringed inside each time he said this, hoping he would stop asking, but he didn't.

So while it was nice to feel wanted and appreciated, I knew I couldn't give Bear what he wanted. I still couldn't get over Bob and reciprocate. I still didn't feel really free. Plus I had a deep fear of being hurt again if I opened my heart to someone again. Thus, the closer Bear tried to become to me, the more I pulled away.

Often we argued about my not reciprocating what Bear was giving to me. This happened several times when Bear pointed out that he constantly "showered" me with attention, such as sending me cards and flowers. Then, he complained, I was so busy at the store that I didn't have enough time for him. Or sometimes he attacked me saying that I didn't want to reciprocate because I was afraid to get involved. Then, when I tried to explain and asked him to understand, he wouldn't listen. So we would go back and forth and the argument would go nowhere, until we both got so tired and frustrated arguing, we would stop and simmer sullenly for awhile.

BACK TO "NORMAL"

Finally, on Friday, December 22th, the Christmas rush ended, and things quieted down at the store. Just as I was ready to close the store and relax over the holidays, everything blew up with Bear—maybe because I finally had time to focus on our relationship. As a result, I realized how pressured and overwhelmed Bear made me feel. When I tried to ask Bear for a little more space, we had a big fight that was the beginning of the end of our relationship. Unfortunately, that meant losing an anchor in my life which I needed, as much as I felt trapped by it, so I felt even worse. Then I got some even more disturbing business news about what else Charlie had done and how my financial situation was even worse than I thought. As I wrote in my diary, which I briefly resumed for awhile:

Friday, December 22, 1989

Friday—December 22! Freedom at last! Finally, after the last customer for the day, it was time to close the store and celebrate. Everything has been so crazy for the past month. Now it's finally over. It was such a relief to shut the door. And knowing I won't have to open it up tomorrow or the next day, I relaxed, feeling it will be quiet and back to normal again.

If only I could say that about my relationship with Bear. Everything suddenly fell apart. Friday night I drove over and picked him up to go to a Christmas party, since his car was being fixed. Then, we came back to my house to have a drink before going to the party.

Unfortunately, while we were having a drink, we got into a big fight. Bear started talking about marriage again, saying now that the Christmas busy season was over, we should do this. When I resisted as usual, saying I wasn't ready, Bear again began telling me that I didn't appreciate him enough, and he began describing all of the things he had done for me. I felt like he was giving me a list of the services he performed for me —such as calling me several times a day, giving me cards everyday, sending flowers every few days, doing something with me every night, and on and on. He made it sound like I owed him for all of this, and when I tried to explain I felt too pressured and overwhelmed by all his attention, he became furious. He stood up screaming at me about how I was ungrateful, and didn't appreciate how much he loved me, and that he had had enough. Then, he stormed out, slamming the door behind him, his drink still on the table. We never did get to the party, and he took a taxi home.

After that, I found it a relief not to go to the party at all, and I spent the evening and the next day at home alone. After all the pressure at the store and the emotional turmoil with Bear, I needed that time to myself.

So that weekend, while I was home, I had time to look at all the Christmas cards and letters my friends sent, which helped to cheer me up and made it a nice Christmas after all. I even got cards from a few friends that Bob and I met in Bora Bora.

Then I started thinking about what to do next in my life. I had become so dependent on Bear, and now I'm alone again. I guess I'll have to show I can do it on my own now. But what? Stay here? Go back to Boston? Move somewhere completely different like California? Take a trip to get away from it all—like Bora Bora, where I was so happy one time with Bob? I don't know. But I guess fate will tell me. It has all my life. I guess I'll have to trust in fate again.

After concluding what to do, I woke up feeling a sense a peace I hadn't felt in a long time and I went to Church with a sense of calm and completion. Unfortunately I missed the last mass, since I thought there was one at 12:30 pm. But the last one was at 11:30. So it was disappointing to go home, after the day started off so well. I really missed not being at Church on Christmas day.

GETTING THROUGH THE HOLIDAYS

Without Bear in my life because of the fight, I had to face the rest of the holidays alone. Though I received wonderful gifts, mementoes, and phone calls from family members and friends who were important to me, I felt sad of being alone, too. As I wrote in my diary:

Monday, December 25, 1989

Christmas day! I got up at 8:00 a.m. and worked out and felt pretty good. But I kept putting off calling my family in Massachusetts, because I knew I would become emotional because I wasn't there. When I finally did call my brother Paul and his wife Cindy, they told me they were expecting another baby. "Great!" I thought, because they had been trying so long. But then I felt a little guilty, because I didn't know about the baby. If I did, I could have arranged to go to Massachusetts to see them. It wasn't my fault not to know, since they didn't tell anyone about the baby, because they wanted it to be a big surprise when the family got together. But I felt guilty and sad anyway, not being there.

What even hurt more was the irony of it all. I had decided not to go visit my family, because I wanted to be with Bear, so I put my own desires first, which was being selfish, instead of being with the whole family as usual. But after all that, I'm not with Bear either. We're not even talking. So I'm really paying now for my selfishness—I'm all by myself and crying. I've been crying hysterically all day. It's as if being alone and miserable is my punishment, and I deserve it for being so selfish at this time of year, which is supposed to be about giving to others.

It also felt strange going through the gifts I got. I was happy to think that people remembered me. But then, I felt lonely being so far away from them. I suddenly felt this loneliness when I saw the beautiful sleigh center piece with a small wrapped-up hot air balloon pin in the middle, which Lennie, the best man at my wedding, and his wife Kris sent me. But I didn't want to call them to thank them, because I was afraid I would start crying, since they were Bob's friends and I had become very close to them after the wedding.

At least I talked to Mom and Dad without crying, when I called to thank them for the big box of gifts they sent. It was hard not to cry, though. As we talked, I told them how nice they were to send the gifts, especially the gold necklace and suitcase, which I needed. But when they started talking about how bad they felt that I wasn't there, I wished I was home too. Still, I managed to hold back the tears. But after I hung up, I was so close to tears, I didn't dare call Gram, my grandmother, though I wanted desperately to call her. I was afraid I'd break down, because I felt so close to her—I spoke to her every birthday and holiday, and saw her every time I went to Boston. So I decided to wait until I felt calmer and more collected emotionally.

Friday, December 29, 1989

The last few days have been such a strange quiet time, when I've been mostly alone in Florida, not doing very much. It was nice speaking to people in Massachusetts I haven't seen in months, thanking them for their gifts, talking about old times. It has been a very reflective time, too. I still feel connected to everyone there. But now I'm here in Florida. My business is here. But feeling so isolated and alone makes me wonder if I should stay here. Still, when I see the setting sun at the end of the day, it looks so beautiful. There's something calming and reassuring about that. But I don't know where I should be. Everything seems so confusing and uncertain now.

Sunday, December 31, 1989

Finally! The last day of 1989 and of the decade. I can't wait to see the end of this day. It has been such an awful year, and such an awful holiday alone.

To celebrate the end of the year—and hopefully a new beginning—I planned a picnic at the beach at 4:00 p.m. with Bear. He called Saturday to say he was sorry about everything that had happened, and said he would try to give me a little more space. He explained he was angry that I couldn't reciprocate the way he wanted, but he realized this was partly because I wasn't over Bob yet. I said I was sorry, too, that I couldn't give him what he wanted, but I enjoyed his friendship and upbeat personality, and said I'd try to be more receptive and understanding of him. That's when he suggested, 'Let's put what happened in the past and have a nice New Year's together,' and I agreed. So we decided to see out the year together. I wanted to try again, because I felt a lot of security having Bear there, despite my strong feelings for Bob, and I still hoped we could work things out. Maybe seeing him again might be a new beginning.

However, as I packed the picnic dinner, I came across a table cloth that Bob had bought for me from the Auberge du Soleil restaurant in Napa, California, where we had the wedding reception and celebration. All of a sudden, I felt flooded with memories from the past and very sad again. How could I see Bear today, when all I could think about was Bob again?

Finally, though, I pulled myself together and drove over to pick up Bear. Then we headed to the beach with a bottle of wine, cheese, a camera, and the tablecloth that was so full of memories. As I laid out the tablecloth on the sand, it felt strangely like Bob was still there, as the memories from the wedding flooded back.

But I didn't tell Bear. Instead, I tried to push the feelings away, as we sat eating cheese and drinking wine. Later, as the sun went down, we talked about how the old year was finally ending and how I was glad to see it go, because it had been such a terrible year. As we watched the sun slowly sink towards the sea, I felt a sense of relief to say good-bye to 1989, the worst year of my life. Before it was gone, I took some pictures of the sun setting behind Bear to mark the end of the day and the year.

Yet, even with Bear beside me, I felt lonely and missed Bob terribly. Though Bear was next to me with his arm around me, I felt so close to Bob. But since he's not here, I know I'll have to do what I can to fill the void. I know I'd like to make this world as good and happy as possible for myself and others. But now, missing Bob more than ever, I think work is about the only thing I can do to fill the void.

But is that enough? I feel like I'm stepping into a void of darkness that comes after the setting sun, where everything is so unsure and uncertain. So what do I do now?

STARTING THE NEW YEAR

Finally, it was January. I looked forward to the New Year with such hope. But the pressure kept building—from the store, from Bear, from the memories of Bob that wouldn't go away. At the same time, making everything worse, the legal and financial problems I tried to push aside became more insistent. So I had no time to write in my diary and put it away for the next six months.

Looking back now, I remember those difficult days.

In January, since the store continued to be quiet with the Christmas rush over, I didn't have to spend as much time there. Instead, Dave stayed on as the manager and handled almost everything, with two helpers.

Still, to check on what was going on, I stopped in for about 6 hours each day. I didn't do much that Dave and the employees weren't already doing. I watched a few transactions, glanced over the log, answered phone calls, logged in a some boxes for shipment, and checked the books showing the daily receipts and expenses. I didn't have to do any of these things, since Dave was very much on top of everything. But I felt that going in each day for a few hours in the morning and the afternoon, helped to keep everyone honest, since the store was operating on a cash basis. If I didn't check, it would be easy for any employee to not record receipts or enter extra expenses and pocket the cash. But since I was there, I feel I prevented that from happening. Even though I felt the employees were honest, it made me feel better to check just in case.

Then, when I finished checking the store by around 3 or 4 in the afternoon, I headed off to the beach. I liked going there as much as a could, since that helped to relieve all the stress I felt. I could lie in the sun soaking up its warm rays, listen to music, take a swim, walk on the beach, enjoy nature, and feel the world go away for awhile.

Soon I wanted Bear to go away, too. I went out with him a few times after our New Year's picnic, but nothing seemed to change. Though we had talked about how I needed more space, Bear couldn't back off. He kept pressuring me about getting married and having kids, and he kept sending flowers and cards and calling several times a day. Finally, on our third date, around the 4th or 5th of January, when we went out to dinner, I told him: "This isn't going to work." Fortunately, Bear understood what I was saying and didn't get mad. He just said he was disappointed, too, and after we agreed to remain friends, he left.

Without Bear around, as much as I needed my space, I soon started feeling lonely again. To help fill the void, I decided to go ahead with some plans Bear and I had made in December to have a big Super Bowl party at the villa at the end of January, since Bear was a big football fan. I had already planned the menu, started shopping for the party, and sent out the invitations to the printers. Plus I wanted to have the party, because I wasn't sure how long I could keep the villa, due to rising financial pressures. So though Bear and I were no longer together, I wanted to entertain in the villa while I still owned it. Since I thought I might not own it much longer, I thought of the event as a kind of last blowout. Then, too, planning for the party helped keep away the growing reality of how bad things really were, as my lawyers Paul Freedman, Joel Kaplan, Mark Bidner, and Bob Rubenstein, began to tell me the grim truth.

Things were getting increasingly worse, because Freedman was still trying to finalize the settlement, although he kept postponing this, since I was still getting medical treatment. So he said he couldn't settle until he knew the final bills and damages so he could get more money. But because of these postponements, there was almost no money coming in now. As a result, I couldn't pay the bank mortgage for the villa, or pay any of the notes due on my several other properties. Though the bank had held off from foreclosing for several months because Freedman explained I would be getting settlement money, the bank officers were getting impatient now to get their money. One bank officer even began calling me every few days at the store to ask when I would be able to start paying the long overdue money for the note due to his bank.

Then, in January, many other creditors started calling, as well. While some vendors called me at the store about getting their money, several other creditors began calling my lawyer, Bob Rubenstein, who was now handling my personal and business matters, after Mark Bidner retired. They were growing increasingly concerned about the overdue mortgage payments I owed them. I now owed these payments, because after the accident, my father, who had made several mortgage payments for me, couldn't afford to pay anymore starting in November. Though Rubenstein tried to hold off the bank officers, he told me they were calling, and I became increasingly worried about my deteriorating financial situation.

At least the party seemed like a respite from this. So, a few days after the breakup with Bear, I sent out the invitations that were already printed. I also called Bear to let him know the event was still on and find out if he still wanted to come. He said he did. So everything seemed set. We agreed he would come as a friend, and I wouldn't invite anyone to be my date either. So I thought the party would be a last good-bye to the villa with lots of friends and Bear.

Unfortunately, though, things didn't work out as planned, resulting in a final big blowup with Bear, which made me feel even worse and less hopeful for an upbeat new year. About a week after Bear told me he was coming, he called to say he had met a girl, and asked: 'Do you mind if I bring her?' I was furious, because we had previously agreed we would each come alone. So I yelled at him: "It's two days before the Super Bowl party, and I haven't invited anyone, and you want to bring a date." I couldn't believe he didn't understand why this wasn't appropriate. But he thought I was being unreasonable. So we had a big shouting match over the phone. Finally we both slammed down the phone. Afterwards, Bear not only didn't come to the party, but we didn't talk for over a month.

At least the party went well. Even though I had to host it alone, I went ahead with it, and it was a glorious final celebration. Everyone watched the game on my 54" wide-screen TV, enjoyed the wine I brought back from the Napa Valley, and feasted on fancy cheese and crab hors d'ouevres. Ironically, looking back now, the party was like the last party on the Titanic—a wonderful night of revelry before the ship hit the iceberg and went down.

BACK TO REHAB AND REALITY

The sinking came quickly. I was sharply reminded of how grim things were a few days after the party when I flew back to Boston to see my rehab doctors so they could chart my progress. So once again, I made the rounds of appointments at the rehab hospital in New Hampshire, taking another battery of neurological tests and discussing any continuing problems.

As before, I saw Dr. Jaeger, handling my overall follow-up; Dr. Cox, the neurosurgeon who operated on my neck, and a few others. After they performed the usual tests for any neurological problems, like the continuing numbness on my left side, they asked about my general health. Among other things, they wanted to know if I still had any headaches or pain; pricked my hands with a pin to see if I could feel the sensation; measured the grip strength in my hands; tested the reflexes in my elbows and knees; and examined my ability to move my neck for any improvement.

While my physical responses generally had improved, unfortunately, my ability to move my neck was only at about 30% of what it used to be, and I still had continuing headaches. When they asked me: "What is your biggest problem?" as usual, I said, "Memory." When I explained it didn't seem to be getting better, they didn't seem to know what to do about it. So Dr. Jaeger simply switched my medication, as they did every time, to help the daily headaches, though he wasn't sure if the new medication would work either. Thus, I felt very much like a guinea pig being tested again and again, until they found something that worked after a long trial and error period.

Meanwhile, on top of these continuing neurological and physical problems, my psychologist Dr. Golub warned me about my growing depression from all the pressure I had been under. She felt I was close to spiraling out of control, and advised me to get some ongoing psychological counseling when I returned to Naples. "You've got to face the reality you have been trying so hard not to face," she advised me. It was a sobering thought to realize I had to do something quickly or face a possible psychological breakdown.

It was odd to hear this warning from her, because while I was in Boston, besides going to the rehab hospital, I had a wonderful time seeing many of the friends I had known for years, and they went out of their way to rearrange their schedules so they could see me. Also, I saw my grandmother, who I was very close to. So the whole week flew by with visits from morning to night.

Afterwards, returning to Florida was so sad, because seeing everyone in Massachusetts showed me how alone I was now that I was back. Thus, Dr. Golub's warning really did make sense, as I kept asking myself, 'What am I doing down here? Why do I have a business in Florida that's so far away from everything and everyone I know? Is it really worth staying here to show I can be independent and make it on my own?

I began asking these questions even more intensely, because now that I was back, the business seemed like more of a trap than ever. Not only had it been hard to manage through the busy Christmas season, but it was a business I couldn't sell, because all the books and records were such a mess after Charlie's embezzlement. It was like I was stuck in another Catch-22. I hated the business and didn't want it. It was keeping me from the people I knew and loved. I no longer had anyone in my life in Florida who mattered. But I couldn't close the business, or even give it away. No one wanted it because of the embezzlement. Thus, I felt more trapped than ever, which made me feel even more depressed.

As a result, I decided to take Dr. Golub's suggestion that I needed some psychological counseling. My depression was getting worse and worse, and there seemed no way to stop it. Thus, I decided to find a psychologist and took the suggestion of a customer who had worked with a psychologist specializing in head injuries—Dr. Woulas. I called him and set up my first appointment at the end of January.

Once I started talking to him, I started pouring out all my pent up feelings, and I realized how so many little things had been building up. So now I really felt ready to explode.

Especially upsetting, I explained, was how my mother-in-law, Mrs. Raymond, had taken over as the executrix of Bob's estate in August 1989, because I had signed a prenuptial agreement in which Bob I agreed to keep everything we had before the marriage separate but share equally what we acquired jointly afterwards. So now, as execturix, Mrs. Raymond was threatening to sue me. She was even claiming that some property I had separately acquired after the marriage, like my Mail Boxes business and villa, might be jointly owned, and if so, she wanted half for Bob's estate.

Then, as I told Dr. Woulas, after her lawyers contacted my lawyers, it was so upsetting to have to give her a list of everything I owned, indicate whose name it was in, and go through my files to find documents of all the real estate and businesses I owned, because she wanted to see the proof for herself. She even wanted to know about the bowling alleys my father owned, because she thought Bob owned one of the alleys in which he was working for my father.

Though it was time-consuming to organize all this material, I had to supply the proof, I told Dr. Woulas, because otherwise, my lawyers said, she could take over my property because of the prenuptial agreement. If anything was in Bob's name after the marriage, she would have a right to it. Or if something was in both our names, she would now own half of it, and I would have to buy her out. So that's why, besides the personal lawyer I had for years and the lawyers dealing with my injuries and protecting me from her suing me on behalf of Bob's estate, I now had eight lawyers. And that's why I felt so angry and scared, as I pulled together more and more documents for them again and again. Although I tried to push them down and ignore them they kept getting worse.

So now, as I spoke to Dr. Woulas, all my feelings of anxiety and pressure came pouring out. I couldn't believe how nasty Mrs. Raymond was, I told him. She was like a witch or vampire, trying to get at everything I owned and take it from me. And each time I produced a document, I felt like I was putting out still another fire. But soon, it would burst into flames again. Now more and more, I felt Mrs. Raymond and the legal problems were engulfing me, taking over my life.

Also, as I told Dr. Woulas, I felt even worse about my own situation, after seeing the stark difference between the full active lives of my friends in Massachusetts and the lonely existence I had come to know in Florida. As I explained, my friends were getting on with their lives. They were starting families, enjoying a wonderful round of social activities. But I was back in Florida, still trying to get over the death of my husband, without anyone else in my life who mattered, knowing I couldn't have a family now. Worse, I had no real friends. So I was all by myself. I had a business I couldn't sell. Plus I had a mother-in-law who was making continual demands and trying to bleed whatever she could from me. So my depression became deeper and deeper.

Now, I felt even more despondent because it was almost February 9th—the first anniversary of Bob's death—another grim reminder of all I had lost.

After two sessions, Dr. Woulas recognized how dangerously depressed I was, literally teetering on the brink of a nervous breakdown. As a result, he decided I should be hospitalized for my own protection and referred me to a psychiatrist, Dr. Huergo, to make the arrangements.

Immediately, I agreed, because I knew I needed help, and I was relieved that I could go to a hospital and have someone to take care of and protect me. I didn't have to struggle alone anymore. But I found it hard telling my parents so they understood why I needed help, because they believed so strongly in the ideal of self-reliance.

They believed anyone should be able to solve his or her own problems, and they couldn't accept the idea that anyone can have psychological problems.

I kept going over in my mind how to break my plans to go to a psychiatric hospital to my parents. Finally, when I arrived home and called my mother, who was spending the winter in Florida, to tell her I had to go to a hospital for awhile, because I couldn't manage the stress on my own, she was speechless for a few moments like she was in shock. I could tell from her reaction how upset she was I was going into a psychiatric ward for a mental illness. Her reaction made me feel like I was the epitome of failure. She had a hard time accepting that I needed to do this to get better, as I had feared when I called to explain. So that made going to the hospital even harder for me, though I knew I needed to go.

GOING TO THE HOSPITAL

Regardless of how my family might react, I felt entering the hospital was the best thing to do. I told Dave at the store what I was going to do, and he agreed to continue managing the store while I was gone. Then, on the morning of February 10th, my mother picked me up and drove me to the hospital.

Even if she was disappointed and disapproved my going there, at least she was willing to help me get there, and I was thankful for that. However, it was a quiet awkward trip, because I keenly felt her disappointment and disapproval as we drove along. Finally, after 15 minutes, which seemed like hours, as I saw the past year pass before me like a bad movie, we arrived at a small community hospital in downtown Naples.

Unfortunately, it was not the peaceful respite from reality I imagined. Instead, going into the hospital was more like entering a prison after we checked into the reception desk. The nurse there directed us to go down a long corridor to the ward, and a few minutes later, we entered the ward's reception area—a long room with a nurses' stand and chairs around it. Once inside, my mother quickly turned to leave, wanting to get away as quickly as possible. "I'll call you," she said, and as I saw her walk out the door, I suddenly felt very frightened and alone.

As I stood there feeling desolate, I noticed a man standing by himself, staring off in the distance, and I began crying. It was a shock, realizing how far down I had sunk myself to be here. I stumbled over to a chair and couldn't stop crying.

Moments later, a nurse hurried over and gave me a relaxer to calm down. As she did, a male nurse in a white jump suit grabbed the bag of clothes I was carrying out of my hand. "Why?" I asked. But without answering, he pulled my bag open and looked through it. When he found a razor I had brought with me to shave my legs, he immediately took it and explained that he didn't want me to hurt myself, so he had to take razor blades or any other objects I might use in this way.

As he continued rummaging around in my bag, I felt like crying out to him: "I'm depressed. But I'm not going to kill myself." But I didn't say anything. After he finished looking through my bag, he did the same with my suitcase, and took out all the bottles of medications I had brought with me. "We'll dispense the medications to you ourselves," he explained. "We'll give you just what it says to take on the bottles." Thus, it was clear the hospital staff didn't trust me to take my own medicines properly. It was like I had become a little child, and I suddenly felt very helpless.

After a few minutes, another nurse took me down another long corridor with doors on either side to my room, where I had been assigned. It was a large room with four beds separated by three white curtains that were pulled back to the wall. Another woman was already in there, lying on one of the beds. I was glad there was only one other woman in the room, not any more, though I would have preferred to be alone.

Then, directing me to sit down on the bed, the nurse said she would check on me later. As she left, she said: "Now just relax." However, I didn't feel very much like relaxing. Instead, once she had closed the door behind her, I flung myself on the bed and broke down crying harder than ever. All I could think of was how low I had come at this point in my life, and I could hardly believe I had come to this. Now, there was no denying it, since I was a patient in a mental hospital, and I felt so helpless and alone.

CHAPTER 10

•

TAKING TIME OUT TO RECOVER

THE WORLD OF THE HOSPITAL WARD

For the next five days, my world was the hospital ward. It was a time of reflection, meeting with therapists, and going to a therapy group. I also spent many hours thinking of the past and the future, and getting centered and grounded again. Perhaps what helped the most was having a chance to pull away from all the terrible things that had been happening, to be in a safer, more protective place. Then, too, realizing how high I had been and how low I had fallen gave me the impetus to pull my life together and strive once more for a better future.

There was a numbing sameness to those hospital days. I had daily meetings with my psychiatrist Dr. Huergo, a few group therapy meetings, and when back in my room, I spent the time quietly remembering and grieving deeply. It was wrenching to let go, though I knew I had to. Remembering and grieving helped me eventually feel a sense of completion and start to release from the past.

I remember the first day I got there. It was already early afternoon, and after the nurse left, I sat in my room resting for a few hours until dinner. I was glad I didn't have to do anything or talk to anyone, because I just wanted to be alone. Later in the afternoon, a nurse stopped by to tell me that I would meet with my psychiatrist the first thing in the morning, and after that I would start a group therapy program.

The next morning, Dr. Huergo, the psychiatrist I would see each day, stopped by to talk with me. He seemed like such a soft-spoken, warm, and friendly man, that I felt comfortable telling him a little about how I felt. I explained how depressed I was, and he told me it was perfectly understandable I felt that way, because of what had happened to me due to the accident, my financial crisis, and the problems with Mrs. Raymond. I felt a little better after talking to him and a little less alone, because I felt he understood. I also realized my deep depression was a normal reaction to all that I had suffered.

Dr. Huergo expressed hope that I could overcome my depressed state by going through a real grieving and letting go process which I hadn't done so far, since I had been caught up with daily events and one crisis after another. "Just give yourself the time and permission to heal and let go of all the things that have happened to you," he said. "It can take time, but keep your eye on that future goal and keep doing what you can to get there. Just think 'Step by step. I'm getting a bit better each day.'" I felt better hearing that. It was like he was giving me a step by step program for hope.

Next, I went to the first of my regular therapy sessions. I had several each day. In this first session, all the patients on the ward met together in one room to discuss why each of us was here. In the second session, like other patients, I met with one of the nurses assigned to me and told her how I was feeling about day to day happenings and problems. For the third type of therapy, I met one-on-one with one of the psychologists, who came to my room to talk to me.

The group therapy session with all the patients was the most difficult for me. Each session was led by a staff psychologist, who encouraged group members to speak and explain their problems. I felt funny talking about my problems in a group, so when it came my turn, I didn't say much. I just said in general terms that I was upset and I described a little about myself, explaining that I grew up in Massachusetts and moved to Florida to run a business.

However, I didn't want to say anything very personal, so I didn't say anything about the things that were really important to me. I said nothing about how much I missed Bob, how my mother-in-law was trying to take everything she could of what I owned, and how I had broken up with Bear and had no one in my life I could really talk to. Looking back now, I know those were the kinds of things I needed to talk about, understand, and let go of to heal. But at the time, everything was so painful, and I had grown up learning not to publicly talk about anything that was personal or that might present me or anyone important to me in a negative light. So I said little.

Meanwhile, when I wasn't in group therapy or talking to my psychiatrist once a day, the hospital had various programs to keep me busy, so I didn't dwell on anything that might make me feel depressed. The hospital's philosophy was that if I was with people or doing things, that would help me stop focusing on my thoughts and feelings, which were making me depressed; then I would feel better. That's why I spent an hour or two going to an art class where we glazed ceramic vases, did oil painting, or made small household objects, like paper towel holders and key rings.

There were some informal chat times, too. Frequently, the nurses on the ward stopped by to chat informally. During meals, I could meet with some of the other patients and talk to them more informally than in the group therapy sessions. Initially, I found these group meals very uncomfortable, since I felt awkward with this group of strangers. Yet over the next few days, after hearing them describe their problems in group therapy, I got to know them and felt more comfortable talking to them.

Although I didn't say much about myself in the sessions or to other patients, I found the meetings and conversations helpful in showing me I wasn't alone in my suffering. In fact, I realized in some ways I was even lucky, because many other patients had it even worse.

I noticed this in my group therapy session. The patients came from all walks of life, and some were in a really bad way. One man was in five different car accidents and had a drug dependency problem. He was addicted to the pain medications prescribed for his injuries from the different accidents, and he was in the hospital to detox so he could break free of his addiction. Another woman was found wandering in the streets, and she still didn't know her name. A girl of about twenty was suffering from anorexia, and she was as thin as a rail and had to be forced to eat. Hearing others share their stories, I started seeing that other people had very serious problems and experienced a lot of suffering, too. As a result, I didn't feel so alone. I realized that I'm not the only one.

Even though I felt less alone, in group therapy sessions, I still didn't feel comfortable admitting how I felt. So when it was time for me to say something, I continued to clam up. I said I didn't have anything to add. Or if I felt the pressure of the group or facilitator to say something, I talked about what I had accomplished in the past. But I avoided talking about my problems, unless someone asked me directly why I was there. Then I said something vague like: "My husband died and I'm very depressed about it." But I didn't talk about the particular things that were really bothering me.

I didn't even feel comfortable describing my difficulties in any detail to my psychiatrist, because he seemed so knowledgeable that I felt he would judge me for having failed. Just about the only people I felt comfortable talking to were the nurses. They seemed so warm and sympathetic, more like me, so I could open up to them.

REFLECTING ON THE PAST TO HEAL

Yet, while I kept my thoughts and feelings largely to myself, what helped the most were the quiet times when I could reflect back. These times of remembering helped me get back in touch with that feeling of joy I had once felt so long ago. Also, thinking back helped me get in touch with and clarify the feelings I had about the accident, Bob, and my mother-in-law, so I could finally work through them and deal with where I was now. In turn, this process of acknowledging, grieving for a loss, and feeling angry about what I felt some people did to hurt me, helped me clear out some emotional baggage, so I could begin to heal. The process was like clearing out all the worn and soiled clothes in a closet to make way for new ones.

THINKING ABOUT BOB AND THE RAYMONDS

Part of the healing process involved simply remembering back to when I first met Bob and recalling my early impressions of my mother-in-law Shirley Raymond. It was a way to recognize the real and destructive Mrs. Raymond, disparage her, and diminish her power, since she had become a threat to me in trying to take over some of my property. Then, as I remembered, I recorded my thoughts in a small notebook I kept by my bed.

REMEMBERING MY MOTHER-IN-LAW

My memories about my mother-in-law were especially terrible and upsetting to think about. Yet it was like a catharsis to face these recognitions. As I wrote in my journal about Mrs. Raymond:

Though I didn't realize it at the time, I now realize Shirley is a very angry, manipulative person, who doesn't have any friends. She didn't even have anyone she wanted to invite to the engagement party or wedding...

She didn't get along with her husband George either, although they put on a good front, like at the wedding, when they were all smiles. But mostly, they didn't spend much time together; they even took separate vacations. Bob told me that the only reason his parents didn't get divorced is because divorce was not socially acceptable.

I can also see now how grasping she has always been—so my estate is one more thing she's trying to grab. I can better understand now what I'm up against. For example, after Bob's death, I remember how I found a letter he had written to his father but never sent. In it, he tried to tell his father he was sorry they had never been close, and he explained that the reason was because he did not respect him since he never stood up to Shirley. But after writing the letter, Bob was afraid to send it, so he never did.

Another time I didn't say anything when I caught Shirley in a lie just before the wedding, and I told Bob not to make an issue of it. Bob had asked her to light one of the candles at the altar to represent the Raymond side of the family, and she replied that she couldn't because she couldn't climb the stairs. But then I realized that there weren't any stairs; she was just making an excuse.

Then, when Bob died, I think she finally showed her true feelings by not coming to the funeral service I held. For now without Bob to persuade her to go, she was able to stay away to show me just how she felt.

I felt better, much better, by writing these memories down. Finally I was able to say all of the things I had held back, because I didn't want to stir up negative feelings in the family by showing my true hostile feelings towards Mrs. Raymond. I didn't want Bob to feel there was any animosity between me and his mother.

Then, the next day of reflecting, I continued:

If only I had taken to heart more of Bob's warnings about his mother instead of trying to smooth things over. Maybe Shirley wouldn't have become so demanding now. I realize now that Bob was afraid to be open with her, since he knew she wanted things to be a certain way or in control of them. And now that she's in charge of Bob's estate, that's her way of trying to still control me—and even stay in control of Bob after his death.

It helped me feel better to record how I felt about Mrs. Raymond's actions after the accident, too. They provided further examples of how mean spirited and grasping she was, and as I wrote, I felt like I pushing another dart into a bulletin board with each paragraph I wrote. It's like each one knocked Mrs. Raymond down a little bit further to a smaller size I could deal with. As I wrote in my journal of reflections:

I've tried not to think about this for so long, because it's so painful to remember how Shirley seemed so petty and disrespectful towards Bob's memory even when she tried to take charge of things. One time was when I was still in the hospital in Florida for surgery, and she decided to have a mass for Bob. She invited everyone to send donations to the National Cancer Institute in Bob's name, and after I got out of the hospital and returned to Boston a few months later, a friend mentioned that she had sent in a donation. When I realized that Shirley had requested donations in my husband's name, I wanted to send everyone a thank-you note. So I asked my attorney to contact her attorney for a list of the people sending in donations, since we were only speaking through our attorneys who were handling details for the estate. But when my attorney asked her attorney for the list, she refused, and I couldn't get the list from the National Cancer Institute, because it only holds the names of donors for 30 days. I was upset at not being able to get the names, because many of the people Shirley had asked to donate were my friends, and I felt they should be properly thanked. It was hard to understand why Shirley would want to prevent me from doing something simple like that; though now I can see it was one more example of her way of staying in control.

Also, she was so strange in the way she handled the videotape of the memorial service and Bob's ashes. I thought it was weird when she had a filmmaker make a video of her own memorial service in Boston while I was still in the hospital in Naples. And then, I thought it even stranger when she gave my mother a copy to show to me. Why would she think I would want to see it? Of course, I wouldn't. It was so morbid to me—just the idea of videotaping a memorial service gave me the creeps.

It also seemed odd that when I was going to hold a funeral service for Bob on a boat and scatter his ashes in the Cape Cod Bay the way he would have wanted, I invited Shirley. But she didn't attend, and later claimed I hadn't invited her, though I had. Then, a few days before I went out on the boat, she had the funeral director visit me, insisting that he wanted Bob's ashes for her, and finally I agreed to split the ashes with her. So I only threw half of his ashes out to sea, and afterwards I wondered why Shirley wanted to keep them, rather than letting me release them as Bob wanted. I felt like this was her way to stay in control of Bob, even after his death.

REMEMBERING THE WEDDING

Perhaps most healing of all was thinking about the wedding. It was a time when I felt totally happy, successful, and complete—a high point of my life. Now to remember this peak was a source of inspiration, even if Bob was gone.

It was such a wonderful magical time when Bob and I symbolized our feelings for each other, our hopes for the future, and the love of our family and friends. That's why it was so soothing and cheering to think about this later. Nothing else in my life was working at the time, and then I remembered this.

It made everything seem possible again. The spirit that Bob and everyone else had brought to the wedding was still there. So remembering gave me a sense of comfort and hope that it was worth trying again.

The wedding meant so much to me because when Bob and I finally decided to get married after seeing each other for three years, we wanted to make the wedding very special. When we traveled to Montreal to celebrate our engagement, a couple we met told us about the Auberge du Soleil in the Napa Valley, and as they described its old-style European atmosphere, like an old-fashioned French winery, we decided this would be perfect, instead of going to France as we were considering. To be sure, my mother and I flew out to look at it and brought back a short video we took to show Bob. A few weeks later, Bob and I flew out to make the final decision and decided this was it. Then, since our family and friends were so important to both of us, we decided to fly everyone to California and make it a week-long celebration no one would forget. We also wanted to show how committed we were to each other forever in front of the people closest to us. Ironically, that vow contributed to making it so hard for me to snap back and let go of my connection to Bob and what I had lost. He was not only so much a part of my life when the accident happened, but our wedding nine months before had been such a powerful experience.

THE FIRST DAYS IN SAN FRANCISCO

The celebration began with a few glorious days in San Francisco, where we arranged for the guests to arrive in three groups—first the members of the wedding party, then members of the family, and finally our closest friends. We planned to greet them as they arrived at the airport, along with Robbi, our wedding planner, a bubbly elf of a man who dressed like a White House secret service agent.

The first day, after Bob and I met Robbi at the airport, we headed to our hotel—the Mandarin in San Francisco—in a long silver limo, which made me feel like royalty. When we arrived at the Oriental Suite on the top floor of the hotel, there were flowers everywhere—gardenias in a big glass bowl by the bed, white roses and cally lilies on the table. As we watched the sun go down and a few sailboats drifted by on the San Francisco Bay, it was the perfect ending to our first exciting day. We had a few last romantic moments ourselves before everyone began arriving the following day.

The next day, we welcomed the first group of arrivals at the airport. As we did, a four-person camera crew with two videos and two still cameras followed us and our guests all over. We had hired them to make an enduring record of the whole wedding celebration from beginning to end. Even our grandchildren would someday enjoy this, we hoped.

The first group included the members of the wedding party— Bob's sister Honey and brother David, and two of our best friends and their wife and boyfriend. After we took the trolley to Ghiradelli Square and Fisherman's Wharf, we spent the day exploring the quaint shops at the Square and seeing the fishing boats docked at the Wharf.

After we returned to our hotel at sundown, we had a party in our suite for the wedding party. As we mingled, sharing champagne and fancy hors d'oeuvres, like Dungeness crab puffs and warmed brie topped with pecans, I felt so good seeing my closest friends here. As we laughed and talked about old times and the future, I felt their support so strongly. It was as if our wedding was not only solidifying the love Bob and I shared, but bringing our friends together with us, as well.

VISITING THE WINE COUNTRY

The next few days at the hotel were like a vacation, and thinking back was a reminder of what it was like to be carefree and have fun. It had been so long since I experienced this. Remembering helped me feel the renewed possibility of experiencing fun and joy again.

Our arrival in the California wine country began with a rehearsal dinner after the members of my family and Bob's arrived. After we walked along a long driveway lined with oak trees past a rolling golf course and rose garden, we stepped inside a stone white building that looked like a magnificent castle. Inside, a man who looked like a French chef welcomed us to the Domaine Chandon restaurant, and led us on a tour. As he showed us rows of wine vats, he spoke of how the restaurant was founded 11 years before to bring the traditions of a classic French restaurant to the U.S., and then gave us some vintage champagne to sample.

Afterwards, we gathered in the dining room, where Bob's father, George, invited everyone to toast Bob and I for organizing this special occasion. As everyone did, I felt the warmth of having my closest friends and family around me. I also felt an especially warm glow seeing Bob sitting with his nephew Scott, showing him how to hold a glass to properly drink and toast with the wine. When Bob pointed out that they were wearing the same pink polka-dotted tie and so had much in common, I felt like I was seeing the connection of the generations, with the older generation teaching the younger one, and thought about how one day Bob and I would be a model for our children, too.

The next day, after the third group with our friends arrived, the highlight was a dinner in a cave at the Auberge du Soleil. We walked or drove in golf carts to get to get there, and arrived to the sounds of a small classical orchestra playing a Bach prelude on saxophones. As I remembered back, I thought about how this dinner was a testament to the power of love of everyone there, and I found it energizing to think about how the spirit of that love was still there, even if physically Bob was not. I recalled how the huge plants with long stems and large leaves at each table were like a symbol of ever-growing life.

Then, during dinner, the presentations of some of the guests were especially touching, such as a poem on romance which a close friend Joy Pierce wrote and recited. It began:

> And now it's time for the story to begin,
> Of the love between our Raymond and Quinn...
> In dating they saw they liked each other's style,
> But they tried hard to remain unattached all the while.
> Even so it seemed the harder they tried,
> The more they became starry-eyed...
> Now the planning is over, there's no need to fret.
> This wedding is one we'll never forget.

I had tears in my eyes when Joy finished the poem, and now, for a moment, I felt I was back at the dinner, feeling that deep sense of connection and joy. Again, the memory helped to charge me up, as I thought about how that feeling might still happen again.

Even thinking about the brief periods of nervousness I felt back then helped me feel better now. Though everything was going smoothly, I kept worrying from time to time that things could still go wrong, especially on the first day when the guests first arrived. But as I saw that everything seemed to be going smoothly and people were enjoying themselves, I relaxed. Similarly, Bob was nervous at times, too, pacing around and making me even more nervous. But then he relaxed as well. After awhile, as all the events we had planned went smoothly, I began to feel like some power up there was protecting us, so I started feeling that whatever happened, everything would turn out all right.

In the hospital, I realized this sense of protection was a feeling I wanted to get back. I felt I needed to put aside my current doubts and fears about whether my life would work again, to just trust and believe. I experienced that sense of certainty and protection so strongly once. So remembering how everything at the wedding worked out in the end was tremendously reassuring. I felt if I could restore that deep sense of trust and faith, I would have that protection back to help me again.

A VISIT TO A MAGICAL ISLAND ON THE BAY

On the fourth day, we went to a man-made tropical island with palm trees in the middle of the San Francisco Bay, which a man built as his home and opened to visitors. Remembering our trip, helped remind me that all things were possible. As I reflected in the hospital, if a man could create an island paradise from scratch, bringing in the dirt and rocks to build it, I could somehow remake my own life.

I remembered our trip starting off on a yacht touring San Francisco Bay on a beautiful sunny day. After we docked on the pebble beach around the island, we walked through the palm trees to a staircase into what looked like the hull of a ship. At the bottom, we stepped into a cozy room with a fire in the fireplace. As we filed by a small bar with colorful pictures of sailboats on the wall behind it, a man with a full beard who looked like Santa Claus—actually the owner—motioned for us to follow him. He led us down the stairs to a wine cellar, where a small classical music group played the piano, violin, and other instruments in the background, as he passed around goblets of wine for us to try. As we sipped the wine, he described his home as the world's only floating tropical island. He had built it himself by hand from over 40 tons of rocks and earth, starting with the concrete hull where we were now.

As I looked around, noticing some of his unique personal touches, such as crossed swords on the mantle and a steel scuba diving suit in the corner, I was tremendously impressed by what he had done. He had started with nothing, and then imagined and created all this. It was like a dream hideaway, which didn't even have a telephone.

As I reflected in the hospital on what he had built, I wished for a similar phoneless hideaway, since I had so many creditors calling that I didn't want to speak to. So the idea that someone could escape to his own private island felt like a wonderful relief to me, and imagining myself there, made me feel a sense of renewal. It was also inspiring to see the creativity that went into imagining this unusual home, and I envisioned how I might use his creativity as a model for myself. Just think what I might do if I could let my own creativity go. It was like another ray of hope through all my troubles.

Remembering our dinner celebration as our boat sped back to San Francisco after the visit was uplifting, too. As we shared our impressions about the island, one member of our group stood up and began to sing the words: "Will You Still Remember?" As I heard his singing in my mind, I kept thinking how significant these days were to me. I would always remember them, too. While he was still singing, Bob and I started dancing, and soon we were rocking to the beat of: "Baby, It's Time We Got Back to the Basics of Love." Then, we had a birthday celebration for Bob's nephew Scott, and after Scott blew out the candles on a big white cake, we watched him break dance in the middle of a circle.

Ironically, it was such a happy time that I even put aside my feelings of distrust for my mother-in-law Mrs. Raymond to link arms with her as we all formed a line and did a line-dance together. So for the rest of the wedding, it was as if there was no anger, no bad blood, nothing negative between us. It was like any bad feeling between us was in suspension, made possible by this magical day on the floating island.

In turn, thinking about these happy memories in the hospital helped me realize that if I could overcome my deep distrust for Mrs. Raymond, I could now overcome other adversities. Also, thinking about the past helped me imagine how I could learn from what happened, so I could feel the terrible things that occurred did so for some reason. Instead of feeling the accident and its aftermath wasn't just some random act of chance, but I could see it as a learning process for me to become a better person, which helped me make sense of it all. So in this way, these memories, too, helped to inspire me and helped me heal.

REMEMBERING THE WEDDING CEREMONY

Then, I thought about the day of the wedding—a time to make a serious commitment after several days of relaxing and partying. As the camera crew wandered around asking my friends and family how much they enjoyed the last few days, I waited in my hotel room like a movie star, getting ready to be made up by a team of makeup artists. They included my own hairstylist and manicurist flown in from Boston for the occasion and another makeup professional from San Francisco. Then, as I stood in my white wedding dress, with cascades of lace and silk, and held a bouquet of roses, while posing for wedding pictures, I felt a little like Barbara Streisand ready to do her big comeback performance. Now, as I reflected, I wondered if I could do my own comeback, too.

Finally, after Bob and the wedding party were ready—the men putting on slick black tuxedos with maroon cumberbunds, the women donning matching maroon dresses, it was time to go to the church. We had chosen a small stone traditional-style church a few miles away in downtown St. Helena, a quaint wine country town. After everyone arrived and the guests settled in the pews, the wedding procession began. It was awesome to think about. After Mrs. Raymond came in with her son David and husband right behind them, my mother followed, leaning on the arm of my brother Paul. Then came the bridesmaids, Bob's nephew Scott with the rings, and finally my maid of honor, my closest friend from college. Meanwhile, the melody "In the Eyes of Love" played in the background. Finally, I came in on my father's arm, as "Here Comes the Bride," accompanied us.

As I reflected now, Bob and I had designed this ceremony to be a traditional wedding, to show how we were both firmly committed to traditional family and religious values. It was reaffirming to think of that commitment and remind myself of my continuing faith even now, although all of this symbolism and pageantry made it so hard to let go of this special time, too.

THE MESSAGE OF THE SERVICE

Thinking about the message of the service helped me release, too. The deacon, Ron Gagne, who was marrying us began the service after Bob and I walked to the altar and knelt down in front of it. After Ron recited a blessing, my brother Paul stepped to the podium and read a passage from the Bible about the importance of the commitment we had made. While I felt a strong sense of sacred oneness at the service, now I realized that my brother's words suggested that the act of loving itself was what was important—that while love might endure, it did not have to enslave. Or as Paul stated it, reading from Paul's message to the Corinthians:

> If I have not loved, I am nothing...Love is patient; love is kind; love is not a jealous love; love does not put on airs; it is not snobbish. Love is never rude, it is not self-seeking, it is not prone to anger, neither does it brood over injuries. Love does not rejoice in what is wrong, but rejoices in the truth....Love never fails. This is the word of the Lord.

Just thinking about the words now had a healing effect, since they spoke of the permission to release, although love might remain. In fact, the words were so meaningful, I felt they were speaking just to me, in that I had pledged an everlasting love. But while it might last forever, it didn't have to hold me back and control me, too. It would always comfort me and be with me, because love never fails. At the same time, it could guide me to something new, including additional love. Then, too, the memory of having that love was inspiring and made me feel stronger, because—the words echoed again and again in my mind—"If I have not loved, I am nothing; If I have not loved, I am nothing." It was a powerful message that gave me strength.

I gained this renewed strength because suddenly I realized that the message of the service was that it was possible to love deeply and feel forever connected to someone, and yet be free. One could do so by drawing on that person's love to feel loved and strengthened, and then, feeling that support, being free and strong enough to move on. It was a message of both holding on and letting go. Though I still didn't feel emotionally ready to let go entirely, the message gave me an image of a new goal to strive for, so I could work hard to overcome my past suffering. I could feel like I was now going towards a new mountain at the end of the dark valley I had just been through. Now, I sat up with a new resolve, finally ready to put the past behind and move on.

CELEBRATING AFTER THE CEREMONY

Then, thinking about our last day of celebration after the ceremony gave me a renewed surge of energy to act on this resolve. I felt like I could direct the excitement and energy of those days to help me do what I had to do now to get my life back on track after I left the hospital.

As I remembered, right after the ceremony, we all went back to the reception room at the Auberge, where a harp and violin were playing. As we gathered near a huge ice sculpture of love birds, with a towering white wedding cake in the center, Bob's best man Lennie, toasted us saying: "May you grow old together and live happily ever after." Then the band struck up a rock rendition of "Suddenly" by Bill Ocean. After Bob and I started dancing, the rest of the guests joined us in dancing, and I recalled a kaleidoscope of memories of how much we all enjoyed the celebration, as the video cameras caught everyone dining, laughing, and dancing to different love songs.

About an hour later, with the beat of "Love and marriage goes together like a horse and carriage," playing in the background, I cut the first slice of cake and fed it to Bob. Finally, after more toasts and dancing, with the reception still going full blast, Bob and I made our way through the crowd to a waiting hot air balloon outside the hotel. Then, as the balloon rose slowly into the air, the guests crowding around on the ground to watch, Bob and I waved goodbye and flew off into the sunset—like the ending of a Hollywood film.

It was a magical moment, and thinking about it in the hospital helped me feel charged up and ready to take on the world again. I recalled how I had spent so much time planning and organizing to create that wonderful week which had gone off so perfectly. From the first arrivals to the ceremony to the final balloon flight, everything had worked so well. My memory of this was like a reminder that if I could put something like this together once, now I could do it again. As I had created this event, so I could recreate my own life. I just had to step into a balloon again and take off, like at the reception. The balloon rising and heading towards the setting sun was a symbol to me that I could rise again, head towards the sun, and land firmly, feeling whole, back on the earth once more.

FEELING READY TO MOVE ON

So finally, after five days in the hospital, I felt ready to take control of my life again. I felt recharged by several days of therapy and inspired by reflecting on the wedding to go back to the real world and try again. I knew I still needed additional counseling to help me stay on course, as my psychiatrist advised. But at least I was ready to confront what lay ahead, even the pending legal and financial problems. I just didn't know how bad it was going to be.

PART IV:
FIGHTING BACK

CHAPTER 11

•

THE BEGINNING OF THE LEGAL BATTLE
AND BANKRUPTCY

When I left the hospital on February 16, 1990, I felt recharged and ready to start fighting. I knew I would have to fight hard and left determined to use every bit of my strength to get back what I could.

The experience was like entering a war on multiple fronts all at once. I had to fight with the insurance companies to get the settlements; fight with my mother-in-law over the estate; continue the battle to stave off creditors; and struggle to keep my business going. I had a half-dozen lawyers to help me, but I had to continually consult with them about what was happening and react to their suggestions about what to do. Usually, I went along with their suggestions, since I didn't know any better at the time whether they were advising me correctly or not. Though they did most of the follow through, emotionally I felt exhausted to be continually under siege. I was still going to therapy, since my stay in the hospital had just helped me get myself back together to go on. But I still had many of the tensions and the problems with thinking I had going in.

To help deal with these underlying problems, I continued going to counseling sessions with Dr. Woulas, the head injury specialist. I also joined a brain injury support group that he had started.

Financially, I was still heading towards disaster, and eventually I did go bankrupt five months later in July. For now, I was determined not to let that possibility get me down. I would fight, I had decided in the hospital, to make my way back.

KEEPING THE STORE GOING

A major fight was the day to day struggle to keep the store alive. To help, Dave stayed on as manager, and a new assistant Rita, he had recently hired, helped, too. As before I went to the hospital, they continued doing much the same work as handling the day to day distribution of mail, and I continued to go to the store for a few hours a day. Perhaps they could have done this work without me, but I wanted to be there to see how things were going. Also, the few hours I was there provided some structure for my day.

When I went in, as before, I checked the books and reviewed the logs. Now it was more difficult, because I had to deal with a growing number of increasingly angry phone calls from long unpaid creditors.

Later, in the afternoon, to unwind, as Dr. Woulas suggested, I went to the beach to relax. I felt some comfort knowing that at least here I could escape from everything else; at least that small part of my life was going well.

For now, going to the beach was about the only time I did have for relaxation, because when I wasn't at the store, I had so many legal matters to deal with. Thus, I had little time for a social life, and Bear was out of the picture anyway. For now, I didn't miss this absence, since I was so focused on this growing legal struggle now heading to the courts.

THE INSURANCE FIGHT

The insurance fight became increasingly complicated. While most of my medical bills were in, except for my bills for my follow-up visits to the rehab hospital, which totaled well over $50,000 so far, my lawyer Paul Freedman assured me I could expect even more for pain and suffering. He expected to get this once he settled with my two major insurance companies— Traveler's and Liberty Mutual, who each offered up to up to $250,000 in coverage. In addition, I had an additional $1 million umbrella policy with Travelers, that kicked in after the other insurers had paid their full coverage.

Unfortunately, though, Freedman reported that the insurance companies were finding reasons to resist paying now or at all. Though he had gotten Liberty to pay $25,000 for excess medical coverage in February 1990, neither Liberty or Travelers was willing to pay any more until all of my medical bills were in and it was clear what all of my damages would be. Also, Traveler's wasn't willing to pay anything on its umbrella policy, until it was determined if it owed anything after the other companies had paid what they owed.

So now a war of legal letters went on. At the end of May, Freedman sent both Liberty and Traveler's letters explaining why each should pay the full policy amount. As passionately as he could, he argued that besides bills over $50,000, I would have to pay for continuing medical treatment, as well as counseling and educational training to compensate for my injuries. Plus now my potential for earning income was less. So my claim would certainly be worth more than my insurance cap, he said.

Later, reading his letters, I cringed. His arguments made my suffering sound even worse than the doctor's more scientific descriptions, such as when he wrote Liberty and Traveler's saying:

> Ms. Quinn has suffered permanent damage to the cervical spine...
>
> In addition to her orthopedic problems, Ms. Quinn... remains with significant memory loss and diminished capacity...She will require treatment on a permanent basis for headaches, depression, stress management and related psychological disorders stemming from her post-brain injury syndrome.

Further, he added, I could expect to continue to suffer from "scarring and disfigurement," "extreme grief and anguish" due to the loss of my husband and the "total upheaval" of my former life." Then, too, I now had a "diminished mental capacity" driving my once flourishing business to bankruptcy. After pointing out that I would experience the effects of the accident the rest of my life, probably at least 40 more years, he concluded with these chilling remarks:

> She can expect to experience physical deterioration of her spine, mental impairment associated with her brain injury syndrome and psychological depression, anxiety and grief for the rest of her life. A healthy and highly motivated young woman has been transformed into an emotional cripple. Deborah has been stripped of her independence and enthusiasm for life.

The irony is that despite my resolve to fight on, Freedman had to make me sound in as bad a shape as possible to collect the most insurance money. Paradoxically, while I wanted to get better as much as I could, my lawyers would do better both for me and for themselves, by making me sound worse.

In any event, Freedman thought the insurance holdup would soon be resolved because of Bob's clear liability and my claim well over the policy limits. "So just a few more weeks," Freedman kept reassuring me, saying he expected the insurance companies to pay the full amount now, as he requested in his letter—$1.25 million from Traveler's, $250,000 from Liberty Mutual.

However, despite his assurances, both companies resisted for months and months. The arguments in back and forth letters became very convoluted, but basically Traveler's Senior Claim Supervisor claimed that Traveler's didn't have to pay anything now, since it had an "excess carrier" policy. This meant that it didn't have to pay me anything until my claims went over the limits of my other insurance companies.

Meanwhile, Blue Cross and Blue Shield refused to pay another one of my claims, which was filed by another of my lawyers, Deborah Feldman in Massachusetts. Why? Blue Cross argued that I wasn't covered for some of the treatment I received, because it didn't meet the company's "level of care guidelines" for rehab services. So Feldman, with Freedman's help, wrote to Blue Cross to reconsider my claim and submitted additional medical information to support her request.

It was a tedious process. Ironically, according to a letter from Blue Cross's legal department, I didn't meet their level of care guidelines, because I seemed to be doing too well when I was at the rehab hospital for the two weeks in question in mid-April. Apparently, I didn't meet these guidelines because I was able to "transfer with minimal assistance" after the first week I entered the hospital, and the second week, I could "transfer independently." In other words, I could get around by myself. As a result, according to the records, I could "function independently in daily life." Then, too, Blue Cross claimed I was only covered for staying in a semi-private room, not for a private room—another reason not to pay the full amount.

I'm not sure where the Blue Cross officer got the idea I could "function independently," since I couldn't at that time. But at least, the officer left the door open, telling Feldman the company might reconsider some of the claims it denied if she could provide more supporting documents. So beginning on May 11, 1989, she started the reconsideration process by disputing their denial, pointing out that the days of service they questioned were medically necessary, and that they had engaged in an unfair trade practice by failing to investigate and settle my claim properly. She even warned of possible litigation, involving triple damages and attorney's fees, and she asked the hospital's CEO to back up the assessment of my first doctor, Dr. Jaeger to show that my treatment was "entirely necessary and reasonable." Finally, after several months of correspondence, Blue Cross did decide in my favor on the grounds I clearly had to stay in the hospital. So they couldn't deny the benefits. It was a small victory in a continuing legal war.

Unfortunately, the cost of victory in both time and money was more than the small amount I gained, because of all the extra legal work involved. However, Freedman and my other lawyers never bothered to tell me such things. They just focused on winning, irrespective of costs—setting the stage for disaster. However, I didn't know enough to see the warning signs at the time.

The problem was that Freedman and my other lawyers sought to play hardball—and they convinced me that the best strategy was to win as much as I could at every stage of the process. Of course, it made sense for them, since they took their fees out of whatever they collected. So they had little to lose. That strategy was disastrous for me because it kept the costs rising more and more, first as the insurance carriers resisted for months, and then when my mother-in-law sued, too—dragging the process out for 2½ years—to 1992—before the insurance companies paid any more. Though I was ready to settle for less much sooner, I believe now the process took as long as it did, because my lawyers resisted settling to maximize the amount collected—which meant much more for them, while I ended up with only a little more at a much higher and disastrous cost.

THE BATTLE OVER THE ESTATE

Meanwhile, on another front, I had a growing battle with my mother-in-law Mrs. Raymond over the estate. I initially turned the matter over to my Massachusetts lawyer, Joe Zaks, since Freedman, pursuing my injury claim in Miami, thought that Bob's estate would be responsible for any additional compensation, since Bob was driving and at fault in the accident. Since all of Bob's property was in Massachusetts, Freedman explained that's where any claim on the estate should be made. Then, I should be able to get compensated from his estate, to the extent there was anything in it.

It sounded like a fairly simple, straightforward matter, as Zaks explained it at the time. Just file my own claim against the estate. As I suspected, it turned out to be anything but simple, since I soon heard from Zaks that Mrs. Raymond had plans to file a wrongful death against me for Bob's death, on the grounds that I was driving, not Bob. Zaks even sent a warning letter about this possibility to Freedman in Florida.

I was immediately worried about this possibility, and warned Freedman and my other lawyers in Florida, handling my personal and business affairs, Bob Rubenstein and Mark Bidner. "She's going to go after me for everything I have," I told them.

Yet they dismissed my concerns. "Don't be silly," Rubenstein and Bidner said. "What grounds could Mrs. Raymond possibly have to file a wrongful death claim against you?"

I said they didn't understand. "You don't know my mother-in-law," I told them. "She wants to control everything. She has never liked me. She'll find a way."

However, they didn't take me seriously, assuring me that Mrs.

Raymond had no claim for wrongful death against me. So they told me not to worry. But I did, expecting the worst.

I didn't have to wait long for the first sign of trouble. It came on February 27th, when Zaks, handling my claim against the estate, received a letter from Mrs. Raymond's attorney, Jack Donahue, asking me to give back Bob's property that was still in Massachusetts. Mrs. Raymond claimed the estate was entitled to this because of the prenuptial I had signed, in which Bob and I agreed not to make any claims on each other's estates for property we each had before the marriage. Therefore, she claimed, all of Bob's property in Massachusetts should be considered part of the estate—not owned jointly by me and Bob.

Zaks thought he could easily take care of the matter and I wouldn't have to appear in court to answer the complaint. As a result, when he wrote to Bidner, he suggested that: "All we have to do is put together an adequate accounting of the estate's assets in Debbie's possession." Then, he asked me to help them put together a list of the property in Bob's estate.

He also pointed out that Donahue's letter mentioned nothing about any wrongful death suit. So he told me not to worry, as did Bidner and Freedman. Just "Relax and document everything," Zaks said. So I did, although I still felt anxious.

Also, I resented Mrs. Raymond's demands, since I was still recovering from the accident in Florida, and now she was pressuring me to give everything back that personally belonged to Bob. She even wanted me to do so right away, though I had to fly back from Florida to do so. That seemed unreasonable to me. So I decided to wait until my next trip to the rehab hospital in New Hampshire in a few months and do it then.

I also felt angry that she was asking for certain items that were very sentimental to me. One was the Rolex watch I bought for Bob as a wedding gift. I didn't want to give it back. Similarly, I felt very sentimental about several Dali prints and an oil painting I bought with Bob the week we spent in San Francisco before we got married. We saw them in a downtown art gallery, and since I didn't have my credit card with me, Bob put them on his card. After we returned to Massachusetts, I paid him back, but it looked like he bought the prints because they were on his card. So now I had to turn over the pictures or pay Mrs. Raymond for them again, until I found my check I wrote to reimburse Bob to show that I bought them. The thought I would have to pay her for them, until I found my check documenting what happened, made me mad, and I saw her request as one more example of how petty and spiteful she could be.

In turn, experiencing this vindictiveness increased my fear that she would really pursue a plan to claim I was responsible for Bob's death. So I kept asking my lawyers: "Shouldn't you take some steps to head off any possible wrongful death claim, in case Mrs. Raymond tries to blame me?" "How could she possibly do that?" my lawyers said, ignoring my concern.

My four main lawyers—Kaplan, Freedman, Rubenstein, and Bidner—discouraged me, saying this wasn't necessary because she had no basis for such a claim. Perhaps objectively there wasn't, since Bob almost always drove; I knew he was driving; and the Florida Highway Patrol homicide report concluded he was, too. However, I worried about having to document and prove this if she made a claim.

At the time, it might have been relatively quick for my lawyers to have written a few extra letters or conducted a few extra interviews to obtain the documents to avoid any chance of her suit. They were so sure of their opinion they didn't think it was necessary.

Then I began to get further indication that my fears were very real. On March 8, 1990, Donahue, Mrs. Raymond's lawyer, had me served with a formal "Complaint for Accounting and Injunctive Relief" that he had filed the month before. It was the first of the many legal documents Mrs. Raymond filed against me. Among other things, she claimed that under my prenuptial agreement all of Bob's separate property should be placed into the estate. She even objected to the funeral arrangements I had made to take Bob's ashes to sea, claiming I had done this "unilaterally," to my "own personal taste," and had excluded her and her immediate family, though I had invited her and she had decided not to come on her own. Additionally, she claimed that I had so far refused her "lawful demands" to get back the assets of the estate, so now she asked for a formal hearing to provide an accounting.

I was furious. I had barely gotten back on my feet after getting out of the hospital for a mental breakdown a month earlier, determined to pull myself together and move on. Now this!

To make matters worse, on March 14th, I received still another legal document from her—a Motion for a Preliminary Injunction, which Donahue had filed two weeks earlier, to make sure I didn't dispose of any of Bob's property. This second document was like adding insult to injury, making me even madder.

Though I had been trying to cooperate and Zaks had been trying to work out a settlement, now Donahue wanted an immediate accounting of all of Bob's assets and all his personal records under my "custody and control" or to which I "reasonable access," as the legal documents put it. The list of items I was supposed to gather was daunting: current and past income tax returns, life insurance policies, savings and checking accounts, bank statements, certificates of title, employment and retirement records, pensions and IRAs, stock certificates or bonds—in short, any records showing any assets or debts. Under normal circumstances it would be hard to gather all this information; and now it was even harder because I still wasn't thinking clearly. Then, too, despite Mrs. Raymond's long list, Bob had very few assets except his clothes, a few pieces of furniture, luggage, and other personal items; so the long list of items I finally compiled actually had little monetary value.

Also, there was no way to talk to Mrs. Raymond anymore to try to work things out. Not only was I so angry, but now that lawyers were involved, I had to respond through them or the formal mechanisms of the court. The process not only produced a growing blizzard of paperwork, but added to the mounting legal costs.

So for the next few weeks—from March through mid-April 1990, my lawyers had to file and I had to sign a series of documents Donahue fired off. If not, I would lose the case by default. Finally, in mid-April, when I flew back to Massachusetts for my quarterly check-up at the rehab hospital, I planned to make this accounting of Bob's assets for Donahue.

It was so sad going back to his apartment in Massachusetts to do this. As I went through Bob's personal belongings room by room, I felt overcome by a deep sorrow. It was so painful not only seeing them, remembering Bob again, but I knew I had to turn everything, including some very sentimental things, back to Mrs. Raymond. How could she be so vindictive to make me do this, I thought angrily? Thinking about how she wanted me to list even the smallest items made me even angrier. Some items were so painful to list, because of their sentimental value.

It took me a day to finish the list. Each item brought back memories of a life not lived. It included: oil paintings, cufflinks and necklaces, a Cape Cod poster, a round antique clock, pillow cases, a Minolta camera, suitcases, ceramic and carved wood ducks, a bowling trophy, a bicycle pump, a dried flower wreath, a cribbage board and backgammon game, a fishing box, a VHS tape of "It's a Wonderful Life," and dozens of other items. Meanwhile, as I went around writing these things down—looking through closets, pulling out drawers, and looking behind furniture, I felt on the verge of crying again and again. I held back the tears as long as I could. At the end of the day, I broke down crying, though I continued on around the house to finish the list. In the end, it even included items worth no more than a dollar or two each, like Mickey Mouse and Minnie Mouse plastic tumblers.

Finally, when I was done, I sent my handwritten list to Zaks, who turned it into a more formal computerized 6-page list of over 200 hundred items that I was transferring to the estate. After he sent it off, he told me that this should be the end of the problems with the estate, since Mrs. Raymond would soon have the property she claimed belonged to the estate, while I had my claim against the estate which would finally be resolved in probate court.

However, even my list wasn't enough for Mrs. Raymond. She questioned whether it was complete. As a result, over the next few months, my lawyers and hers sent letters and legal pleadings back and forth over what should and shouldn't be in the estate. Looking back now, I'm amazed at the pettiness of all this wrangling and at the vigor with which the lawyers on both side pursued the matter.

After all, since the amounts involved were relatively minor. I was just asking the estate to reimburse me for about $600 in funeral expenses, while Mrs. Raymond wanted me to turn over about $12,000 more in property—most of this being the value of the two prints and an oil painting Bob and I bought in San Francisco the week before the wedding.

In the end, my lawyers ended up billing me far more than either of these claims, while Mrs. Raymond's lawyers billed her much more, too. At the time, not knowing enough to do so, I never questioned whether it made sense to carry on this protracted litigation. It really didn't, since there wasn't any money in Bob's estate, because he died in debt. I needed a lawyer to represent me, since the lawyers on Mrs. Raymond's side fought on, and my lawyer had to respond. So the lawyers battled on, because Mrs. Raymond was so determined to win, although it would have been more sensible and far less expensive and exhausting for them to simply sit down together and work out a fair settlement. Even though Zaks was trying to settle, he told me he couldn't, and I didn't know enough to insist or get another lawyer to represent my own wishes. So instead, the war over the estate went on.

The wrangling even went on over whether Bob was a partner in some of my business ventures, and I had to show proof he wasn't involved. Just my word and everyday records weren't enough. I had to dig up detailed records of everything. For example, in 1986, Bob and I had created a company called the Ray Quinn International Corporation, thinking we might set up a business together to distribute a special type of paint. But in 1988, when we decided not to pursue this venture, because we couldn't get the manufacturer to agree to our terms, Bob resigned and transferred any interest he owned back to the corporation. This way, I could use the corporate shell we created to buy my own Mail Boxes business, and I didn't have to go to the time and expense of creating a new corporation to own it. However, since Mrs. Raymond didn't accept my explanation for this, I had to find the records to show this was true.

Then, I had to respond to her further request for me to turn back a variety of items which I knew nothing about, such as Bob's wallet after the accident (which might have been taken by the heli-copter pilots), and scuba and fishing equipment she claimed he owned.

The process was even more difficult because I had to respond with legal papers called "affirmative defenses," which had to be filed by Zaks and served on Mrs. Raymond. I couldn't just say the com-plaint was unfounded, because I had already provided her with a list of all of Bob's assets in my "possession and control." Instead, Zaks had to turn my response to her written requests into a legal denial, and this documentation process continue for months, since Mrs. Raymond seemed relentless, unwilling to give up. It went on even though Zaks tried to stop the process when he wrote to Donahue in early May, "With the exception of the newly added items, we have previously addressed our knowledge of the existence or nonexistence of these items both verbally and in writing several times."

When Donahue repeated her demands, Zaks came to realize that any prospects for settlement were dim, as he wrote to Donahue at the end of May, "It seems you are determined to litigate this mat-ter." That's when he brought in Deborah Feldman, who handled litigation for his law firm, to assist him.

So what should have been reasonably settled turned into a long drawn-out lawsuit that went on for two and half years and cost far more than the items at issue.

Though Feldman tried to resolve Mrs. Raymond's claims by pointing out that I had far more serious claims against the estate than the claims she was now making—notably the expenses for Bob's funeral, for my medical bills, and for the $12,000 loan I made to Bob, Mrs. Raymond didn't back off. Donahue didn't even try to set up a meeting to discuss conflicting claims. Instead, at the end of June, he responded with a formal "First Request for the Production of Documents." Among other things, he now formally asked me to produce information about a Rolex watch, Dali print, and Neizvestny painting, in 30 days—on August 3rd, though I had pre-viously included these in a letter about this property. So, on August 1, Deborah Feldman filed her own formal complaint on my behalf, seeking reimbursement of the $600 funeral expenses and $12,000 loan to Bob.

Over the next few months, the legal quibbling went on—some of it amazingly petty, over very small amounts. Efforts to work out a compromise went nowhere, such as when Feldman and Donahue tried to work out a compromise settlement in September and October, 1990. Initially, Donahue asked for two art pieces and the Rolex or a cash equivalent of $10,000. Then, while Feldman countered with my offer to pay the estate $5000, since I already owned the art as marital property after Bob's death and since the Rolex was worth less than Mrs. Raymond claimed. I even agreed to give up my own claims of almost $13,000 against the estate. But in mid-November, after Mrs. Raymond asked for both art pieces plus $5000, and I agreed to pay that, return one print, and pay the estate for the other, negotiations broke down.

Unfortunately, there were two hang-ups. First, Mrs. Raymond wanted a Certificate of Authenticity to value the paintings. Secondly and more importantly, I was still waiting to receive the insurance settlements that were in limbo, so I could pay the $5000 settlement. Then, ironically, I couldn't get that, because Mrs. Raymond threatened and subsequently filed her wrongful death suit against me, claiming I was driving. So this action tied up my settlements now and for two more years.

Meanwhile, with my settlements up in the air, the suit over the estate couldn't be settled either, since I had no money to pay the $5000 to settle it. Thus, the estate suit went into a kind of limbo, though Feldman made one last effort to settle it in September 1991 as part of a "global" settlement of claims in both Florida and Massachusetts. However, when that global offer was rebuffed, Feldman dropped the suit for the time being.

Then, the suit remained in this inactive status and wasn't finally settled until a year later in September 1992, when Donahue offered to settle for Mrs. Raymond's original request—the return of both paintings plus $5000, in return for her dropping her wrongful death claim against me. I considered his offer legal blackmail, because her wrongful death suit against me was "wrongfully" keeping me from getting my insurance settlement. So this offer was like asking me to pay Mrs. Raymond to stop hitting me on the head, when she shouldn't have done this in the first place. That's why I resisted paying at the time, though in retrospect, perhaps I should have, because my refusal to pay this blackmail contributed to her decision to continue her suit against me which cost me much much more.

PURSUING CRIMINAL CHARGES AGAINST CHARLIE

The next legal quagmire involved Charlie, a once trusted long-time friend who ran my business while I was in the hospital. Or at least I thought he was a long-trusted friend. As it turned out, he brought my business and me to near ruin. What made it even worse, is he did this at a time when I was most down and vulnerable.

I made my initial embezzlement report in early February, 1990, shortly after I made a trip back to Florida and discovered his theft. Still it took several months, until June, while the police investigated, before they decided to take further action. By then, Charlie had left Florida and I wasn't sure where he was. Now the police were ready to arrest him, because over the months, Detective Ralph Ciancia of the Collier County Sheriff's Office in Naples had continued investigating based on my initial report of missing money. Finally, he concluded that Charlie probably had embezzled about $25,000, and he filed an affidavit at the county courthouse stating that Charlie (or more formally Charles A. Levesque) had committed grand theft embezzlement, and he asked the judge to issue an arrest warrant.

As he described in his affidavit, after I was in a serious accident and not expected to live, Charlie began making out American Express Money Orders to himself and his creditors—starting the day of the accident—February 9 until October 1989, when I was well enough to discover and stop the fraud. As Ciancia described it, Charlie used his authority to sign company checks and take American Express Money Orders for himself. How? Charlie would deposit the Amex Money Orders, which are like blank traveler's checks at a bank, into the Mail Boxes' operating account. Then he made the Mail Boxes checks to himself and his creditors, and he never paid American Express for these money orders. So eventually American Express considered these checks and money orders a debt which I owed them.

All told, Ciancia found that Charlie had deposited 92 money orders worth nearly $25,000 into the Mail Boxes account, and from that account, he paid for his auto loan or simply issued a check to himself for that amount. Charlie even made out a half-dozen MBE checks to his landlord and to local retailers to pay for groceries and haircuts. So now I owed American Express all this money. It was such an obvious scam—but presumably Charlie thought I would never get well and discover it.

Now, with the affidavit filed by the police, the justice system was quick to go after Charlie. I felt relieved that at least that part of the legal system was working. Two weeks later, on June 28th, the Collier County circuit judge issued a bench warrant for Charlie's arrest, with bail set at $10,000. Though Charlie had fled the state, Detective Ciancia took steps to get him back, asking the State Attorney's Office to extradite him from anywhere in the United States. The judge approved that extradition request, too.

About a month later, the police found Charlie in Topsfield, Massachusetts, living at his mother's house. They quickly arrested him, took him to jail, and in late July, he was extradited and sent back to jail in Naples.

On Monday, July 23, at Charlie's first court appearances, the judge advised him of the charges against him and his right to have counsel. When he appeared in court again the next day, he requested a trial by jury, put up a bond for $10,000, and said he would get a private attorney to handle his case. The judge set it for trial in three weeks—starting August 20.

I was glad that the case against Charlie seemed to be proceeding so quickly, although it soon began to bog down, and I began to feel the same frustration I did in going through the civil litigation process. As I soon learned, such delays are common in the criminal justice system, and it was disturbing to discover this, because I felt so angry and betrayed by what Charlie had done and wanted to see him judged guilty and punished as quickly as possible.

Still I could do nothing to make the case go any faster. First, it

204 • CONQUERING THE DARKNESS

was postponed for another 3 weeks until September 10th, when Charlie finally was assigned a public defender to represent him, since he couldn't afford a private attorney. Then, he entered a "Not Guilty" plea, which is typically what defendants do, even if they are guilty. This way, they can try to get a better deal from the prosecutor by making the prosecution prove their case. I felt discouraged hearing Charlie make this plea, knowing what he had done, though I knew it was also his right to have my charges against him proved in a court of law. I just wished he had pled guilty, been sentenced accordingly, and then the process would end.

Then, there was still another delay until September 24th, and another until October 15th. "Why?" I wanted to know, and Assistant State Attorney Dave Whiting reassured me by explaining what was happening.

As he explained, one reason for the repeated delay is that despite the money he had taken, Charlie was now broke. So he couldn't afford a private lawyer. As a result, though he originally told the judge he would get a private attorney, he didn't. Instead he filed what's called an "Affidavit of Indigency," claiming he was broke. As he explained in this document, he now had no income, cash on hand, real estate, or personal property of value. He also claimed he no longer had a job or other source of income. While I was glad he had at least suffered financially for his actions, I felt frustrated real justice in the courts was taking so long.

Then, there were further delays to give the Assistant Public Defender handling his case time to prepare. Finally the case was set for trial on December 17, 1990.

I attended that trial, and I was glad to see Charlie finally punished for what he had done. There was little he could say in his defense, since the proof was clearly against him when I testified about what he had done. And what made his crime seem even more serious to the jury was that before his theft, he had been my friend for 30 years and I had treated him with such trust. So the jury quickly found him guilty, taking less than 2 hours to decide.

Then, when it came time for Judge Jay B. Rossman, who heard the case, to sentence Charlie, Rossman felt he deserved the worst. Although Charlie showed no remorse and claimed he didn't do anything wrong, Rossman was not impressed. He said he didn't believe it when Charlie claimed he had a right to do what he did because he was a corporate officer and he acted in his role as secretary for the company. As Charlie tried to explain, the jury hadn't understood this. Rossman also was not convinced, telling Charlie that he, Rossman, was even less persuaded than the jury had been.

As a result, a few days later, when Rossman handed down his judgment, he sentenced Charlie to not only pay full restitution of almost $25,000, but to serve 22 months in the Florida state prison and pay a $10,000 fine. Then, after he got out, Charlie would have to spend 13 years on probation, and during this time, pay back the money he owed to me and the state, or he could return to jail.

The penalty was the maximum Rossman could give, and he explained that he showed no mercy, because he felt that Charlie's theft was made even more serious because of the way he took advantage of me when I was down and out and so completely trusted him. Although Rossman's words did little to take away the pain I still felt at Charlie's betrayal, at least they made me feel relieved that Charlie would finally be getting some justice. Or as Judge Rossman put it in the court record:

> The case is a very serious grand theft.... At a time when the victim was extremely helpless and needed assistance, Mr. Levesque, the defendant, was called on to assist the business...Approximately nine months later, over $24,000 was embezzled according to the verdict of the jury...
>
> As the primary purpose in this sentence, I'm going to order restitution. The victim...should be made whole...
>
> I also believe that there should be a sentence to ensure that ...people do take white collar crime very seriously, especially when a friend of the family is called upon to assist and...not only do they not help but they take advantage of the situation.

So in a way, his sentence was a complete victory for me in what had been a very sad situation. Though I didn't really feel like a victor, at least I felt vindicated that Charlie would be punished, though it might be a long time before he could actually be expected to pay me back—if indeed he ever would.

CHAPTER 12

•

THE WRONGFUL DEATH BATTLE: THE LONG STRUGGLE OVER WHO WAS DRIVING

While the estate battle was just petty, Mrs. Raymond's wrongful death suit against me was devastating. Though she had no credible evidence, she countered my wrongful death claim against Bob's estate by claiming I was driving, not Bob. Therefore, she claimed, I was responsible for the accident and should pay the estate for Bob's death, not the other way around. I believe she did this not only to get as much money as she could from me, but also to express her long-held hostility towards me. Then, too, I felt she was using this as a trump card against me, to convince me to reduce or drop my own claims against the estate.

Ironically, and even more painfully, Mrs. Raymond filed her suit on February 7, 1991, two days before the anniversary of Bob's death, which had been February 9, 1989. I know now she filed then due to legal reasons, since she had to meet the two years statute of limitations for filing such a suit. However, at the time, this anniversary filing date made the suit even more emotional and devastating for me. I was already a jangle of nerves remembering Bob's death two years before. Now the papers for her suit arrived on my doorstep like an ironic valentine.

Beside the emotional turmoil, the suit created financial havoc, too, because it put all my expected financial settlements with the insurance companies on hold. That's because now the companies weren't sure if they owed the compensation for the accident to me— or maybe to the estate. So before they could pay me anything, they had to make sure I was, in fact, the victim.

Though eventually I was shown to be exactly that, it took two years to prove this. In the meantime, before the settlements came through, I lost almost everything, with no way to get it back. I had no recourse against Mrs. Raymond, against the lawyers, against the insurance companies, against the courts—against anyone who caused all these unnecessary expenses. The money just disappeared into a legal pit.

Altogether, I lost about $2.1 million directly, and about $4-6 million more in immediate future earnings, because these other losses caused me to lose my Mail Boxes area franchise, worth about this. So my total loss was about $6-8 million, due to this single suit that Mrs. Raymond had no basis filing, though to settle it, I had to give up any hope of suing her for my losses. I lost almost everything I had at the time. I ended up in bankruptcy, almost became homeless, and was forced to file for food stamps, while trying to prove her suit was unfounded from the beginning.

Ironically, the suit wasn't even filed against me directly. Instead, it was filed against the company that owned and leased me the car in the accident, First Service Credit Corporation, and against a trust in charge of my various real estate investments, the Mt. Pleasant Realty Trust. However, I was named as a Trustee of the Mt. Pleasant Realty Trust, so that meant I was the primary party responsible in the suit.

The nightmare began shortly after 8 a.m. on February 14th, when I was just waking up and heard the doorbell ring at my home in Naples, Florida. When I opened the door, a uniformed trooper from the sheriff's office was standing there, and he handed me a summons in a thin manila envelope. I didn't know what the envelope was at first, but as I sat down at the kitchen table, half-stunned, and opened it, I felt a sense of shock and foreboding. As I began to read, the words on the document, which had a court stamp showing it was filed February 7th, bore this frightening news:

> On or about February 9, 1989, defendants placed the 1987 Mercedes Benz (owned by the First Service Credit Corporation and co-owned or leased by the Mt. Pleasant Reality Trust)...into

the hands of Deborah Quinn Raymond, who on that date operated the said motor vehicle with defendants consent...Robert
George Raymond, deceased, was a passenger in said motor vehicle...

At that time and place Deborah Quinn Raymond negligently
operated or maintained the motor vehicle so that she lost control of said vehicle...

Then, the summons went on to describe how badly Bob had suffered. He had experienced: "bodily injury, pain and suffering, disability, disfigurement, mental anguish, loss of capacity for the enjoyment of life, loss of earnings...and lost his life." I could barely go
on reading, I was shaking so hard. It was bad enough that I was
already suffering from Bob's loss and remembering it on this anniversary. Now the summons was falsely accusing me of causing his
death. Mrs. Raymond was seeking a trial by jury as well.

After I calmed myself enough to call my lawyer handling my
personal injury claim, Paul Freedman, I asked him what to do. Then,
over the next few days, I tried to respond quickly with his help,
hoping the suit would soon go away. "You just have to clarify the
facts," Freedman assured me. "Then the suit will be dropped."

Even though Freedman wrote to the insurance companies explaining the fact that Bob was driving and I was the passenger, the
insurance companies said they couldn't pay me, since they were now
aware of the suit against me. Now, they said, they had to wait until
the courts settled the matter. They had to know for sure who was
the passenger and therefore who to pay before they could pay anyone—a process that took two years—until 1993.

Meanwhile, everything became complicated—very complicated—as my own lawyers, Mrs. Raymond's lawyers, and various
sets of insurance company and other lawyers battled it out in what
eventually turned into four separate lawsuits. The fight took so long
to settle and was so exhausting, that it took over most of my life for
the next two years, at a time when I was still struggling to overcome
the lingering effects of my brain injury.

THE FIRST MONTHS OF THE BATTLE

At first, I thought I would have the support of a number of parties—my auto leasing company, First Service Credit; the Mt. Pleasant Realty Trust which was the entity owning the car, though I was a trustee; and the two insurance companies providing various levels of insurance—Liberty Mutual and Traveler's. I thought we would be working together as a team when these companies jointly selected an attorney Michael J. Corso, in Ft. Myers, Florida, to represent them. Supposedly, we were all on the same side, and so he would protect my interests, too. Presumably we were united, because if Bob was driving, his estate and his insurance carriers were liable. So initially, Freedman thought it was just a simple matter of making that driving arrangement clear to everyone involved.

Even so, Corso suggested that I should have my own attorney to work with him, and as it turned out, I did need one, since our interests were soon at odds. Then, Corso had to act to protect the insurance companies, representing the leasing company and trust. In fact, soon I was not only fighting Mrs. Raymond, but Corso and other insurance company attorneys, too. At first, though, I cooperated with them, and as requested, I signed and verified various documents Corso or the insurance companies sent me, and I was available for deposition and trial proceedings.

I found myself on the opposite side of the fence from the insurance companies representing First Credit and Mt. Pleasant, when Mrs. Raymond produced her single piece of evidence claiming I was driving and therefore at fault. This was a March 14th affidavit which Thomas Biggs, her lawyer handling her wrongful death claim, obtained from one of the emergency paramedics, Susan LeMay, who treated me at the scene of the accident. He had gotten this affidavit from her, because of what she had written on the EMS trip ticket—the brief report of the accident recorded by the emergency services unit at the accident scene. As her affidavit explained, on the February 9th trip ticket, she had written down that I told her that I "was the driver of the 1987 Mercedes coupe." Even though all the other documents gathered back then—the homicide reports from police investigators, the reports of an accident reconstruction expert, and the statement of a witness—described me as a passenger, her affidavit was like a monkey wrench that changed everything. Though her statement contradicted everything else, it threw everything else into question. It meant I now had to provide proof that I wasn't driving and that Bob was, just as all the other documentation showed.

Unfortunately, LeMay made this original statement, because she incorrectly interpreted my half-incoherent comments when I was severely injured, didn't know where I was, or what had happened. When she asked her question about who was driving, I did not fully understand it, so I gave the "I was driving" answer she reported in the EMS trip ticket. Eventually, an investigation explained all this. Regardless, it took two years of legal fighting to do this—though in retrospect, it seems that this issue could have been resolved much sooner, ending the costly battle.

It wasn't, and I didn't know enough to resolve this situation myself or get Freedman, my lawyer handling my injury and wrongful death claim, to deal with this issue more quickly. So then, once her affidavit was treated seriously, making who was driving an issue in our conflicting wrongful death suits—mine and Mrs. Raymond's, the insurance companies decided they weren't going to pay until this issue was resolved.

I think now their hesitation to pay, until they knew who to pay, was quite correct. Instead of trying to resolve the who was driving question, Freedman challenged the insurance company's refusal to pay, continuing the legal battle. So while I was left struggling financially to survive, since I couldn't collect my settlements, successfully run my business, or even do much work at all because of the continued effects of the brain injury, the lawyers' clocks went on ticking. Freedman and my other lawyers continued to add up their fees against a future settlement, reducing the value of whatever I would eventually collect.

Meanwhile, the local press made it sound like Mrs. Raymond really did have a valid case. The first article about the accident in the *Naples Daily News* simply reported Mrs. Raymond's claim that she was seeking damages from the firms that owned the car, since they let me drive the car and my negligence caused the car to go out of control leading to Bob's death. No one ever called me or my lawyers for a response, and it would be a long time before I would present my own side of the story in court or to the public.

I find it hard now, looking back, to understand why Freedman didn't challenge this recently obtained affidavit to get Mrs. Raymond's suit dropped. But instead, he responded by trying to persuade the now reluctant insurance companies to pay. For example, on February 12, a few days after Mrs. Raymond suit was filed and after Liberty Mutual wrote that it couldn't pay until the question of who was driving was resolved, Freedman wrote back stating that I wasn't the driver and I could provide sworn testimony to that effect. Instead of trying to work out what Liberty would need for additional proof or challenging the affidavit directly, Freedman charged that the company's refusal to pay was a breach of contract, which would lead to court action against the company if Liberty didn't pay. Perhaps Freedman thought this hard-nosed response might scare the company into paying. Now I believe, his approach helped to create a climate of hostility that pitted me against the insurance companies, representing First Credit and the Mt. Pleasant Realty Trust. So on top of Mrs. Raymond's legal challenge, Freedman turned the insurance companies against me.

Additionally, he used the same kind of aggressive pit-bull response to Biggs, Mrs. Raymond's wrongful death case attorney, which I think increased the hostility there, too, and made the case even harder to settle. The lawyers were like two bullies fighting on a playground, neither willing to back down for fear of losing face, so they fight on until exhaustion. At the time, Freedman persuaded me what he was doing made perfect legal sense. "We know what we're doing. We're looking after your best interests, Deb," he told me. Not knowing any better, I simply went along with him, not realizing how wrong his strategy was.

Freedman began his response to Biggs on February 14th, when his associate, Joel Kaplan, wrote a reply that sounded patronizing in suggesting that Biggs did not know what he was doing in filing the suit. First Kaplan suggested that Biggs did not fully investigate the merits of the allegations in the suit, since he rushed to file it on February 7th before the statute of limitations expired. Or as Kaplan put it, he "blindly" filed it with "baseless and frivolous" allegations. Thus, Kaplan demanded that Biggs should act to dismiss the case immediately, since it was interfering with my own claim for damages from my insurance companies.

Kaplan's pit-bull efforts persuaded no one. Mrs. Raymond pressed on with her suit. In retrospect, perhaps a more conciliatory approach might have been more effective in producing a settlement; at least it might have been worth trying initially. But from the beginning, Freedman and his associate Kaplan set the course for confrontation. Since Mrs. Raymond was already so hostile and vindictive towards me, I believe Freedman and Kaplan made the fight even worse, while their bills against the eventual settlement mounted.

THE EARLY DAYS IN COURT

Then, with the insurance companies and realty trust now adversaries, and Mrs. Raymond unwilling to back down, Freedman took his adversarial approach to the courts, initially by trying to force the insurance companies to settle. He did this by asking Judge Hayes, who was handling the case, to hold an emergency or expedited hearing on a petition he filed, called a Petition to Enforce Settlement. In it, he argued, that Liberty's failure to settle was placing me in a precarious financial position that might even lead to personal bankruptcy, and the company should pay, because six months earlier in August, 1990, they agreed to pay and were ready to sign the documents on February 11th. But then, they backed out of their agreement. Unfortunately, this ploy by Freedman didn't work either, and just contributed to even further delays, though I didn't recognize this at the time.

Meanwhile, I continued to accept Freedman's assurances that he and Kaplan knew what they were doing and that the settlement would only be delayed for a few months. However, I was growing increasingly disturbed by danger of this suit and the delay it was causing. In spite of my brain injury, I still realized that the delay might cause a "domino effect" leading to more and more losses. That's why I repeatedly called or wrote Freedman urging him to settle. Again and again, I warned him that Mrs. Raymond was a merciless enemy and he should resolve her claim as quickly as possible. I even asked Bob Rubenstein, the lawyer now handling my personal affairs, to persuade Freedman to take the threat more seriously, telling him that "Mrs. Raymond will stop at nothing in her vengeful pursuit of compensation due to her son's death."

Still, the delays continued. For one thing, the emergency hearing was put off, at first for three months, and then reset for March 14th, after Freedman emphasized how urgent the hearing was. Secondly, Biggs showed that Mrs. Raymond wasn't willing to back down, when he claimed he did investigate the matter and didn't just file to beat the statute of limitations deadline, since he did have some "evidence" I was driving. This turned out to be the EMS trip ticket LeMay had written at the accident scene, and later Biggs would obtain LeMay's lengthy affidavit to support his claim.

Meanwhile, Michael Corso, representing the two insurance companies tried filing motions for them on February 25th and March 5th to dismiss Mrs. Raymond's suit—a usual first step in responding to a lawsuit. In the motions, he stated that she didn't have a legitimate claim, since she was claiming the opposite facts than those in my wrongful death suit against the estate and her as estate administratrix. He even described her claim a "sham pleading" with "inaccurate and improper" facts to counter my own claim, pointing out that I had already filed an affidavit that I was a passenger to support my claim. Plus, he asked to combine our two suits, since both depended on who was driving, to save time and money and avoid inconsistent decisions in the courts.

Unfortunately, though, his motions weren't enough to stop the suit, and the financial problems I feared were fast descending. I was already facing angry creditors, had several creditor suits pending, and was trying to deal with two actions to foreclose on my residences in Florida and Massachusetts. The previous year, in July 1990, I had hired another lawyer, Louis X. Amato, to set up a Chapter 11 bankruptcy reorganization to get my Mail Boxes business back on track, and now I needed the settlement funds to keep my houses, me personally, and the business from going into a full Chapter 7 bankruptcy. Amato was concerned that I was fast approaching bankruptcy, and he wrote to warn Freedman how serious my circumstances were. After describing the current problems I was facing, he warned of the dire possibilities ahead, explaining that if Freedman couldn't quickly get my settlement proceeds, I was likely to lose my two homes, my business, and have to file personal bankruptcy. As he urgently warned: "These settlement proceeds represent her only chance to avoid financial ruin. The situation is now quite desperate."

Just about the only effect of his letter was that Freedman was able to persuade Judge Hayes to hold the emergency hearing, then scheduled for May 14, in March. Even so, it took months for Hayes to issue his opinion and when he did, he concluded this wasn't an emergency, so I lost everything after all. It was as if I was caught up in a slow-moving legal treadmill, and it was hard to get it to go any faster or get off, once it was set in motion. Once Mrs. Raymond's suit had started the train rolling, the lawyers and judge were running the train.

Thus, while my own financial problems mounted, so did the blizzard of paperwork and my legal fees in response to her suit. The big problem was the opposing allegations. Once they were resolved, Liberty Mutual's Claim Adjuster, Steve Renner, promised to pay. Yet as long as Mrs. Raymond's suit was active, he explained he couldn't. But Freedman still didn't try to resolve this underlying issue.

So plans went forward for the March 14 Emergency hearing. Meanwhile, Freedman tried to collect additional evidence to support my version of what happened, such as the original report of accident reconstructionist, William Fogerty, a Professor of Civil Engineering at the University of Miami. He had concluded that it was probable Bob drove the car after he visited the scene of the accident, obtained measurements and photographs, and reviewed various reports, such as a vehicle inspection by Florida Highway Patrol officer, Trooper R.K. Coburn and a Traffic Homicide investigation report. In reply, Biggs could only offer Susan LeMay's newly obtained affidavit based on her original EMS trip ticket. Nonetheless, as long as that affidavit was still on the table, it was enough to keep Mrs. Raymond's case alive.

In hindsight, I believe—and other lawyers I have spoken to have told me—the best strategy would have been to immediately attack the credibility of this affidavit on which Mrs. Raymond's based her claim. If Freedman had, perhaps he could have gotten my suit quickly dismissed. Probably, he could have easily done so with some additional investigation to show that LeMay was wrong, because she either misinterpreted what she heard me say or that my statement was not reliable since I was barely conscious at the time. Or if he couldn't get the case dismissed by the judge, perhaps he could have used this information to work out a settlement to get the suit dropped.

Instead, Freedman focused on trying to get the insurance companies to pay. Accordingly, at the March Emergency Hearing and at a series of motions and hearings held after this, he continued to argue that the insurance companies had breached a contract and were not acting in good faith, so the judge should force them to settle now. The judge never agreed with this argument—though Freedman continued to appeal and reappeal and was defeated in the end.

In retrospect, it seems like he should have been defeated, since the insurance companies really were acting in good faith as long as Mrs. Raymond's suit was still pending in court. As long as it was, there really were two contending claimants to a single settlement, and as a result, the judge couldn't force them to settle. The companies had to know who to pay first—and this is just what Freedman didn't do—showing I was the passenger to get rid of Mrs. Raymond's suit by undermining the one piece of evidence on which it was based.

Instead, Freedman waited for two years to undermine her testimony, when the trial approached. By then, it was too late to avoid the financial and emotional disaster I experienced. By then, I had already lost millions and gone through bankruptcy, while my costs to keep the litigation going mounted.

Meanwhile, while Judge Hayes took two months considering

my emergency motion and finally decided it wasn't an emergency, Mrs. Raymond delayed responding to the who was driving issue. Though Corso had sent her interrogatories soon after she sued to learn the witness she expected to call to support her claim that I was driving, as well as find out about Bob's assets, it took her almost three months to reply. It was as if she was stalling, knowing she didn't have a valid suit, but wanting to keep the process going as long as possible as her way of attacking me.

Whatever her strategy, it worked, and my lawyers couldn't do anything to stop the process. So the legal battle went on.

STILL MORE SUITS

Then to further complicate matters, Lewis F. Collins, Jr., the attorney for the Mount Pleasant Reality Trust, filed the first of a series of interpleader actions on April 8th, another on April 15th. These were designed to take the trust out of the litigation while Mrs. Raymond and I resolved in our own suits who was driving and therefore at fault.

As a first step, he got First Service Credit released from liability in either suit, since it was only the lessor of the car, and its lease required me to have liability insurance and indemnify First Service from any losses. After the judge agreed, First Credit was out, while my insurer, Liberty Mutual was liable for any claim.

A week later, Collins' second interpleader complaint was designed to get Liberty Mutual off the hook until Mrs. Raymond and I settled the who was driving issue. To this end, he asked the court to put Liberty Mutual's $250,000 insurance settlement in a registry with the court and let me and Mrs. Raymond fight it out among ourselves as to who was driving. Then the court would pay this money to me or Bob's estate based on whether I or Bob was determined to be the passenger.

His argument certainly made sense. I'm surprised that Freedman still continued to argue so hard against it, rather than focusing on resolving the dispute. As Collins pointed out, there were now two conflicting suits filed by me and Mrs. Raymond disputing who was driving and both made a claim on the full policy limit of $250,000. Plus, as a further complication, my Blue Cross insurer, which had already paid me benefits, had filed a lien against any additional recovery I collected, so they could be repaid out of this settlement. So that, Collins argued, was another reason to put the funds in a registry until the correct recipient could be determined. This way, until a court could decide these matters, Liberty Mutual wouldn't pay the wrong party and be exposed to "double or multiple liability," due to possibly conflicting results in the three lawsuits filed by me, Mrs. Raymond, and Blue Shield. Then, too, Collins argued, because of this situation, Liberty had not breached any contract or acted in bad faith in not paying me now, as Freedman claimed. Thus, in conclusion, Collins wanted the court to hold the $250,000 until the other suits were settled, release Liberty from further liability after paying this full policy amount, plus award the company costs and attorney fees for having to file this action.

Yet, despite this seemingly reasonable position, now argued by still one more lawyer for the trust and insurance companies, Freedman pressed on. Rather than try to defeat the LeMay evidence underlying Mrs. Raymond's suit, Freedman repeatedly tried and failed to defeat the interpleader suit, further increasing delays and costs.

He first tried to defeat it on May 9th when he asked the judge to dismiss it on the grounds that Liberty was responsible under its policy to *both* the driver and passenger, so regardless of who was driving, it owed up to $500,000, with $250,000 of that due to me. Moreover, he argued that Liberty's responsibility to settle didn't depend on resolving any factual question related to the accident, since Liberty had already entered into a binding settlement agreement to pay, so it had to pay me, regardless of Mrs. Raymond's claim. Finally, he argued against paying any attorney's fees, claiming Liberty had wrongly filed this action to delay me from pursuing my breach of contract and bad faith action against the company. It should have already paid me with no strings attached.

Unfortunately, if the trusts and Liberty were acting appropriately in light of the conflicting claims, Freedman's losing cause was already doomed, though he kept prolonging the legal battle and increasing the costs, because of the numerous motions and procedural delays. Though I began to hope the case would simply come to trial and be over, there were continuing extensions over seemingly unimportant legal niceties, even as Freedman kept assuring me everything was going forward.

For example, on April 13, when Judge Hayes finally ruled on the emergency hearing, he granted my motion to dismiss Mrs. Raymond's suit. But at the same time, he permitted her to amend her complaint by adding a few additional sections to more clearly describe the damages she sought, which she did a few weeks later. Meanwhile, in mid-April, since Freedman was stalled getting any money from Liberty, because the interpleader held up any action, he tried to get a payment from the Traveler's Company, that provided the next layer of insurance coverage. Again, it was a no-win strategy, but he wrote to Traveler's requesting the company pay anything over the $250,000 on hold in the courts, up to it's own liability cap. He claimed Traveler's should pay, since it was liable for anything over $250,000 and any settlement would certainly be more than that. So again, Freedman's effort seemed futile, though I just went along with him at the time.

Then on May 6, more bad news, when Thomas Newcomb Hyde, another lawyer representing Mrs. Raymond, joined the legal fray to answer my allegations of blame for the accident. His counter-argument was that I caused the accident and damages due to my own negligence in driving. Plus now he also claimed I wasn't wearing a seatbelt, which was the "sole and/or contributing cause" of my injuries.

THE WARRING WRONGFUL DEATH CLAIMS

So the next few months involved still more briefs, motions, and affidavits on both sides. At one point, Freedman even argued before Judge Hayes that he was being unfair to me, to persuade him to reconsider or step out in favor of a new judge. In retrospect, why was he unfair? After all, it would seem he was correct to let the suits go forward, as long as the underlying LeMay claim was still alive.

Then, in mid-May, there were further delays, when Hyde asked for more documents about the accident, such as any information showing that Bob was driving, including the expert accident reconstructionist's report and my affidavit. It's surprising he didn't already have this information, though perhaps he didn't because he was new to the case, or because Freedman hadn't sent it to him, because of his focus on challenging the insurance companies and Judge Hayes. Whatever the reason, having to provide these documents just meant more expenses and delays.

Then, on May 29th came Freedman's challenge to Judge Hayes, when he accused him of a conflict of interest because of his previous adverse rulings. To this end, Freedman asked me to sign an affidavit in which I described how I feared I wouldn't receive a fair trial, because I didn't think Judge Hayes could be objective due to his conflict of interest.

At the time, I simply went along with Freedman's challenge and signed, believing Judge Hayes was biased, as Freeman said, though now I realize he wasn't because he had to rule as he did to resolve the conflicting claims first. So now, looking back, I don't think challenging the judge made much sense, in that the challenge only made an already complicated case more complicated and made for more delays. Also, if Judge Hayes really was biased, why would he admit this, and wouldn't making the motion to challenge him make him even more hostile towards me and Freedman? In any case, after Freedman made the challenge, eventually Hayes, not surprisingly, turned him down.

Meanwhile, by the end of May, the Traveler's Company, which was previously set to settle, decided to take the same wait and see position as Liberty. Traveler's first learned of the "who was driving" issue, when Freedman contacted them about paying while the Liberty interpleader case was pending. Now their Senior Claims Supervisor wanted to make sure I was, in fact, the passenger before paying. So, on May 31, he wrote Freedman: "I am holding the offer of $250,000 in escrow. If it is found that Ms. Quinn was the passenger and not the operator, our offer *stands*."

Still, instead of trying to settle this "who was driving" issue quickly,

Freedman asked for a stay of proceedings in my wrongful death suit to focus on getting the interpleader suit thrown out and finding Liberty in breach of its earlier settlement agreement. Ironically, Judge Hayes, who Freedman had recently challenged for bias, would be the one to decide. It seems so hard to fathom now why Freedman continued to pursue this already losing strategy. But that's exactly what he did.

Although Freedman soon did win a stay on my suit so it went on hold while he challenged the interpleader, he had to respond to still another suit—the counterclaim filed by Blue Cross to place a lien on the $250,000 Liberty put in the court registry, so they could get back any money they had already paid, once the "who was driving" and "who should be paid" questions were settled.

Thus, over the next six months, through January 1992, while the wrongful death litigation with Mrs. Raymond was mostly on hold, Freedman and the insurance companies battled it out. Freedman tried to get them to pay now because of their contract, while they argued that the interpleader should be settled first to determine who they owed. It was like a continuing legal *deja vu*—rounds and rounds of the same arguments back and forth.

Meanwhile, my own life went into a financial free fall, as the creditor suits mounted. Even though I had begged Freedman and his assistant Kaplan to settle the case for over nine months, and my accountant Steve Goldberg had repeatedly called them to urge them to do so, Freedman pressed on. Repeatedly, he insisted that I shouldn't settle for so little—I should hold out to get more, and he and Kaplan wouldn't listen to my fears I could lose everything. So weakened by their resistance, I had backed down again and again. Thus, repeatedly, I signed the legal documents as they requested, since they told me they needed my signature, though I didn't really understand what was happening.

The case itself turned into a kind of legal chess game, as Freedman and the insurance and trust lawyers argued over multiple procedural issues and fine points of law. Freedman even filed a motion in September, arguing formally now, that Liberty owed $500,000, not $250,000, although simply reading the contract with Liberty would show that Liberty only owed one $250,000 payment to whoever was the passenger, which is just what Liberty and the trusts argued. Still Freedman pressed on, until ultimately Judge Hayes turned him down in January 21, 1992.

Meanwhile, a continuing battle went on over whether the trusts and Liberty could place funds in the court registry and force myself and Mrs. Raymond to interplead and resolve the issue of who was driving ourselves. Since Freedman was trying to prevent this and asking for a payment now, Collins, representing Liberty, filed still another a motion on October 3, 1991 asking the judge to let Liberty do this, because the policy only provided coverage for the passenger—not for both occupants. In fact, as he pointed out: "There are no proceeds which could be claimed by the driver of the vehicle as the driver would have to sue himself or herself in order to recover—which is a *legal impossibility*." So again, Collins urged the judge to order the defendants to work it out by interpleading among themselves, and then, Liberty could pay the appropriate party, with this money held by the court.

It's amazing, looking back to think that this same argument was still going on after six months, since it had already been rehashed repeatedly in several exchanges of legal documents, and this position of the trusts and Liberty certainly seems quite sensible. But on December 3, Freedman continued the fight with a memorandum of law asking the court not to place any funds in the registry, until my breach of contract action against Liberty was resolved first because, he claimed, Liberty had made a binding agreement to settle and owed me the $250,000 whether I was a passenger or not.

It's an argument Freedman had made before, and it wasn't any more successful now. That's because if Freedman was incorrectly interpreting the contract and Liberty owed the $250,000 only to the passenger, his continued effort to fight the interpleader was a waste of time that needlessly prolonged the suit and upped the legal fees.

I didn't know about these legal pitfalls at the time, but I believe now that Freedman made these serious legal mistakes, particularly after I saw the affidavit that Liberty's Claims Supervisor filed on December 10, along with a copy of the policy, which showed that it included a $250,000 limit for the passenger. The copy of the policy was available from the very beginning of all this legal wrangling. It seemed very clear what it said, as I read it now. So why wasn't it clear to Freedman then? He was the lawyer, not me? Why did he keep fighting? If only I knew then what I know now.

In any event, with all this legal wrangling over whether there was a contract, who was the passenger, and who owed what to who, by the end of 1991, my claim for compensation was still in a legal limbo, and as the wrangling went on, my own world continued falling apart.

Making this collapse even worse is that some of the people who were once trusted friends began taking advantage of me when I was most vulnerable. One was a man I had known for about seven years and even dated briefly, Conrad Ramakers. I had met him back in 1984 and we went out a few times before I met Bob, and afterwards I lost touch with him for a few years. But after I moved to Florida and read about him being in the crash of a small plane in Fort Myers, about 10 miles from me, I called him to see how he was feeling, and after that we spoke by phone from time to time, so I considered him a friend.

I turned to Conrad after I learned in the fall of 1991 that the bank was going to foreclose on my house in Florida and the lawyer handling my business affairs, Bob Rubenstein, told me I had a day to move everything. Otherwise, he said, the bank would take my furniture, too. I didn't have the money to pay a moving company or the time to make arrangements since it was already 4 p.m., and the two liquidators I called after finding their names in the phone book only offered me at most $5000. But the furniture was worth about $50,000. So I called Conrad, since he had lived in Florida much longer than I had, to see if he knew anyone who might want to buy my furniture, and he said he might be interested himself since he had just gotten married and was furnishing a new house. After he came to look at it, he offered to give me $7000. Since I felt I didn't have much choice, I agreed he could take it if he could get it out before the bank came at 8 a.m. in the morning and locked the doors. At least, I thought, his offer was $2000 more than the liquidators were offering, and at least my furniture would be going to someone I considered a friend.

Thus, later that night he came over with a truck and took the furniture, promising to pay me in a few days. However, after a few days, I hadn't heard from him, and when I called, he promised to pay but didn't. Instead, he kept making promises to pay me for about six months, and then he left the area and never returned, though he owns a house here. Apparently, I learned later, he shipped my furniture out of state to the home of his new mother-in-law, and then he literally dropped off the face of the earth. Eventually, after spending over a year trying to find him, I sued him in March 1993, and after advertising the suit in the newspaper, because we couldn't find him to serve him, I finally got a judgment against him for $40,000 and placed a lien on his house.

The one bright spot in the midst of all this legal wrangling while I was still seeing several doctors each week is I met John Daly, a man that would be like my anchor for the next two years.

I had initially encountered John briefly at my engagement party with Bob back in the summer of 1987, though I barely remembered him, since he was just one of about 100 guests at the party, held at the Salem Country Club in Peabody, Massachusetts. My father had invited John, since John had constructed a pool for my parents at their new house in Naples a few months before, and afterwards, my father had become very friendly with John, treating him almost like a son. They were drawn together since John had grown up in Haverhill, Massachusetts, about 10 miles from where I grew up in Topsfield, so there was that close connection due to family roots. At the time of the party, John planned to fly to Boston and be in the area visiting his family, so my father invited him to the party. Thus, our original meeting was all so casual and happenstance, though I wasn't even aware John was there until later.

However, John's continued contact with my parents made all the difference. That's because in the summer 1991 when I was in Florida and my mother was there, while my father was back in Boston, she was taking John to a local restaurant, Buffalo Chips, and invited me to go along. "Sure," I said, glad to meet someone who wasn't a lawyer or a doctor, because of the legal and medical nightmare that had become my life.

After my mother and I met John at the restaurant, as we ate

buffalo wings, my mother and I began telling John my story, describing the accident and what happened afterwards. As he listened, John seemed very sympathetic and supportive, commenting how he was "overwhelmed by all I had gone through". He could barely believe I was still "up and walking after everything", as he put it, and after dinner, he asked if I wanted to go to the dog track to watch the dogs race. I had never been before, but was intrigued and said "I'd love to." After we left the restaurant and my mother drove home, John took me to the track, a small circular area on a grassy field around the size of a football field, and we sat in the stands, several rows from the track. John still had so many questions about what happened to me, and I wanted to know all about John, too. So even after the dogs started racing, we barely watched them. We were so engrossed in talking and getting to know each other. In fact, we were still talking after the track had closed and everybody else had left. One of the security guards came over and asked us to leave.

We laughed about that on the way to the car, and after John drove me home, he asked to see me again. Then we started dating, seeing each other about six or seven times a week. We found we had so much in common, and I was especially drawn to John because he is such a good, funny conversationalist. He kept up on the news, liked to talk about current events, and had an ironic, dry wit that helped to cheer me up. His way of commenting on or laughing about the absurdity of everyday things made me laugh, too. So much was going wrong in my life at the time, that I found it a real respite to get away from it all by spending time with John. It was fun doing everyday things like going to the beach and looking for sand dollars or going to a local restaurant for dinner, and I felt a renewed enthusiasm that I could be attractive and desirable to a man again. It was one more sign of progress in getting back to normal.

Over the next few months we became closer and closer, and in the fall when I moved into a rented house, because the villa was foreclosed on due to financial pressures and the bankruptcy, John helped me move in.

CHAPTER 13

•

GOING TO TRIAL AND
SETTLING THE CASE

MOVING ON TOWARDS TRIAL

By early 1992, I was thus facing four separate lawsuits over the insurance proceeds and estate, plus the first of the three dozen creditor lawsuits that were filed against me as well. My life was becoming a seemingly unending legal nightmare, in which I spent most of my days meeting with lawyers and responding to legal documents, and the rest of my time seeing rehab doctors, health practitioners, or psychologists to try to get well.

As difficult as everything else was, at least John was still there. In fact, we were seeing each other so much that John moved into the house I rented and we became even closer.

I also started a part-time job in February 1992 working for a real estate broker, Mary Goeckeler. I helped her by filing, making copies, and occasionally sitting in at open houses on weekends for about a year until March 1993. It was simple work I could manage, and I was glad to be finally back to work again, though I still felt depressed because of all the lawsuits and continuing medical problems. Meanwhile, John was working in real estate, too, as an agent, so we had that in common to share about. It was nice having someone to come home to, someone with whom I could share about my experiences on the job. It felt almost like being an ordinary married couple, and we continued to do fun things like going to the beach or seeing a good movie.

Yet the pressure of the legal process was starting to build, adding to my continuing medical problems, and eventually this pressure would contribute to tearing apart our relationship.

Despite the extra work and confusion of dealing with four separate suits, Freedman hadn't been successful in getting the judge to consolidate them back in September. But in early January, Michael Corso, representing the insurance companies, again tried to consolidate my wrongful death suit and Mrs. Raymond's, since both hinged on the same factual issue—who was driving. Like Freedman, he argued to the judge that combining the cases would avoid inconsistent rulings, and save court time and expenses for everyone involved.

Meanwhile, I was feeling more and more desperate at the snail's pace of the pretrial proceedings because I was so close to poverty, that I felt I had to do something to speed up the process. As a result, I finally took my story to the local press—to the Naples *Daily News*. I hoped if the press told my story, this might put some pressure on the judge to move my cases forward.

Although in retrospect, I don't know if the *News* article really did lead Judge Hayes to move any faster. At least I felt some solace when the newspaper printed a supportive article about me. I felt the article helped me gain the sympathy of the newspaper and its readers for what I was going through. To get the story written, I spoke to a staff writer, Jaime Castillo, and on January 17, 1992, he published my story, beginning with words that expressed exactly my sentiments:

> Debbie Quinn Raymond just wants the slide to stop. Four and a half years ago, she was a successful real-estate broker worth an estimated $2.2 million. Now she periodically goes through her things to see what she has left to sell.
> 'The computer is my next saleable thing,' she said recently at her rented North Naples home. For Raymond the statement carries particular poignancy because the machine has been a key element in her rehabilitation from a near-fatal car accident...Children's computer games—on a computer just like the one she now contemplates selling—have helped her retrieve a fraction of her memory.

Then Castillo went on to describe how my statement to LeMay was holding up the insurance settlement money and was why I felt, as he wrote, "like I've been financially and emotionally raped...It's a black-and-white case—I wasn't driving." But instead, I had ended up experiencing a seemingly never-ending court process with continual delays and postponements. And most recently, the Judge had ordered a mediation meeting for the end of January. "But why?" I complained at the end of the interview: "There's nothing to mediate. Either my husband Bob was driving or I was driving. It's time to let the court decide."

I was so glad to see someone finally describe the frustration I was feeling, although soon after the article appeared, the only thing that occurred in the case was more legal maneuvers resulting in a postponement in the mediation date and another stay in my own wrongful death case against Mrs. Raymond.

Meanwhile other proceedings were proceeding slowly. One reason is that Mrs. Raymond still hadn't answered the interrogatories originally sent to her back in March 1991. As a result, in late January, 1992, Corso, the insurance companies' attorney, filed a motion to compel her to answer them, produce certain documents, and answer additional questions.

Then, one major roadblock was broken on February 9th, when Judge Hayes finally granted the trust's interpleader motion permitting them to place the $250,000 at issue in the court registry, while Mrs. Raymond and I resolved among ourselves who was driving. The trusts and Liberty had been arguing for this result for almost a year, and at last Judge Hayes agreed that only my lawyers and Mrs. Raymond's lawyers should be involved in the interpleader trial to decide who was driving. So Freedman's efforts to argue otherwise and force the insurance companies to pay first had been in vain. All he did was delay the trial and increase expenses.

So with all that side skirmishing out of the way, at the end of March, Judge Hayes set the interpleader trial for April 27th to once and for all determine the question of who was the driver. Additionally, he finally set a date for the main wrongful death trial for May 4th to May 21; and he ordered that all discovery for it be finished by April 17th.

I was ecstatic to hear him announce these dates. At last, I thought, everything will finally be resolved. At last, I told my friends and lawyers, "I can finally start moving on with my life. I'll have the money to pay off my debts. I'll be able to start pulling my life back together."

Meanwhile, in response to these new developments, Paul Freedman put together his pretrial statements. In one, he listed the key issues for the court to determine—who was driving and whether there was negligence. In the other, he indicated the many expert and lay witnesses he planned to call to testify—about the accident, my before and after condition, and my continuing damages and prognosis. All told he listed about 80 witnesses and 20 exhibits.

But then, within days of Judge Hayes setting these dates, I discovered that none of this was to be either, because Mrs. Raymond's lawyer Thomas Biggs unexpectedly died on March 22—only 3 days after the pretrial conference. It was like the hand of cruel fate brushing everything away. It was a crushing blow that meant having to start the trial setting process again. Fortunately, John was still in my life to cushion the blow, as I poured out my feelings about how upset I was by this new turn of events. But even though John helped me gain the strength to go on, the experience put additional strain on him.

DEATH AND TURMOIL

The process was brought to a dead halt, because when Biggs died, this meant Mrs. Raymond needed a new attorney, meaning additional delays and expenses. On April 1st, Judge Hayes gave her 30 days to find a new one, and two weeks later, she did—Jonathan Stidman, who filed a Notice of Appearance to let everyone know he was on board.

However, he also asked for a continuance, so he could get acquainted with the case, since Biggs had been handling the case on his own. Thus, he couldn't learn about the case or Biggs' strategies for it from any other lawyer. Additionally, he complained to Judge Hayes that he had to do additional discovery and depose a new expert witness Freedman had recently added. So he couldn't be prepared by the 27th—just two weeks away.

I felt like I was hit by a 2x4 when Freedman told me the news. I felt what occurred couldn't have been any worse. Not only did this mean the trial was being postponed yet again, but this postponement meant I still couldn't get any settlement money at a time when staying afloat was becoming more and more difficult. Two months earlier in February, the banks had started foreclosure proceedings on the villa and the house in Topsfield, because I couldn't pay the mortgages. I felt like I could soon be out on the street if some money didn't come through very quickly.

Freedman tried to fight the continuance, making a motion in early May in which he urged Judge Hayes to schedule the trial "in the immediate future...in the interest of justice," since the only issue was the identity of the driver. Unfortunately, given the slow pace of the courts, any immediate future was far off, since Freedman's motion wouldn't be heard until June 22nd. So even if Judge Hayes set a trial date then, it would be months more before the trial actually occurred.

CHALLENGING THE EVIDENCE

About a month after the postponement, Freedman finally challenged the validity of Susan LeMay's evidence—over a year after Mrs. Raymond filed her suit. In a motion he filed on May 6th, he argued that it should be excluded as "inadmissable hearsay," and once it was, Mrs. Raymond's would have no evidence supporting her claim. He argued that my conversations with LeMay occurred when she was providing emergency medical service, so that any statements I made about the accident weren't made for "the purpose of providing medical care." Thus, since they were "not pertinent to the diagnosis" of my condition," they were legally hearsay that couldn't be admitted in court. For added support, he attached two recent cases— one from 1986, the other from 1991—where a judge had previously excluded such evidence. So now Judge Hayes had to decide his motion.

Why did Freedman wait so long to try to exclude this statement, I wonder, looking back now. Why not attempt to do this much earlier to persuade Mrs. Raymond's attorney that the statement might not be allowed in as evidence, therefore getting rid of the case? Why was Freedman challenging the statement on a technicality as hearsay, rather than just challenging the validity of the statement itself, since I was nearly comatose when I gave it? Now I feel this belated and questionable motion is one more reason I was represented improperly at the time, though I didn't know enough to question anything my lawyers were doing then.

In any event, the next week, there was at least the hope of a settlement, after Mrs. Raymond's lawyers requested still more documents and then came back with an offer from her. She was willing to drop her own suit, she said, if I would pay her $50,000, plus settle the estate probate matter by paying her $5000 and giving her the two paintings she wanted—just as she had requested in her last settlement offer before the settlement negotiations went on hold.

I was very tempted to accept the offer to end all the litigation, though I felt outraged, because I considered the offer a kind of extortion. After all, Mrs. Raymond had started the process by bringing a frivolous, unfounded suit that had sent my whole life into disarray and financial free-fall. But finally, angered by her high demand, I said "No." Then, as negotiations went on for over three months, she dropped the amount she wanted from me to $20,000; then to $10,000, and by early August, she wanted $5000.

Would I reconsider, Freedman asked me? I was still angry, but I now felt that however unjustified, paying her off would at least buy the end of the litigation, and I would finally get my insurance money. Still, hoping she might settle for less, I asked Freedman to offer her $1000. He didn't want to, telling me "that's an insult," and offered her $2500 instead, which she accepted. Though the amount was more than I offered, at the end of August, I reluctantly told Freedman, "Okay, go ahead and pay her." Though he had ignored my request and offered more, I felt so tired of all the haggling, I wanted it over. Another compelling reason is I had learned a month before I had cancer and was facing a hysterectomy a week before the trial was scheduled to begin. So I didn't feel up to going to trial in mid-September, a week after major surgery. I felt I had to focus on getting well. So my feeling of fight for now was gone, and I agreed to pay her the $2500 legal bribe to drop her wrongful death case.

After that the outcome was quick in coming. On September 1, Freedman asked Judge Hayes for a summary judgment in the interpleader, on the grounds that there was now no issue of material fact, since discovery had clearly shown that I was the passenger. As he pointed out, this was supported by my own affidavit and the depositions of various witnesses, including William Fogarty, the accident reconstruction expert. At last, on September 2, Judge Hayes agreed, granting the summary judgment in my favor.

So finally, a success! It was a long time coming, but with this decision, Judge Hayes could soon release the $250,000 in the court registry from Liberty Mutual. I felt relieved I could finally start paying off my many bills, although I had lost the business and the villa by then. Also, I had to sell the house in Topsfield and a condo on the East Coast of Florida at a loss to keep them from foreclosing. I even lost my property in New Hampshire because I couldn't pay $2000 in taxes.

First, like a ghost that doesn't go away, Mrs. Raymond made one last effort to derail the order. It was like she couldn't let go; she had to fight to the end. This last ditch attempt came on September 8th when Stidham, her new attorney, filed a motion for a rehearing. He argued that the parties had agreed there would be no summary judgment until the details of the settlement had been worked out, and they hadn't done this yet. Thus, she wanted a rehearing.

To counter her move, Freedman had to engage in still more negotiations back and forth, and afterwards, to finally put Mrs. Raymond's suit away, I had to promise that I wouldn't pursue any further claims against her or the estate because she had filed this suit. It was her way to make sure I would have no recourse against her later for her legal blackmail.

However, I felt I had no choice but to sign to end the process. Once I did, finally, the case with Mrs. Raymond was over. In return for my signing, Mrs. Raymond agreed she wouldn't oppose Judge

234 • CONQUERING THE DARKNESS

Hayes' summary judgment in my favor and would seek no other action against me.

While I was relieved to get rid of her suit, so I finally could pursue my own suit against the insurance companies, I steamed thinking that I would have to write a $2500 check to her after I got my settlement money. All I could think was "legal extortion," because I agreed to pay her this money to drop a unfounded suit that had delayed my own settlement for over 18 months and cost me so much. Yet since the agreement said that each side had to bear its own costs, I could never make any claim against Mrs. Raymond, the estate, or her attorneys. And I couldn't use this agreement to affect any of the claims Mrs. Raymond and I were still making against each other in the estate probate battle that had been on hold while these lawsuits in Florida were resolved. So despite all the havoc her suit caused, Mrs. Raymond could now just drop it with no real penalties for her, beyond paying her own legal fees for bringing it. Meanwhile, because of it, I had lost millions and was back to Square 1 in pursuing my original claims for the insurance money for my injuries in the accident.

Yes, it was unfair and I felt furious agreeing to pay her. But I felt I had to do so—the only way to get rid of her suit.

GETTING PAID

At least, Mrs. Raymond's suit against me was almost over, except for a few loose ends to tie up over the next few weeks.

One was settling the estate probate battle back in Massachusetts that had been on hold while the wrongful death suit was going on. Unfortunately, the long delays in resolving this suit meant that I now had to give up my claim to about $12,500 in estate property funds. I discovered this after Deborah Feldman tried to write me and then called September 16, explaining that she had postponed any probate action against Bob's estate for repaying my funeral expenses and refunding my loan until the Florida actions were resolved. But now, because of the long delay, the court had dismissed my probate case against the estate on August 25. So now I had only

30 days from then—until September 25—to reinstate the action.

So what did I want to do? At this point, I felt so defeated, I felt it best to give up. I felt drained by the battle in Florida, drained by the surgery, and didn't have the heart for another fight. Besides, Feldman recommended against reviving the action, since it would be so expensive, compared to the limited benefit to be gained. So it wasn't worth it. As Feldman explained so convincingly in her letter:

> The court would most likely order an immediate trial date, maybe even within the month, requiring your presence in Massachusetts and active participation. Proceeding with the Action could be an additional strain mentally, physically and financially. Further, should a judgment be obtained, the Estate, most likely, has no funds available to satisfy it.

So, I decided to let the matter drop, seeing it as one more loss due to Mrs. Raymond's wrongful death case.

Again it was nice having John there to help me feel better about this loss. After I told him, he reassured me that at least her suit was over and she would soon be out of my life. Also, he was there for me after my surgery, this time for the hysterectomy in 1992.

At the time, I just laughed about his comment. In retrospect, it was a signal that our relationship was becoming more distant. Then, too, during this time, when John and I went to a romantic dinner one night — a respite from all the turmoil — I made the mistake of turning to him and suggesting: "Well, why don't you marry me? We've been together so long and are so close." Unfortunately, it was absolutely the wrong time to ask this, because I was suggesting marriage out of desperation in a moment of brief joy to cling to him even more tightly, because of the maelstrom that had become my life. However, I'm sure my proposal scared him, making him feel like I was pulling him into a permanent trap. He simply said: "No. I don't want to. I'm not ready for this now." And we never talked about getting married again. But I think that request contributed to his pulling away from me even further.

This happened because John is a very patient person, and he had stuck with me so far because of his strong sense of commitment,

236 • CONQUERING THE DARKNESS

and because in the beginning everything had been so good. But now, there were increasing problems and my inopportune request only helped to highlight them. For example, John worked about seven days a week in real estate, while I stayed home most of the time and sometimes went to the beach. Though he didn't say so at the time, I think John worked so hard as his way of getting away from our close yet increasingly distant relationship, without having to formally leave. I think he didn't want to confront this change in his feelings and let me down, though we didn't talk about this then, and he still isn't sure why he stayed now.

In any case, while my personal legal case dragged on, now that Mrs. Raymond's suit was out of the way, John and I muddled along from day to day, each day pretty much the same. John worked; I went to the beach, rode around in my Jeep, or stayed home feeling depressed. And so it went.

Then, in mid-September, after he got the formal release from Mrs. Raymond stating she wouldn't appeal the interpleader agreement, Freedman asked the court to reinstate my original wrongful death and personal injury action, as well as releasing the $250,000 in the court registry.

Unfortunately, a second loose end before I could get this money was dealing with the Blue Cross lien on any payments to me for medical services. It took another month until the end of October to resolve this lien, since Blue Cross claimed it wanted back the $44,000 in medical fees it had paid out, while Freedman argued that Blue Cross should only get $22,000, because that was its pro rata share of the $250,000 he recovered, after the payment was reduced by the company's share of my attorney fees and costs—which totaled about $123,000 at this point.

So there was yet another court hearing on October 28th to resolve this—the same date set to hear Freedman's request to reinstate my original wrongful death case against the estate, trusts, and Liberty Mutual. Yet while Judge Hayes quickly agreed to reinstate my original case, he set still another hearing in November to hear the Blue Cross matter. But then, at last he agreed—Blue Cross should pay its share of the legal fees and only receive $22,000. It was one small victory, in a long and expensive war.

So finally, the last hurdle to getting the long delayed settlements from Travelers and Liberty Mutual was cleared. I was to receive the $250,00 in the registry from Liberty and another $250,000 that Traveler's was holding, while waiting to see what Liberty would do— for a total settlement of $500,000.

Then, in late December and early January, the insurance settlements finally arrived—though I only ended up with $208,000 by the time the attorneys took out their fees.

When I looked at the statement they sent me, I sat down on my bed in a state of near shock, looking at the small amount and trying to figure out why it was so little, after so much time and so much fighting. There it was in black and white—$208,000. Not only did the lawyers deduct their 40 percent in legal fees, but they had paid out $22,000 to Blue Cross, $13,000 to Mrs. Raymond for the probate settlement which was now finalized, too, and about $50,000 in payments and costs to other lawyers who helped on the case.

At least, I reminded myself to feel better, with Mrs. Raymond's wrongful death suit finally settled, my own wrongful death suit could go forward, so I could get additional funds from my third level carrier. As Freedman had explained to me, this was coverage on my car, that was provided by an additional $1 million umbrella policy from Traveler's, and he was confident it would now be a simple matter to get that. As he reassured me: "Now it's clear and indisputable that you were the passenger, and your injuries and expenses are so high."

However, getting this money turned out to be anything but a simple matter. That's because Traveler's was prepared to fight, claiming that my injuries were not as severe as I claimed and that I was negligent in contributing to them, since I didn't use a seat belt. So now there were more delays and costs as the battle went into still another phase.

PURSUING THE WRONGFUL DEATH SUIT

But at last, my original personal injury suit for an additional $1 million insurance could proceed. Beginning on February 24, 1993,

Freedman began arranging for me and my doctors, who would testify about my injuries, to give depositions the following month. Meanwhile, since Traveler's decided to fight paying any more, its own attorney, Robert E. Bugg, began scheduling his own depositions. He was trying to seek evidence to counter my own claim.

Unfortunately, all of this pressure from the lawsuits and medical problems finally became so great that I couldn't work for Mary Goeckler anymore, so I told her I had to quit in mid-March 1993. I was just too upset and nervous.

At the same time, my growing sense of tension and desperation was putting more pressure on John. I could feel the growing distance, but didn't know what to do about it. I felt like John was reaching his limits and the relationship was near the breaking point. Perhaps John stayed as long as he did, because he was always a very solid, patient person, devoted to making and keeping commitments. He clearly felt deeply stressed and burdened by what was going on in my life and our relationship. Later he told me he kept hanging on because he felt like he had created a committed link, rather like the old saying: "For better or for worse", and so he continued to honor this commitment. Still more and more, with each new crisis, he felt a growing desire to leave.

However, I didn't know what I could do to make our relationship any better, because the legal process, like the medical procedures I kept having to undergo, had taken on a life of its own. John even kidded me after I arranged to have two more surgeries later that spring: "You have surgeries like I play golf."

Later, I had to appear for one of these depositions on March 29th. I had already given a deposition nearly a year earlier, on April 2nd, 1992, but now Bugg wanted to ask me further questions about my condition in the past year and my future prognosis. I was nervous, afraid I might say the wrong thing. But Freedman told me he would be by my side while Bugg questioned me to monitor the session and make sure the questions were appropriate. If not, Freedman could object, he explained.

As much as I hated giving another deposition, because it was such a long, grueling process, I had to do so to show how much I had suffered and lost, while Bugg wanted to show I was as normal as possible to minimize my damages. It was depressing to think about having to present myself as a loser and victim once again.

Finally, the day of the deposition arrived. We held it at a court reporting office in Naples, that was set up for taking depositions in a neutral setting, so both sides could feel equally comfortable. As we walked in, a trained court reporter was waiting for us with a transcriber on the desk in front of her so she could take complete notes of everything we said.

Bugg began by asking about my present situation, and I explained how I was now living in a rented house in Naples, with John Daly, who had been my boyfriend for a year and a half. Because I didn't have any money myself, I said, he was supporting me, paying $1000 a month for rent and buying our everyday food and other supplies.

"So what about work?" Bugg asked, and I described how I had worked on and off for about a year starting in February 1992 for a real estate broker, Mary Goeckeler. I did assorted clerical work, like mailings, filing, and making copies for her. But I only worked for about 8 hours a week, I explained, because I got tired very easily due to my injuries, and many months I couldn't work at all because I had several surgeries in late 1992 and early 1993. Then I stopped working for her entirely a week before the deposition, because I felt too much pain after a few hours to work the hours she required. And I only got $5 an hour, I told Bugg, explaining that this was a far contrast to the millions I once controlled as the owner of a number of businesses.

Then, to show how different things were now and before the accident, I described the business and properties I once owned, from the Mail Boxes franchise to the four real estate properties I had bought, but all gone now. It was so painful to talk about how I had once been very successful, because the contrast showed how far I had fallen, how much I had lost.

Next Bugg wanted to know what I was doing now. This part of the deposition was especially difficult, because it painfully reminded me of my current situation. For example, when Bugg asked "Do you have any goals or plans to go back to work or start any businesses?" I started shaking, as I replied: "I don't know what I can do and that's the problem I'm having."

When Bugg asked how I was currently supporting myself, it was hard to hold back the tears as I explained how bad things were. "At the present time, I'm just borrowing from family, friends," I told him. "I've sold everything that I own...I'm concerned how I'm going to support myself. I'm still trying to figure out something that I can do out of the house, because some days I can't drive because of vertigo and pain."

Then, I talked about my various surgeries—feeling a shooting pain go through me as I did, like a reminder of the past. As I described them, I felt like I was listing a surgical chart—a hysterectomy about 6 months earlier; an operation to repair my nose after I fell and broke it because of the vertigo; and more surgeries on both elbows after I pinched the nerves due to sleeping in a half-sitting position when I had to wear the halo. Now, I told Bugg, I expected still more surgeries, including one to correct a previous surgery done incorrectly on my nose and several cosmetic surgeries to remove earlier scars.

As I continued on, describing the various scars I still had from the accident and the surgeries and the pains I still felt in my neck, head, and lower back, it was all I could do to keep from shaking.

Bugg still had more questions. Next he wanted to know about the doctors who were still treating me and the support group I was still attending for chronic pain and brain injury patients. And then we talked about how hard I found it to accept the continuing limitations from my brain injury. Although I mentioned a few bright spots, like the computer I got, which Dr. Woulas suggested for brain injury patients, and the memory and concentration exercises I still practiced on this computer, mostly I told him about the problems.

"Because of my limited financial situation, I can only see Dr. Woulas once a week," I said. "I can't even participate in hobbies, because of my physical situation, though I used to be very active in aerobics before. But since the accident, I haven't been able to find anything to replace it. ... Either I end up in pain... Or I have to walk at a very slow pace because of the weakness on my left side....I've tried swimming. I can't swim. I can't jog... I've tried everything, and for a very active person, it's very frustrating."

Then, once again, I had to relate what I recalled about the accident and describe my current physical problems. But it was not like telling a sympathetic doctor. Instead, as Freedman had warned me, I felt Bugg rating and evaluating me, as I reported each continuing symptom: "Chronic headache, neck pain, spasms in my neck, forgetfulness, numbness on my right side which comes and goes, and then there's the vertigo...I never know when it's going to hit. I'm always walking into walls, that sort of thing. When it really gets bad, I can't get out of bed or I'll just fall to the floor. That happens maybe a couple of times a year and I often feel depressed and anxious. So I'm taking medication for that."

I gave several examples to illustrate. "For example, if I'm having a phone conversation with someone, I won't remember it the next day. If I see something, I'm more likely to remember it than if I talk about it...I found working for Mary Goeckeler...very hard...because...she'd tell me something to do and I'd forget it."

I was relieved when the deposition was finally over, and wondered how I did after we left. "Fine, you did fine," Freedman reassured me. "You made it sound really bad." I felt unnerved by Freedman's coldness and calculation, though I knew I needed to present myself in this negative way to do well in the trial. I felt depressed, because as I told Freedman, "That's really how it is."

Over the next month, Freedman continued getting records to show the additional medical procedures and costs I incurred, and at the end of April, he wrote Bugg to follow-up on my deposition, emphasizing that the accident had a "devastating effect" on me in numerous ways. His letter was designed to persuade Bugg to recommend the full settlement to Traveler's, rather than proceeding to trial. So after pointing to the many deficits and difficulties I had experienced—"physical disability, intellectual/brain impairment, grief, emotional strain and economic upheaval,"—and noting that my problems were well documented from my many doctor visits and surgeries, he urged Travelers that there was no need to further investigate or continue the litigation process. As he concluded his letter:

> Ms. Quinn should not be forced to agonize through protracted litigation especially since the policy limits do not approximate her damages...Further discovery can only be cumulative of the facts already in the company's possession. It is patently unfair to cause Ms. Quinn to incur additional expense and delay in prolonging this proceeding.

Thus, he asked Travelers to pay the policy limits of $1 million within 30 days.

Unfortunately, when they didn't, my precarious emotional state become even more precarious. I also began to worry whether my boyfriend John Daly would stay, since I felt he was the one person who helped me hold my life together. So far, he had stayed on, helping and caring for me, despite all my legal and medical problems, because he understood and sympathized with them. But as the suit dragged on, each new hurdle made me feel anxious and afraid that this one anchor in my life might not last. I was so afraid he might leave if things weren't settled soon—and in fact, he did. A month later, in June, he left, telling me he couldn't take my emotional upheavals anymore, because I continually acted like an emotional powder keg—frequently either depressed or angry, living from delay to delay, after being caught up in the legal system for so long. Meanwhile, I felt helpless to do anything, as Freedman kept me informed of each new delay.

Freedman didn't even consider trying to negotiate for a smaller amount to promote a quicker settlement, which is what I once said I wanted months before. But by now, I realized how little I had gotten from the first $500,000 because the attorneys took so much, so I wanted to go for the full $1 million left, even if it meant going to trial. As a result, since Freedman was still determined to play hardball and said he thought I deserved the full amount and expected to get this, I readily agreed. So he continued to fight on. Now I think it would have made more sense to try to work out a compromise settlement, but I didn't know enough to press Freedman to do this at the time.

Meanwhile, when an article appeared in the *Miami Review* describing the great successes that the Mail Boxes Etc. company was having, I felt even worse. The article was one more reminder of everything I had lost, though Freedman felt it useful for the case, and he sent Bugg a copy to show how much I might have made had I not been forced to sell the business. But I had to sell, as Freedman reminded him, because I had lost so much money and couldn't run the business anymore, since I now lacked the abilities to handle a franchise, as my various doctors would testify.

Unfortunately, this last blow legally and financially contributed to the final blow that helped topple my already teetering relationship with John. I was no longer working for Mary or anyone, and was spending even more time at home doing nothing except responding to legal requests and constantly feeling in pain, so I was increasingly difficult to live with.

Then one night in May 1993 I simply flipped out. John and I went to meet my mother for a small dinner to celebrate her birthday while my father was back in Boston, and I forgot I had taken some pain medication that I shouldn't mix with alcohol. So during dinner, I had a couple of sakis, and when we got home, I was in a strange, hyper-state. Suddenly, for no apparent reason, I started becoming upset and yelling at John, though now I don't even remember why. I think it's because I felt John slipping away, and afraid I would lose him, I started becoming more and more excited and hysterical. When John tried to calm me, I yelled more loudly and more irrationally, until finally I pushed him out the front door and locked him out of the house. After I finally opened the door, he came back in. However, we didn't speak after that, and he packed up and left the next day.

I felt devastated, seeing him go. I had come to rely on John for so long and for so much, and now he was gone. And his leaving had occurred on top of all the legal and financial losses I had just experienced, plus the continuing medical nightmare. For days, I felt helpless, hopeless, and could barely pull myself out of bed. I just wanted to go back to bed and sleep forever.

Looking back, it's hard to see why John stayed as long as he did, because our relationship was so shaky the last few months because of all my problems. But John kept hanging on, perhaps out of a sense of commitment and guilt. Then, I think my explosion gave him the impetus he needed to finally leave. And what was so upsetting was that John had been like my anchor, and now that anchor was gone. So I felt lost for a time, like I was completely alone and drifting at sea again.

NEGOTIATING AND PREPARING FOR TRIAL

Finally, in June, Freedman got a trial date for October 6 from Judge Hayes. So that meant up to five more months of delay in getting any settlement. In the interim, Freedman advised the doctors and witnesses he expected to testify to be available. The roster included my psychologist Dr. Woulas; neuropsychologist, Dr. Raffa; William Fogarty, the accident reconstruction expert; Trooper Whiddon, who was first on the scene; George S. Kendrick, the truck driver who saw me as a passenger; and others. I was glad they were still available and willing to testify, though I knew each witness added additional costs that would come out of any expected settlement.

Even though I was now determined to go for all or nothing, since I had lost almost everything due to all the delays, I still had to go through a court-mandated mediation program. This was required to get all the parties to meet together with a mediator a few months before their court date to try to settle the case. Then, if they could settle, this would reduce the legal costs for everyone, since there was no need to go to court. So I had no choice. I had to go through the process.

At least, I could share my concerns with John again. We had become friends once more after John had a month to cool down after our blow up, though we decided our relationship had become too intense to work romantically. John was surprised, because I had told him I was now determined to go to trial. But I assured him the mediation was just a required step in the process, and afterwards the trial would go forward.

Besides, it was hard to imagine Freedman and Bugg sitting down to work anything out, since they sent each other such bitter legal letters. For example, on June 14th, Freedman attacked Bugg's lack of faith in responding to his April 26th letter requesting a full policy settlement, when he wrote: "...Your failure to respond to our offer of settlement indicates a total disregard for Deborah Quinn's serious injuries and financial peril. There is no justification for such lack of good faith in this matter." A week later, Bugg wrote back in kind, expressing offense at Freedman's tone, as well as disputing the evidence of damage Freedman claimed, when he responded:

> I am surprised by the tone of your letter in that I thought we were working together in trying to resolve this case by scheduling a mediator...
> While I wish to continue to work together toward resolving this matter before trial, letters referring to 'bad faith' and 'total disregard' can only be received in a manner that they are dealing not with a serious resolution of this matter but rather are attempts to put 'pressure' on me or my client to settle at an unreasonable amount.

Freedman only attacked back, stating:

> A million dollar settlement does not begin to compensate my client for her losses.
> Your client's decision to delay a resolution of the claim has to be based upon factors in its self-interest and not in the best interests of the insured.

Needless to say, Freedman's and Bugg's exchange discouraged any settlement, and so the matter seemed headed for trial, which I wanted at this point. As I told Freedman, "I'm ready to roll the dice," and he continued preparing accordingly. He continued to collect updated medical and billing information from my psychologist Dr. Woulas, my vocational rehab counselor Dr. John Russell, and others. Plus, he sought depositions from two additional doctors I continued seeing twice a year—Dr. Cox, my neurosurgeon, and Dr. Jaeger, my overall rehab doctor—to show how extensive my physical and mental losses continued to be and how long it was taking me to regain my past abilities.

At the same time, Bugg prepared for trial, too, bringing in some of his own experts to give opinions on my condition that might show less damages and losses than Freedman charged so Traveler's would have to pay less. As I later learned, lawyers often go through this exchange process—gathering and showing each other the evidence they have before a trial, so they each have a better idea of the likely outcome. Then, they can work out a settlement with this in mind. The process is like collecting an arsenal and showing off your weapons to judge who is stronger; then there's no need to actually go to battle. Meanwhile, my life was like the battlefield where this battle was occurring, and it continued to fall apart.

In mid-August I had to take still another grueling medical examination which Bugg requested, because he wanted an independent medical examination to counter the records and testimony of my own doctors. He set the exam up with neuropsychologist, Dr. Glenn Larrabee, on August 19th and 20th, and arranged for him to give me a comprehensive neuropsychological evaluation to examine how well I functioned in many different areas. So I had to take tests of verbal learning, visual memory, word association, facial recognition, mental control, finger-tapping, form perception, cognitive behavior, and other abilities. Larabee additionally planned to look at my mood and emotional functioning, using tests like the MMPI and Beck Depression Inventory.

At first, Freedman tried to resist my taking the test, writing Bugg that it would be "burdensome, overbroad, and unduly taxing." In the end, I had to take it since Bugg insisted on having a detailed medical profile of my current condition. When I did, Freedman did little to prepare me on what to expect or how to best respond to the questions to support my case. As a result, I unwittingly tried to perform as well as I could by answering the questions to show how well I could do certain skills and how normal I appeared—my usual reaction to any test. I try to do the best I can. But ironically, the better I answered, the more I undermined my claim for continuing damages and losses.

Meanwhile, in case the mediation now scheduled for September 14 didn't lead to a settlement and the trial occurred, Bugg sent Freedman a proposed amendment for a joint pretrial statement to the judge detailing major admitted facts, expected witnesses and exhibits, and issues for the court to determine. He did so because if they both could agree on a statement, they could skip having a time-consuming pretrial conference to work out these issues.

Overtly, this proposal seemed like another routine procedure. Looking back, it's clear that Bugg now felt he was in a stronger position after doing the investigation and testing, since the revised statement he proposed reflected a strong attack on my case. This meant that the assurances which Freedman had been giving me all along about how strong my case was weren't true. I think now Freedman made this mistake in judgment because he was so determined to absolve me of any blame and so focused on the damages I had suffered that he failed to consider any other conflicting factors and prepare to counter them. But now Bugg suddenly brought them to Freedman's attention, like poking holes in an overblown balloon. Unfortunately, Freedman had led me to trust in that balloon.

That's why, for almost four years since the beginning of the case, Freedman had urged me not to settle and go for the full $1 million on top of the first and second tier settlements of $250,000 each. But now, Bugg undermined Freedman's earlier assessment.

Freedman didn't even tell me any of this at the time. He just acted like everything was going ahead as usual, but instead everything had changed dramatically. My case was suddenly much, much weaker than Freedman had told me all along. Now, looking back, it seems like Freedman should have been prepared for this. He had kept me from settling much earlier, because of what he told me about the strength of my case early on. But now, my case didn't look so strong after all. It was another major blow, and in retrospect, I feel like Freedman had kept me hanging on a dangerous cliff for so long not realizing the risk. But I didn't know enough to realize what was happening back then.

In any event, Bugg quickly countered Freedman's claim for full damages by contesting the nature and extent of my damages. He argued that my claim for injuries and damages should be reduced to the extent they were compensated by or subject to compensation from other sources. Additionally, he said my damages should be reduced because I was negligent in not wearing a seat belt, and the court should decide how much this reduction should be. Plus he now wanted to add several more expert witnesses to support these claims. Besides Larrabee, the neuropsychologist who had tested me, he wanted to bring in an economic expert to discuss my economic damages, if any; an accident reconstruction expert to discuss my failure to use a seat belt; and a witness to discuss the condition of the tires. In addition, he wanted to add other witnesses to talk about my Mail Boxes Business and my medical status; and he might want to name his own vocational-rehabilitation witness to counter any claims made by the expert Freedman wanted to use to review my job prospects. In short, if the matter came to trial, Bugg showed he was well prepared to counter Freedman with a duel of the experts to undermine Freedman's experts.

Then to show he meant business and prepare for the mandated mediation, over the next few weeks, Bugg and a lawyer assistant sought all sorts of documents about my educational background and medical history. If I didn't have the records, Bugg asked my medical providers for them. He queried about two dozen of them. In fact, his investigation was even more extensive than what Freedman had done originally when he assured me what a strong claim I had. In turn, I felt this investigation was one more example of what Freedman hadn't done, while convincing me I had a strong case, so I should keep fighting. Now, Bugg had seemingly taken him up on his bluff, and my case was suddenly in trouble, though Freedman didn't admit this to me then. Instead, he responded by assuring me everything would be fine and requesting more medical records and bills.

GOING TO THE MEDIATION

Finally, the mandated mediation occurred as scheduled on September 14th at the offices of the selected mediator, Robert Hagaman's, in Naples, Florida. When I arrived at 8:30 a.m., Freedman hit me with a bombshell about the real strength of my case—the first time I heard this. For almost 2 years, he had been telling me I had a strong case and should expect to get the full $1 million, so it was worth fighting on. That morning Freedman suddenly did a 180 degree turn, telling me I didn't have a good case after all, so I should settle without going to trial and get what I could.

What had changed? At the time, I couldn't understand it. I felt flabbergasted, devastated, like Freedman had just pulled the rug out from under me. But why? Though now I believe what happened is that Freedman hadn't fully investigated my case and now recognized the weaknesses because of Bugg's investigation, at the time, his change of heart was a complete shock. I think this is what occurred, because Bugg's investigation really did turn up information that undercut Freedman's claims, so now at the mediation, Freedman had to negotiate from a weaker position. Thus, when I came in to the mediation, he had to make the best of this bad situation and get me to agree to what he worked out.

Of course, now it is too late to do anything, since the case is over, the money is lost, and it's too hard to go back and prove anything. Now I believe that if only Freedman knew about these weaknesses early on in the case, he might have seen the wisdom of settling months or years before, as I had repeatedly urged him in the beginning. Yet at the time, I didn't know. I couldn't know.

At the mediation I could do little. I simply felt shocked and helpless to discover things were not what I thought. But I had no control, no ability to do anything myself now. As my lawyer, Freedman was acting for me; and I still didn't have all my mental abilities back.

Thus, I sat quietly for most of the mediation listening. First, the lawyers began by presented their sides of the case, arguing their strengths and weaknesses and what they were initially prepared to offer. Then, the mediator had them meet in separate rooms, and he moved back and forth between them, as their offers went back and forth. It was a long, tedious process, and it became even longer, because after each round, the insurance company lawyers had to call their home office for an approval.

Initially, Freedman asked for the full million, while the insurance company offered $100,000. Then, through the morning, his offer gradually went down, and their offer gradually inched up. Meanwhile, as the time approached 11 a.m., Freedman looked nervous and began pacing. "We've got to get this settled today...We've got to get this settled soon," he kept saying.

Why the sudden rush to settle, I wondered? Was it only because Freedman now recognized the weaknesses of his case? Or was there an additional reason, since he had scheduled an afternoon mediation starting at 1 p.m. on the other side of the state? Was he ready to settle for a lower amount than otherwise, because he had to be at this second mediation? I wasn't sure, although I suspected he was under pressure because this second mediation was scheduled. For example, several times Freedman called the office of the mediator handling the second mediation to tell him he would be delayed. Each time he called, as the delay became longer, Freedman seemed more tense.

Finally, at about noon, the mediator came back with what he said was the insurance company's last offer: $500,000. Freedman urged me to take it, telling me to forget about getting anymore. However, when I was reluctant to do so, saying I was concerned about having enough for my ongoing medical care, he seemed unconcerned and replied almost flippantly: "Don't worry. President Clinton will take care of your extra health bills."

I was furious when he said this. I had been waiting about 2 years because Freedman had urged me to wait to seek the full settlement amount, and now he was offering to get me just half. Even then, I knew I would get much less after the lawyers' fees and expenses were deducted—perhaps only $250,000 more than if I had settled two years earlier without the long struggle and great personal losses.

Thus, I firmly refused. I told Freedman, "Forget it. I'm not settling. I'm out of here, unless the company is willing to pay $100,000 more."

Freedman looked at me with amazement. "Oh, come on, Deb. Let's get this over," he said.

I felt he wasn't taking me seriously, that he expected me to cave in again, just as I had in the past. So, instead, to show I was quite serious, I got up and started walking towards the door.

Freedman tried to dissuade me, urging me to come back. I insisted. "No. I'm going. That's it," I said.

Then, I started out the door, and saw that Freedman was extremely upset as he raced after me to hold me back. I think now my ultimatum upset him so much because if he didn't settle at the mediation, he would have to take the case to trial, and after Bugg's investigation, the case no longer seemed as strong as he had thought. Also, I don't think he was fully prepared to go to trial, since he hadn't collected all the records or depositions he needed and the trial was three weeks away. Still, regardless of the risk of going to trial, I was ready to walk out, and I told Freedman that he either presented my demand or I was leaving. So finally, reluctantly, Freedman presented my demand to the mediator and called the afternoon mediator to explain he would be further delayed.

I came back in the room, and a few minutes later, after the insurance company lawyers conferred briefly among themselves, they agreed to exactly what I wanted without having to call their home office. So just by standing up to them myself, I got $100,000 more as a settlement.

Ironically, when Freedman later figured out his bill, he still paid himself his 40% in fees out of this additional amount. Though I told him I felt this payment was unfair, because I had gotten this extra amount myself, he held firm, saying our agreement stated that he would get his fee based on the total settlement. Still, I resented him, because he wouldn't have gotten this additional $100,000 without my threat to walk out. I couldn't get him to adjust his fee to take less. Now it's too late.

THE END OF THE BATTLE

In any case, once the insurance company lawyers agreed to pay the additional $100,000, the insurance battle was finally resolved, and the mediator, Hagaman, filed his Mediation Report with the court, announcing success.

Yet was it? I felt strangely drained after I left the mediation, feeling like I had given in because I was so tired of fighting and because I felt so alone there. I felt abandoned without anyone to support me when Freedman suddenly changed gears and told me I didn't have such a strong case after all. The process might have gone differently if John, who I was still close to as a friend, had come with me. He had planned to go, but decided not to, because I had told him I had made up my mind we were going to trial. So he thought this would just be a routine procedure and didn't go.

Thus, he was very surprised when I called him that night when I got home from the mediation and told him how upset I was about Freedman pulling the rug out from under me, so that I settled because I didn't know what else to do. "What? You settled!" John said shocked, and then he told me how angry he felt about what my lawyer had done. His reaction contributed to my growing anger about what had happened as I continued to think about the mediation later. But for now, I just felt mostly tired and drained, yet relieved that I didn't have to think about the lawsuit anymore.

Then, a few days after Judge Hayes signed Bugg's request to dismiss the case, since the mediation was successful, on October 8th, I finally got my money.

So finally, the long-drawn out case was over. And I was relieved for that at least, though I ended up with so much less than I had expected. After Freedman deducted all his fees and legal costs— since under the mediation agreement, each party had to pay its own costs—my $600,000 settlement was whittled down to only a $365,000 payment to me.

A few years later, as I began to weigh the costs and gains, I realized it was a very expensive win. That's because, I realized too late, the long fight was not only not worth the small amount of additional settlement money I gained but far more costly in the long run. Though I had gained about $365,000 more after lawyers fees and expenses were deducted, I had lost about $2.5 million due to bankruptcy, foreclosure, and other proceedings against me.

Only Freedman and his associate Kaplan had come out ahead, because they earned about $235,000 more than they would have if I had taken the $500,000 settlement as I wanted over two years before, instead of listening to Freedman telling me to go for even more. At the time, I didn't understand how to look at the benefits and costs, but as I gained back my mental abilities through rehab therapy and counseling, my questions grew. I began to ask questions about how Freedman and Kaplan represented me, and what he had done to hurt me—questions like: Why wouldn't they settle as I asked? Why did they insist that battling on was the best thing to do? For them maybe—I realize now. However, weren't they supposed to be putting my interests as their client first? Why couldn't I have paid off Mrs. Raymond six months earlier to drop her unfounded suit for $10,000? Why did the lawyers keep things going?

In the months after the settlement, not understanding fully what happened, I only thought that Freedman had charged too much and eventually I sued him and his firm for excessive fees. In my suit, I disputed many of the costs he added to my bill as well as the interest I didn't receive on the funds which Liberty Mutual placed in the registry. Finally I did get back $20,000 from him and his firm in an out of court settlement.

Unfortunately, as I have learned more, I realize I settled for far too little, since now I realize he made so many serious mistakes, though hard to prove. And even if I could, there's little I can do, since as part of the settlement, I agreed not to hold Freedman liable for anything further. It was an agreement I should never have signed, and certainly the lawyer I hired to sue Freedman and his firm should have never advised me to sign it. Not knowing any better I did, because I didn't realize the extent to which Freedman had taken advantage of me in pursuing a losing strategy that ended up paying him well while costing me millions. But at the time, all I could think of was this was over and I had gotten a final bit of justice, so I could put the case to rest.

Now, with the case over, I felt I could finally get on with pulling together my life. I still had to continue my rehabilitation for a few more years. I still had to resolve some lingering creditor suits—about three dozen of them—by working out a settlement to pay off the creditors. At least I felt a heavy burden lifting; I felt I was leaving the darkness and could now see the light ahead of me. I could move on.

EPILOGUE

•

After the mediation ended in September 1993, I felt a big release of emotions. Though I felt a heavy burden lifting and could now move on, I also felt anger towards my attorneys, because I didn't feel I got a fair settlement. I felt they suddenly changed gears, telling me to settle now, whereas they had previously urged me to hold off settling for about two years because I had such a strong case. But now they said I didn't. I was also upset, because a year earlier in September 1992, I had felt another sense of defeat when I agreed to settle with Mrs. Raymond and pay her $2500 to drop her wrongful death suit. I caved in because I felt too weakened by all the lawsuits plus the threat of still another surgery, this time for cancer. So now I felt a growing sense of anger because of both settlements, and that anger lingered until it eventually propelled me to take some action, which included writing this book.

The sense of finality was overwhelming, too, while the sense of being released from a legal prison into a new freedom was very scary. What would I do? Where would I go? As terrible as they were, the lawsuits had been such a complete part of my everyday life, so now I felt strangely bereft and abandoned. As I left knowing everything was over, I started to cry, and in the car, I couldn't stop crying.

Then, over the next few days, I started to find my anchor again. Though I was no longer living with John and we weren't romantically involved anymore, we were still close friends, and he was someone to talk to. When I got home from the mediation and called him, he sounded shocked, because I had been telling my attorney and him for so long that I was going to trial. He had even offered to come to court with me to lend me moral support, as well as be a witness. However, that morning, he decided not to go to the mediation with me, thinking it was just a routine mandatory court procedure before the main event. So John was very surprised when I told him of the settlement. "What do you mean, you settled?" he gasped. Then I explained how I had felt so tired and alone and deserted by my lawyers, which contributed to my settling.

At least, the legal nightmare was over, and to help put aside my anger and feel better, I went out and bought a Jeep. It was my way of giving a gift to myself for everything that I went through. It was my symbol of strength, freedom, and independence—all the things I felt or wanted to feel, now that the nightmare of lawsuits was over. There was still some paperwork to complete to sign off on all the agreements. But otherwise, the suit was finished, done. Driving around in my Jeep helped to remind me of that and make me feel better.

Yet, even though the lawsuit was lifted, I wasn't completely back to normal mentally or physically, and still felt very depressed. The Jeep helped to lift my spirits a little, but the grim reality was that I still couldn't work on a full time basis and still felt ongoing pain, especially around my neck, shoulders and back. I also had recurring headaches and vertigo, experienced flashbacks about my former life of happiness with Bob, had trouble remembering and thinking, and didn't know when the rest of these problems would, if ever, end.

GETTING BACK TO NORMAL

To cope and try to get back to normal, I spent a lot of time going to the beach. Going to a good movie helped, too. Also, three times a week I went to the local rehab hospital for massage therapy and for cranial sacral therapy, in which my neck and head was massaged while in traction to help with the continuing pain. But mostly I stayed home, not doing very much. I had already sold the Mail Boxes area franchise in June 1991 as a result of the bankruptcy, and after I discovered I had cancer in July of 1992, shortly before my settlement with Mrs. Raymond, I had closed the store, as well.

I decided to try to write a book about what I had gone through. I had vaguely thought about doing this a few months after the accident, after an aunt and uncle suggested I should keep a diary so I could write a book. However, after the first ghostwriter I found through a friend died after several months, I had dropped the idea, though I kept writing the diary. But now, I considered the idea of doing the book very seriously. In a way, writing it would be my way of overcoming my feelings of frustrations and anger, especially at the lawyers, and finding some rationale for what happened. I felt a growing mission that this was what I should do to make sense of what had happened. And later, the process of writing the book turned out to be extremely healing. It helped me better remember and organize my thoughts — not only about what happened to me, but generally in everyday life. Having a project to work on helped pull me out of my depression and prepare me to go back into the business world again.

I started looking around for a ghostwriter, and by mid-October, 1993, I found one who lived near me in West Palm Beach through a writer's organization. I thought she would be especially good for the book, because she told me she had her own difficulties with back pains due to a spinal cord injury. She had suffered it when she fell into a store basement through a trap door on the first floor and broke her back. She even had a fusion operation done in her back and had had screws placed near her spinal cord, much like I had experienced with the fusion in my neck.

Unfortunately, the very qualities that drew me to her made it impossible for her to write the book. After I packed up several boxes of my medical and legal records, and even sent her my wedding and engagement photos, so she could begin pulling together my story, she had a series of relapses. As she explained, they occurred because the screws were not holding, which laid her up for weeks and months at a time. Then she had an auto accident, resulting in a brain concussion. So working with her was slow going, and ironically, the slow down occurred because this writer was the victim, though she was supposed to be writing about me. At first, I tried to be sympathetic and supportive, thinking just a few more weeks and she would be back on her feet. After 16 months or so of repeated delays, I felt so frustrated and stalled, I had to move on, as painful as it was to tell her. Afterwards, I started looking for another writer.

Meanwhile, in October of 1993, I started pursuing an idea for a new business venture—a golf ball retriever, which is like a long rake with curved prongs for retrieving golf balls. I had first seen the retriever the year before when I visited my parents, who were living nearby in Florida for the winter, and we had gone to the golf course, since both are avid golfers. Though I never played any golf myself, I went along to keep my parents company as they played, and as they drove around with the retriever on the side of their golf cart and used it to pull balls out of the water, people were very curious about it. They kept coming over to my parents asking about it, because it looked so different than other retrievers, which are more like regular rakes or have egg-cups on the end of a long-handle. Also, they noticed that this unusual retriever design made it easier to retrieve the ball, because the unique angle of the tines, throws the golf ball into the rake and holds it there. And many of them were eager to get such a retriever for themselves.

Initially, I had just observed this interest. Yet now, since my father was close to retirement, and I was looking for projects to occupy my time more productively, I asked my father if I could take his idea to the patent office and try to market it. "Sure," he agreed, and so at the suggestion of a long-time friend and financial advisor Steve Goldberg, I contacted a patent attorney in Massachusetts, Don Halgren, on what to do, and my mother drew up some drawings following his guidelines. I talked with Halgren several times as he put together the documents needed to file the patent, such as getting engineered drawings and a detailed description of the retriever.

Finally, the patent was ready for filing in January 1994, and then I waited for it to come through before trying to actively market the retriever, since I wanted to be sure it was fully protected. The process took three years, until January 1997, because Halgren had to make a half-dozen additional revisions until the patent was finally accepted—which is common in submitting patents. Once it cleared, I started gearing up to market the retriever, pulling together a team of investors and business managers. Meanwhile, as I worked on improving my mental and physical skills during this three year period after the January 1994 filing, I gained the ability to actually run this new company.

One development that really helped me gain this ability is working with a computer—and writing the book helped, too. I had originally gotten a new computer in the early summer of 1993, right after I broke up with John and he moved out, since I had more time alone to work with a computer. But now, with the big lawsuit settled, I had even more time. So I threw myself even more seriously into learning how to use the computer. I spent about 6-8 hours a day doing it.

At first, learning the computer was slow going. Though I had used an old 286 computer to work with the Captain's Log mental exercises program a few years before, I first upgraded my computer to a 386, then finally to a 486, while continuing the use the software. Now I wanted to learn so much more, including how to work with word-processing software, e-mail, AOL, and the Internet. Initially, though, I was slowed down by many problems because of my poor memory, so I was continually hitting the wrong keys and crashing the system. Or I had trouble getting the program to work. As a result, I often called the various tech and support lines, though I soon found the support people weren't very patient with me. Though I went through the manuals that came with each program, I still had too many questions and I was often slow to understand, because I started off knowing so little about computers in general.

However, I was determined to learn, and so in October, I finally found someone to help—Alan Malone, who worked at a local company where I bought my computer. He was very helpful when I called again and again for help, and I decided to hire him as a kind of "computer guru." He was so patient, and I needed someone like that for support.

Working with the computer was extremely healing. For one thing, all the attention to detail helped improve my memory and thinking ability. Additionally, I looked for brain injury support groups and did a lot of research about brain injury on the Internet and AOL. I used some of the search engines, like Altavista, to help me find useful Websites and newsgroups, such as sites put up by colleges, support groups, psychiatrists, hospitals, and the Brain Injury Association, formerly known as the National Head Injury Foundation. I found the information very helpful in better understanding my own experiences and in getting ideas about techniques for improving memory and thinking. Also, in exchanges with others on line, I contributed my own ideas about what people might do to improve their situation, drawing on my own experiences. For example, one time I suggested that they might turn on a light in the laundry room to remind them they have laundry in the washer or dryer, after several people wrote that they were continually forgetting they had put their laundry in the washer or dryer and would leave it there for days. Eventually, after following these conversations a couple of times a week for a few weeks, I moved on, since I found that many people who stayed in the support groups continued to complain about their situation, instead of trying to change and improve things, say by learning how to compensate for deficits. However, after finding out about it on the Internet, I joined the Brain Injury Association of Florida.

Then, in November of 1993, feeling increasing strength and confidence, due to working with the computer and setting the golf ball retriever patent in motion, I decided to take on my lawyer Paul Freedman for taking advantage of me. Not only did I feel the settlement was unfair, but I felt he had helped himself to excessive fees. He had charged me a full 40% in legal fees plus costs, which was close to 50% of what I got, though the case had settled and hadn't gone to trial. In addition, I felt he hadn't paid me the interest due on the $500,000 in settlement money that had been put in the court registry while the discovery and settlement process went on.

So I contacted still another attorney, Ted Zellman, to handle this suit. Had I known what I know now, due to writing this book and realizing all the mistakes my attorney made which caused me to lose millions, I would have sued for a lot more, based on malpractice. At the time, I didn't understand the full extent of what he had done, and I didn't recognize this until the writer I later hired analyzed all of the court records from my many suits and pointed out what had happened. Even Zellman, the lawyer I hired to sue Freedman, didn't recognize this, since he didn't examine the earlier court records closely. Thus, the suit Zellman filed against Freedman and his firm was only for excessive fees.

The suit was finally settled about 8 months later, in July 1994, but I only got $20,000, less, of course, Zellman's own fees, and unfortunately, I agreed this settlement was in full settlement of any further claims. So I couldn't sue again when I realized what had happened. But at least, at the time, this suit was another mark of my progress back towards a normal life. It helped me direct and release the feelings of anger I still felt in a productive way, which helped me feel better, too. Plus it was one more experience of victory that helped inspire me to do even more.

Another important milestone in November 1993 occurred when I started working part-time at The Office, a mail boxes service like Mail Boxes, Etc., but private, and worked there until April 1994. My job was to load data like address records into the computer for the store owner. Though the work was a step down from what I had done before in running my own business, it gave me a way to use some of the skills I still had and get my foot back in the door of the business world.

Meanwhile, I was trying to get back in shape, working with various personal trainers on an exercise and weight lifting regimen to build up my strength after my last surgery in the spring of 1993, when I was still living with John. I still felt a lot of pain, and didn't realize that the weight lifting was not what I should be doing, since it was reinjuring many of my earlier injuries. Still I kept going, determined to get back as best I could the physical abilities I had earlier when I was something of an exercise junkie.

SAYING GOOD-BYE TO THE PAST

Finally, in February 1994, I made a personal breakthrough in being able to put the accident behind me, so I could truly move on. That February was the 5th year anniversary of the crash, which was very symbolic to me. So I wanted to do something special to say goodbye to Bob, as a way to finally release from the past.

To do that, I decided to take a cross to the site of the accident where Bob died. I saw this as a memorial to him and to the love we shared which would live on, even though I was finally ready to let him go. I felt it would be fitting to put a cross at this site, because many people in Florida put up crosses by the side of the road or on the median strips where family members or friends are killed as a way to remember them. After I described my plans, I asked my next door neighbor, who works as a handyman, if he would make a wooden cross for me, and he was glad to do so, especially since he had known and liked Bob. He made a 2'x3' cross with two boards and painted it white, and afterwards, my mother surprised me by hanging some red silk roses on the cross. They finished it a day before I planned to place it at the site.

The next day, February 9th, I picked my mother up and drove her to Alligator Alley. She had never been to the crash site before, and it was a very emotional time for both of us, going back, remembering. On the way, we were both very quiet, as we reflected on the past and fought back tears.

At last, after driving a half-hour, we arrived at the site. It was the first time I had even been on this road in five years, since I had avoided it since the crash, even though it took me an extra hour to cross this area between West and East Florida, taking side roads so I didn't have to pass the crash site. The original two-lane road had been expanded to four lanes because there had been several crashes there, both before and after mine. Now there was a wire mesh fence there, too, though there wasn't one when Bob died, since the fence was put up after the alley was widened.

I pulled up on the dirt shoulder by the fence, and my mother and I slowly approached the fence. I led the way holding the cross, my mother just behind me. Then, we put the cross up on the fence, attaching it with some wires. After it was up, I read the same poem that I read when I scattered Bob's ashes on Cape Cod Bay: "And through all the tears and the pain comes the one thought that can make me internally smile again: I have loved." This poem by Melba

Colgrove, "How to Survive the Loss of a Love," had meant so much to me then; so it seemed fitting to read it again now.

As I read it, I felt a sense of completion, because I never felt a sense of finality about Bob's death before, because there never was a funeral with a casket and body I could view. After I scattered Bob's ashes, I never felt that was final either, because there was no grave site; his ashes were released at sea. Thus, by planting the cross and reading the poem, the accident site became my grave site to Bob, and I could finally say goodbye. I was finally able to drive on Alligator Alley again, and know what had happened was now in the past.

After we finished the brief ceremony, my mother and I went to Bob's favorite restaurant at the Ritz-Carlton hotel for dinner. It was my final gesture of remembering how things had been when everything was so wonderful, and now I felt at last I could move on.

MOVING ON

After the ceremony, in April 1994, I made another big step when I began working for Westec Security selling security systems and worked for them for the next six months. It was still another marker of progress, because now I was working even longer hours, 50 and sometimes more hours a week, plus I had more responsibility and contact with people. I had a sales and business background, and now I was truly feeling my wings again.

About six months later, in September 1994, while still at Westec, I also started working on a legal book about unethical lawyers, since I still felt so angry about what happened to me and wanted to warn others. Because of my first writer's medical problems, my book on my personal experiences was on hold, so I found another writer and threw myself into this legal book. The experience helped me learn even more about computers, too, because I did the research myself, learning how to maneuver through the Lexis-Nexis legal data base to get examples of cases of lawyers who had been sued for malpractice, charged with criminal offenses, or brought up on a complaint before the American Bar Association. I was eventually able to complete a proposal in early 1995, and then, since my first writer wasn't be able to complete my personal book, in early 1995, I asked my legal book writer to help me write my personal story, too. And that's this book.

Meanwhile, I continued to monitor what had happened to Charlie after he was convicted and spent only 4 months in jail, although he had been sentenced to 22 months. He got out early due to "gain time" for good behavior in jail. After he got out, he was put on probation and was supposed to pay me a monthly court-ordered restitution until he paid off the $26,000 he had stolen. For a time he did. After he got out in August 1991, he sent me about $2000 a year, but in late 1996 he stopped after paying me about $10,000. After he ignored a reminder letter I sent, I followed up with his probation officer to find out what happened. Supposedly, she explained, he had told her he was having hard times and the judicial system gave him until 2006 to pay in full, so unfortunately, she explained, I would just have to wait until he paid me again and didn't have any recourse, like having him put back in jail for non-payment. So since then, I haven't been able to do much—just wait and hope.

Similarly, I checked in from time to time on the status of a civil case I had filed about six months before my mediation against Conrad Ramakers, who left with my furniture two years earlier in 1991 and never paid me. In this case, when he didn't show up at court, I had gotten a default judgment of $40,000 in April of 1993 and had put a lien on a house he then owned and still owns in Florida, although I haven't been able to collect. That's because I'm not sure where he is, since he has been moving all over the country, apparently because he has other people after him. These even include the Immigration and Naturalization Service, since he immigrated to the U.S., but never became a citizen. At least I was able to get that lien on his house after I got my judgment, though I can't force him to sell it because of Florida homestead laws. But if he ever tries to sell it, I can finally collect—so I started monitoring that judgment, just in case.

HEALING PHYSICALLY

As I learned new skills and became more productive, I concentrated on healing physically, too. Doing so was still difficult at times, because after recovering from my hysterectomy in September 1992, I had to have two other surgeries in the spring of 1993 and another in January 1995—the first two an ulnar nerve transplant and the third because I fell and broke my nose because of poor balance due to vertigo. I had to have the ulnar nerve transplant in each elbow, because when I was in a halo for three months after the accident, I had to sit sleeping up which inflamed the nerves in my joints. They never healed properly, so even more than five years later, the pain was still excruciating at times, especially when I tried to exercise. Now that I hoped to get back to a more active routine, something had to be done.

After I recovered from these various surgeries, I was determined to get in shape again. So besides seeing a chiropractor a few times a week, starting in December 1994, I worked with a half-dozen different personal trainers to guide me in an exercise program. I felt I needed a trainer, rather than just going to the gym and working out however I wanted, because I had had so many injuries. I didn't want to exercise incorrectly or too strenuously, to make these old injuries worse. But, unfortunately, I kept experiencing setback after setback with each of these trainers, often feeling a great deal of pain after I exercised. Later, when I finally did find a trainer who helped me, I realized that these other trainers had been pushing me too fast by having me lift weights. As a result, I kept reinjuring my old injuries, which is what I thought I could avoid by working with a trainer. I just didn't have the right trainer to work with at the time.

By June 1995, after 18 months of exercising, it was very frustrating, because I was still in so much pain during and after sessions that I told my then trainer Doug Splittgerber that I would have to stop. After I did, I felt really depressed at not exercising, which made it hard to work on the books and other projects I had started with such hope after I planted the cross and experienced a personal breakthrough. Was I doomed to keep from becoming close to normal again?

Doug called me to motivate me again. He suggested I see a physical therapist, Debra Corbo, who specialized in a technique called myofascial release, which puts pressure on the densely woven connective tissue, called "fascia," which covers and interpenetrates every muscle, bone, nerve, artery, vein, and all our internal organs, including the heart, lungs, brain, and spinal cord. "You can use this total system approach," he urged me. But at first, I ignored his referral. I was so depressed, and the thought of working with still another trainer and failing made me feel even worse.

Still, Doug kept calling to urge me to try going to Debra, and finally, in October, because of his persistence, I agreed to make one last try. And that turned out to be exactly what I needed, although it took me several months to notice the difference.

When I first went into see Debra one morning in late October, 1995, she asked me to undress. "Now stand in front of a wall," she said, "so I can look at how your body is aligned." The first thing she noticed was that I was out of alignment. As Debra explained to me: "Your whole body is twisted. Your one arm is internally rotated and the other arm is externally rotated. So it's no wonder you're hurting."

Then, she proceeded to explain that I wasn't crazy or having psychosomatic or imaginary pains, because none of the doctors I had seen could see any problems on an X-Ray or in an MRI. Rather, I had pain due to my lack of alignment which put a strain on the fascia or connective tissue throughout my body. "That's why any exercise contributes to further strains and leads to even more pain," Debra told me.

The way to deal with this, Debra explained, is through a long intensive program, lasting at least 9 months to a year to reshape and realign my body. Then I probably would have to follow an ongoing regimen of visits and continue exercising for years afterwards to stay in condition. "I work very slowly," Debra explained, "because I have to actually move the connective tissue internally and that way help to release the pain. It's a very slow process, but it's better that way. The approach doesn't just deal with the symptoms, but with the underlying basis of the pain."

Then, Debra asked me about my operation after the accident,

and I showed her a picture of me in the halo. After studying it, she explained that the fusion to heal my neck had resulted in my head being slightly rotated. "If it wasn't rotated, you would have been paralyzed for life. But this rotation contributes to the alignment problems you have."

After that, Debra literally went up and down my body noting the areas that were especially sensitive and painful, which at the time included both my shoulders, my upper and lower back, both knees, and my feet. I was literally a walking "paincushion," as Debra told me. As a result, when I did certain exercises, like squats for strengthening my knees, this was exactly the wrong thing to do, because this exercise only made the fascia in my knees more inflamed, so I could hardly walk. Debra was also appalled when I told her how one massage therapist had decided my neck should be more mobile, and had tried to move my neck, producing intense pain. His manipulation even caused me to see stars and feel much dizzier than usual. "You can't move something that's fused," Debra said. "No wonder it hurts so much."

I felt reassured that Debra really knew what she was talking about as she explained in detail what was wrong and what she would do to correct it. "I want to get rid of the most severe pain first," she said, "even though that's not usually the source of the problem." And eliminating the worst meant starting with moving the cranial bones, which is called "craniosacral therapy." Though I originally had some of this therapy several years before when I was at the rehab hospital in Naples, the therapy hadn't worked, perhaps because the therapist there didn't use enough pressure to provide the necessary release.

Debra began by deeply massaging the bones in the back of my head while I was lying on the table, since these bones had been knocked out of alignment when I wore the halo. "That's why," Debra explained, "the cerebral spinal fluid in your system doesn't move the way it should. Instead, it's blocked from flowing easily through your joints, much like a blocked river results in a much smaller flow downstream, so some lands become parched and dry." Another parallel might be when a mechanical device doesn't have enough oil, so the parts rub together, get stuck, and can rust more easily when exposed to water.

Whatever the reason, it was a slow, painful process. Though Debra started with only light pressure, I still felt some pain, and as she worked on me, pressing and shaping here and there, she kept asking: "Is that too much?" because she didn't want to go above my pain threshold. At the same time, she reminded me that there had to be some pain, because she was pushing against the bones to change their alignment.

Usually, I tried to endure as much as I could without saying anything, since I kept wanting to see change as quickly as possible. So Debra watched for signs the process was becoming too painful by observing my body language. If my hands and feet started twisting or "dancing," as Debra called it, or if I seemed to be tensing or tightening too much, she would pull back.

Afterwards, at each session, she used myofascial release to press and release the fascia in the rest of my body. So she could do this, I took off my clothes and stretched out on the table. Then Debra moved her hands over my body, pushing down with one hand and pulling back on the muscle with the other in each area, so she created a tension. After she did this several times, the tissue would start to move, and I could feel it like a rolling sensation or a glow of warmth. Sometimes it felt like a wave moving through me, though at other times, I just felt a sense of heat at the point of tension and release. Meanwhile, as Debra felt the tissue start to stretch, she would press against it a little more, following the tissue movement to encourage it to flow. This flow occurred because when she released the connective tissue in one point, the effects of the release spread to connective tissue in other parts of my body, much like what happens when one presses against a balloon or piece of rubber in one point. The pressure creates movement throughout the balloon or piece of rubber. For example, Debra might cause a release to occur on the right side of my back, and all of a sudden, I would feel the wave of movement coming down my leg or perhaps I would experience the front part of my arm hurting. Or another way to look at this process is to see this fascia as a little like a spider web of tissue that spreads through the whole body—pull on one part of it, and you affect the whole network.

Debra also felt that my whole system had knotted up because of the many pressures I had experienced since the accident, not just the physical injuries. Besides the emotional trauma of the accident, I experienced the trauma of losing my husband, losing my business, having trusted friends steal from me, and having to start again. In effect, all of these stressors became stored in the connective tissue, contributing to its tightness that translated into physical pain. As Debra told me after a few sessions: "You have all this tension inside you, and there are times when you are angry or crying, and you don't know why you are. You might feel this emotion at any time, such as when you are walking or exercising, because you have put pressure on where this tension is stored. And in a session, you may feel it, too, when I am putting pressure on you, because I'm releasing the tissue, so the emotion comes through."

So, reassured by her explanation of what she was doing and what to expect, I continued on, seeing Debra three days a week over the next few months, even though each session was so incredibly painful as she moved around the bones and tissues. But Debra kept reassuring me: "You have to experience some pain for long-term release." Then she further explained the source of various pains, such as when I was experiencing a recurring low back pain and she told me: "That's because your low back is so tight and your pelvis is rolling forward, so you get a tense sciatica pain down your leg. It's because your back is pulled in pinching the nerve in your back and buttocks."

So I kept on, feeling like Debra was my last hope, since I had been through so many other trainers and doctors without success. Even so, in the beginning, the changes were so slow, I hardly noticed any difference. But Debra kept priming me to expect this, explaining: "You're so tight all over. It takes time to start the loosening process, because it's too painful to try to do it too quickly. However, the tissues have memories, so gradually some movement is occurring though you may not notice it right away. We just have to keep pressing and stretching gradually. Then as you become looser, you'll start to notice the difference."

After two months I finally did. Though I still hurt all over in most of the same places as when I started, the pain wasn't as intense. Before I had rated my pain level at about an 8-10 level on a scale of 0 (no pain) to 10 (very high intensity pain), but by mid-December, I felt my pain had declined to about a 3-4 level. As my pain declined, my spirits lifted. I felt more hope and enthusiasm; more interest in participating in activities; more confidence that I could. I even sent Debra a fruit basket for Christmas that December of 1995 with a card that said: "Thank you for my renewed interest in life." And that's how I felt — like my life had somehow been given back to me.

Still, though I noticed a little less pain and more flexibility after six months, I felt frustrated the process wasn't going faster, so I decided to work even more intensely, and in May 1996, I started going five times a week instead of three. I did that for one month, before going back to a three-times a week regimen. It seemed to be just what I needed.

A key reason is that I needed the more frequent reinforcement to know what to do because of my memory problems due to the brain injury. For example, when I was going just three times a week, I sometimes forgot appointments, and many times Debra would explain an exercise and even give me pictures and written notes about what to do, but afterward I wouldn't remember what to do or I would lose the picture or explanation. I often forgot because I felt so much pain that this was all I could think about, and I would push out thoughts of anything else, as well as become depressed. It was as if a blanket of pain and depression had come over me, cutting me off from everything else.

Once I started going five times a week, this provided the repetition I needed to ingrain the physical and neurological changes Debra had made in my body, as well as reinforce her exercise instructions. The effect was like having a new habit pattern imprinted in both my body and mind. So I was able to better follow through and the change was more enduring.

After a month, in June, the new pattern was imprinted, and

incredibly, for the first time in years, I had my first pain free week. It was like the blanket around me for so long was finally lifting, and it felt wonderful to feel I could be normal again. I felt uplifted, ecstatic, and after I told Debra about this development, she felt I could go back to three times a week. When I did, I found the pain still stayed away. So finally, I felt on the way to a real recovery.

After that, I was able to move ahead even more rapidly, though I was seeing Debra less. Since I was looser and more flexible now, I could even do more stretching and movement exercises, and the results of the stretching continued even when I wasn't doing it. As Debra told me: "After you do a static stretch, lying down in a stretched position, you begin to change the tissue's memory, so it will continue to stretch and unwind itself. It knows where it needs to go once we give it the incentive to start moving." Then, after several months, with the tissue loosened up, she could have me do more dynamic stretches, in which I would stand up, stretch, and move my joints to release them even more. After that I worked on strengthening my muscles, though I still had to be careful not to lift weights that were too heavy, since they might put too much strain on my muscles and trigger old patterns.

The results were amazing. I felt like I was really starting to return to the way I used to be, when I had been an exercise and fitness buff. At the same time, those changes helped me become more alert mentally, as Debra herself noticed. I was much less forgetful. I remembered appointments better. And Debra didn't have to explain the exercises I should do in as much detail and with as much repetition. I understood what she wanted much more quickly.

Too, this alertness helped me know what I did when I experienced any pain, so I could adjust my position to stop doing whatever was causing the pain. At one time, I couldn't remember what to do. I just suddenly felt pain, and I couldn't tell Debra more than that, so it was hard for her to recommend what I should do to change. As a result, without any input from her, I would keep doing whatever was causing the pain, and the continuing tension would become part of the tissue memory. Thus, the problem would continue until Debra was able to independently discover what was wrong and work on that area.

Now I could remember enough to explain what I had done before the pain, so Debra could directly work on that area or I knew enough to change my position myself. For instance, say I was sitting at my computer with my phone to my ear and had my shoulder up as I talked. After an extended period, say 15-30 minutes, this awkward position would create an unusual tightness, which would spread throughout my whole system, creating pain. Or another time, when I visited Sea World, I realized I had been putting too much weight on my right side to compensate for a weakness on my left side due to the brain injury, resulting in feelings of pain that night. At once, I recognized the cause, realizing I had been out of alignment causing the tissues to swell.

Thus, from June on, with much less pain, and some days with no pain at all, I was able to do much more. After three more months, I dropped down to seeing Debra one day a week, since I could now do even more work on my own in what would become a continuing program to stay aligned throughout my life. I would have to continue, because as Debra told me: "You have to keep stretching regularly, just like everybody else, to maintain alignment. Then the strengthening exercises, like weight lifting, are designed to stabilize your system and keep everything that's been realigned in place."

There were still certain types of exercises I might never be able to do, such as aerobics at their usual fast pace, because my brain injury made me slower to react and that could lead to injury. Or as Debra put it: "The wave of thought coming from your brain to your muscles, especially on your left side, doesn't connect the way it should for you to respond quickly enough. The connection is good enough for functioning on a day to day basis. However, when you start doing rapid-paced activities like aerobics, it's hard to maintain the proper alignment and you can easily lose track of what you are doing, because your brain has to work so much faster every single step you take. That's why you need to take any exercising more slowly or watch yourself on a treadmill with mirrors to keep that alignment. You can't just go to an ordinary gym and work out, because you need that continual monitoring by yourself or by a trainer."

Now I know. So since then, seeing Debra once a week, I have continued this workout and alignment program. I still do it today.

GAINING SUCCESS AT LAST

Meanwhile, as my physical condition improved and as the pain gradually decreased and almost completely went away, I regained the spirit of entrepreneurship and independence I once had.

After I had left selling security systems for Westec Security at the end of 1994, I had experienced a period of depression for about a year when it was hard to motivate myself to do anything. Though I had started on my legal book and was working on my personal book again with a new writer, it was slow going, as well as very sad, because I had to go back and remember old painful memories. As a result, as I went back and forth with my writer, trying to put years of experiences, medical records, legal suits, and other documents in order, I sometimes felt overwhelmed by it all. It was still hard for me to think logically, especially about events that happened after the accident because of my difficulty in forming new memories. Yet I knew I had to remember, if I wanted to write the book, and so I pressed on. Though I didn't realize it at the time, this process of repeatedly reaching back to recall, ordering my thoughts, and correcting and recorrecting revised drafts of the manuscript helped my mental healing, too. Though the process often left me frustrated, discouraged, and depressed, it was like a continual challenge to improve my thinking, so I could finish the project, much like Debra's pressure on my muscles and fascia was painful but provided the necessary release.

Thus, by December 1995, as the curtain of pain around me started lifting, I felt increasingly eager to get back to work, and I continued writing my personal story. At the same time, I filed additional papers in response to patent office queries to get the golf ball retriever through the patent office.

In early January 1997, the patent for the golf-ball retriever finally came through, so at last I felt free to market it. And mentally and physically I finally felt ready. I had prepared myself to take the lead in running a business again.

Three weeks after the patent came through, there was a PGA (Professional Golfer's Association) Merchandise Show for professional golfers in Orlando, Florida, and I made arrangements to be there. Though there was no time to get a booth, I prepared brochures describing the retriever, and I walked the exhibit's floor handing them out. Meanwhile, I got a small management and marketing team together to lay the groundwork to launch the product. Besides calling on the help of my long-time accountant Steve Goldberg and the patent attorney he recommended, I found a golf-pro eager to support the product and two other people excited enough about it to participate in the new company. We started off by doing a survey in the Naples area using 50 prototypes of the retriever to get reactions and we got back very enthusiastic results on the survey. Now, as of this writing, the next step is to raise financing to manufacture the retriever and start selling it in a local test market area, and then go national. The plan is to combine the retriever with other products that golfers might find of special interest, such as golf accessories, a liniment for sore muscles, and golfing software programs. Perhaps by the spring of 1998, everything will be ready to go, once the business plan is finished and the financing for manufacturing and distribution is in place. It's a major project, but now, eight years after the accident, I feel ready.

In a way, I feel like taking on this project is a culmination of everything I've been doing to get back to the normal life I led before the brain injury—and perhaps even surpass it. For me, the past few years have been almost like a mission to show not only that I can achieve this goal, but others can, too, as if I want to show the power of the human will to master and overcome the obstacles and challenges that fate might put in our way. I know there are times I could have given up. There are times I truly wanted to; times when I felt I couldn't take one more setback, one more personal betrayal; one more day of pain.

Yet, somehow, I found the strength and the willpower to keep going. I'm not sure exactly how, but perhaps some of the determination came from my strong faith, perhaps some from the support of my family and friends, perhaps some from the early spirit of independence and entrepreneurship I've always had. But whatever it was, this inner power kept me going.

So now, finally, with a small team around me, I feel I've met the challenge and am ready to go on. In turn, I hope this book will be an inspiration to others who have experienced a brain injury or any other disability, or have loved ones who have, to help them know there is hope. I want them to know that if they just direct their will and their desire to overcome their difficulties that they, too, can make it; that they, too, can prevail.

In a sense, then, this goal to reach out to others has become my next mission. Besides heading up this golf ball project, I want to take this message of healing, recovery, and hope to others, and for me, this book is designed to bring this message. Originally, when I started this book, I wasn't exactly sure why I felt it was so important to write. I just felt a need to write it to heal myself. Although now I see it as more—as a way to help others, as well, by showing what can be possible, how much we can really achieve, and how we can surpass obstacles and limits that stand in our way. I have written this book in this spirit—and this is why I see what has happened as truly coming out of the darkness and into the light.

Debbie Quinn wearing a "halo."

At the time that this picture was taken, I had already been wearing this 9 pound device, called a halo, which was attached to my head in 4 different places by screws that were drilled into my skull, for approximately 3 months. I was anxiously awaiting my next doctor's appointment which was scheduled five days away to find out if it would be removed or if I would be confined in it's restrictiveness for yet a longer period of time.

My hopes, at the time, were that the halo would be removed and that my life would begin to regain some sense of normalcy.